WE CARRY GOLD

A CHRISTIAN MEMOIR OF ONE WOMAN'S WRESTLE WITH GOD

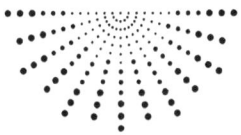

CARLENE SINGLETON

CONTENTS

Disclaimer	v
Acknowledgments	ix
Foreword	xi
Introduction	xiii
1. Babies And More Babies	1
2. Caleb	17
3. Matthew	41
4. Micah	67
5. Nathan	113
6. Aaron	137
7. John Mark	164
8. Ben	191
9. Daniel	216
10. Dai	250
11. Thuy	281
12. James	291
13. Sarah	310
14. Abigail	344
Afterword	379
About the Author	389
In Memoriam	391

COPYRIGHT

© 2013, 2016, 2019 Carlene Singleton

We Carry Gold: A Christian Memoir of One Woman's Wrestle with God (3rd Edition)

All rights reserved. No part of this book may be reproduced or modified in any form, including photocopying, recording, or by any information storage and retrieval system, without permission in writing from the publisher, except as permitted by the U.S. copyright law.

ISBN: 978-1-950036-02-8 (Paperback)
ISBN: 978-1-950036-03-5 (eBook)

Library of Congress Control Number: 2019932410

Proof-reader and Line Item Edit – *Audrey Moran*
Book Cover by *Lisa Frederickson*
Special thanks to the Editor of previous editions - *Janet Taylor-Perry* B.S., M.A.T. author, editor, educator

Focus7 Publishing 2019
Las Vegas, Nevada
www.focus7publishing.com

For questions, permissions, or comments, please contact:
focus7publishing@gmail.com

DISCLAIMER

Although the following accounts are true, names have been changed to protect the innocent.

In no way is this writing meant to pass judgment, but to relate my personal journey and maturation in the Lord.

Publisher's Disclaimer
    This book is a memoir. Some names and characteristics have been changed, some events have been compressed, and some dialogue has been recreated.
    Carlene Singleton is relating a true story that took place in Mississippi decades ago. Her reference to babies (boy or girl) being 'black' is in nowise intended to be politically incorrect, prejudice, a racial slant, or anything else that might offend someone.
    Instead, it is merely to represent a problem of the times, where

it was unusual for a white woman to be traveling around carrying a black baby.

Carlene's desire, is for her experiences and revelations to help bridge gaps of prejudice. She knows that we are all God's children. Her stories are intended to demonstrate how the Lord tenderly watches over all of His children. She hopes to bring to light His miracles for these little ones and a respect for all life.

If you have any questions about anything, please send an email to us at focus7publishing@gmail.com.

-Lisa

DEDICATION

**This book is dedicated to the glory of
God for His heart for His little children.**

*"If my father and mother forsake me,
then the Lord will take me up,"
Psalm 27:10*

We stood on that scripture a lot, especially when we were waiting to see if we would get the baby we had been called about.

Besides the great blessing of our own three precious children there were few blessings as great for Hamp and me as to be handed a little child which the Lord had taken up.

---

*To this have I been called, to walk hospital corridors alone, and
cry for children who are not my own...*

ACKNOWLEDGMENTS

I would like to acknowledge my husband, Hamp, or Hampy, as his family, close friends and I refer to him, for pushing me and hounding me to work on the book. He literally pestered me into beginning, working on it for three years through several babies, and finishing it while we had James. Oddly though, he would never look at a word of it. I wrote the whole book having no idea what he thought of it. He never gave me a reason.

I would also like to acknowledge the love and support of the Red Dog Writers, Judy Tucker, Lottie Boggan and Janet Taylor-Perry, all three wonderful writers, who encouraged me to revise and update the book for the last two babies we had, who were not in the first book. They almost have me convinced I am a writer.

A special acknowledgement goes to Janet Taylor-Perry, who came alongside me as an instrument of the Holy Spirit and took up where Hampy left off. She lent me her energy, her enthusiasm, her vast store of knowledge about English and writing, and also pushed me to get the book finished. If not for her this book would almost certainly not have been published in its present form. The pain and fatigue of fibromyalgia would have not allowed it.

FOREWORD

I doubt there is any physician of long experience who, if he is indeed honest with himself, has not witnessed a miracle. What happened to some of these children was truly miraculous; also miraculous was the love, patience, hope and faith embodied in Carlene as she cared for these children.

My mission as a physician was to supply the "conventional wisdom" and scientific skepticism about prognoses, but as a believer, I tried never to quash Carlene's optimism. The stories are true; the author and I have witnessed these events and rejoiced in them. She is truly a servant of the Lord.

Robert H. Thompson, M.D.
former Chief of Pediatrics
Mississippi Baptist Medical Center

INTRODUCTION

> *"For we are His workmanship, created in Christ Jesus for good works which He ordained beforehand that we should walk in them"*
>
> — EPHESIANS 2:10

His ways are above our ways, His purposes beyond our understanding, and so, for reasons of His own, God called our whole family to care for his orphaned, sick and handicapped babies, most of which turned out to be little black boys. This ministry is how Jesus chose to reveal Himself to us, and without it, I can't imagine what our lives would have been. The journal entries, which are interspersed with the narrative, are not always specific to the story of the baby in whose chapter they appear. Hopefully they won't create confusion, but rather show there were struggles and other aspects of spiritual growth occurring at that time.

God's presence and His miracles are with us in the midst of the grime and sweat and the joys and losses of our lives. So even when God is pleased to show powerful manifestations of Himself, life is still filled with those things which bind us to the earth and remind us of our humanity.

If anyone had told me as a teenager in the 1960s I would spend my adult life mothering sick and handicapped black babies, I would have run the other way as fast as I could. In addition, there was nothing in my background to prepare me for mothering my own three children, much less dozens of other women's.

The only child of somewhat Bohemian parents, I grew up with very little formal Christian education. There were only cultural Christian influences in my life besides my hit and miss attendance at Sunday School with neighbors and friends. The only devout Christian I knew was my great grandmother, for whom I was named. She was the official family Christian, and I know she prayed for me diligently, and was concerned about the haphazard upbringing I received from my very young and unconventional parents.

At the age of nine, I prayed alone to receive Christ after watching a Billy Graham crusade on television while my very young parents slept off an afternoon of sherry drinking. From then on I was aware of the reality of Christ, but as my parents were nominal Christians, I had very little instruction in my faith. I was an adolescent in the early 1960's, which may partially explain why as I grew older, except for periodic flashes of conviction which flooded my heart, I even lost track of the reality of sin. Right and wrong became moral concepts open to my intellectual interpretation.

When I met my husband, Hamp, in 1964, he was very moral and seemed almost religious. I was surprised those qualities attracted me. I wanted a moral man, but not a godly one, or a Church-going one. They were no fun. My parents' indifference had turned me away from Church. Like me, Hamp had received Christ as a child, but had been undiscipled. He only knew Jesus was real. Before we married, I prayed often that God would bless our marriage, and even though there was virtually no Christian activity in my life, I was sure this was God's man for me and the Lord was very much involved in our relationship.

Hamp and I married very young by today's standards. He turned twenty-two weeks before we married, and I turned twenty-nine days after that. Three years later our first child, Stacey, was born. I had planned to return to my job when my baby was six weeks old, as was the custom of my peers. But as soon as I saw her I knew I could never entrust her to anyone else. I stayed home. Sixteen months later our son, John, was born and on his second birthday, our daughter, Laura, arrived. Since neither Hamp nor I had experience with babies or small children, three children under three and a half was overwhelming, to say the least.

Stressed out with three children, unable to communicate, and rapidly growing apart, by the time we had been married eight years, we were in serious trouble. As our relationship deteriorated, I turned to the church, hoping to find the God of my childhood. I found a church near our home and suggested to Hamp we attend. While he went with me gladly, I became very active there, but it was not what he needed. We fell into a deadly pattern. I was growing in the Lord, but my husband was not.

In 1973, when Laura was eighteen months old, Hamp built us a new house in an area, miles away from our part of town. I didn't want to leave the house I had brought my babies home to and which I loved. Hamp was immovable on the subject and I was too busy changing diapers and washing baby bottles to mount an offensive. After we moved, Hamp began attending the little Presbyterian Church a few blocks from our new home. I continued at the old church, where I taught the senior high Sunday school class. I was very attached to the kids there, and felt I was making a difference their lives. Jimmy McGuire, the pastor of Hamp's new church, lived up the street from us. He and his wife were about our age and had a new baby. Hamp and Jimmy were soon good friends, and Jimmy, sensing Hamp's desire to rekindle his relationship with the Lord, spent all the time with him he could. At my church one day after directing Bible school, and feeling desperate to hold my family together, I poked around the church library, having no idea what I was looking for. I found a book on Christian marriage, and discovered God's order for husbands and wives. This book affirmed everything I had thought families should be, and ours wasn't. It described just the relationship I wanted to have with Hamp. Since I had no one to talk to, I tentatively began to pray and try to apply Christian principles to our relationship.

At first things didn't seem to change, but one night in our living room, Jimmy explained salvation in a way neither of us had ever heard before. He held up his hand to depict me. Then he held up his wallet to depict Jesus.

"When you received Jesus, He came to stand in front of you. Now when God looks at you, He sees Jesus."

I was stunned. "That's it? It's that simple?" For the first time, I understood Jesus had done everything needed. There was nothing for me to add by my own effort. I only had to accept Christ's sacrifice for my sins, and ask Him to take control of my life. Hamp and I both grasped the reality of the gift of Grace that night in a way which changed us forever.

As we began to allow Christ to take control of our lives, the sharp differences in our personalities that had torn at our relationship for years, began to lose their edge. Hamp and I began to see for the first time that our marriage was to be controlled by Christ, not us, and as we began to allow Him to soften and draw us after Him, our attitudes toward each other changed.

As I asked the Lord to make me the woman He wanted me to be, He focused me on my role with my husband first. He led me to leave my church and take the children to the church where my husband felt comfortable. This is a scriptural principle our culture has made extremely hard to follow. It seems most young men and women don't know what marriage is supposed to be now. While this changed my attitudes and feelings for him, it also made him more aware of his responsibility before God for the family's spiritual welfare. I was especially blessed in this area, because Hamp was a decent, honest man already. It seemed easy for him to assume his role of spiritual responsibility for his family once he understood it was God's will for him.

When he learned that his role was not only to provide for us and protect us, but his spiritual authority also made him accountable for our spiritual growth, he took his responsibilities seriously.

The children and I had been having devotions at bedtime for several months when one night Hamp appeared in the doorway and said, "I think I am supposed to be doing this." He came in and led our devotions that night, and from then until the children were older teenagers, he led us in family devotions each morning and night. We sang songs, read and memorized scripture and read wonderful books together like *The Cross and the Switchblade*, *God's Smuggler*, and *Little Pilgrim's Progress*. It was supernatural how anger and resentments that might have built up during the day melted away, at least for me, as we prayed for each other. And nothing has ever touched my heart so deeply as hearing my husband pray for me. Leading family devotions and prayer is the most powerful thing Christian fathers can do for their families, especially if they have sons. It was largely due to the teaching the children received at family devotions which brought them all to salvation while they were still quite young.

As my husband became more and more the steady, dependable, head of the family God wanted him to be, I found myself experiencing a peace and enjoyment in being a wife and mother I had not known before. And it did not come from giving control of everything to my husband, as people often suppose. I didn't. It came from my growing relationship with Jesus, and the knowledge that He was ultimately in control. Hamp never thought being responsible made him king of our home. He knew if he lorded himself over me, God would not answer his prayers (I Peter 3:7), and I wouldn't give him the time of day. I respected my husband's intellect and trusted his mind and heart to bear burdens I could not. As he saw he could trust in my love and respect for him, he also gained a new respect and love for me. We always discussed everything about the business, the children, the church, and anything else touching our life. Often he changed his mind when I gave him my opinion. This is the way God has told us to live in marriage, and he never took advantage of his physical strength over me, or demanded that I obey him. A husband wants a loving and generous wife, and he won't have one if he constantly stands over her reminding her she is under him in God's sight. He understood his responsibility for my spiritual good would not be accomplished by forcing me to do something which would grieve me terribly or make me miserable. In almost everything, I willingly went along with whatever he thought was best, even if I wasn't as sure as he was about what was right. My trust in Christ was the foundation upon which my trust in my husband was built. In I Corinthians 3:10 and 11 Paul says "...as a wise master builder I laid a foundation, and another is building upon...it, for no man can lay a foundation other than the one which is laid, which is Jesus Christ." We should always be trying to let the Holy Spirit move in us to draw us closer to His perfect will for us.

Once we had laid a firm foundation for our family in Christ, even though we were young and inexperienced in Him, He wasted no time, but quickly started us on our journey with His babies.

1
BABIES AND MORE BABIES

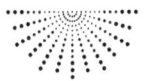

God opened the door for His babies coming into our family through my spiritual mother in the Lord, Camille Barranco. I had sung in the choir with her at the first church Hamp and I had attended. Camille's husband was Catholic and she often went to church with him.

I went to Camille one day for advice about a spiritual matter, and found she had a beautiful newborn baby girl staying with her. The baby was to be adopted through Catholic Charities and she had been asked to be a temporary foster mother, because all of their usual foster homes were full. Camille watched me holding the baby and said, "You would make a wonderful foster mother." The idea appealed to me instantly, but I said I was sure Hamp would never agree. Laura was just two, and I didn't think he would want another baby around the house. It was chaotic enough with a five-year-old, a four-year-old and a two-year-old.

In spite of that, I couldn't put the idea of foster parenting out of my mind, and by that night I knew I had to ask Hamp. I asked the Lord not to let me get into something that would overwhelm me. I knew I was just a baby in the Lord, and lacked discernment to know what was foolish and what was obedience to God's word. I worried about the children's reaction when the baby had to leave, and I was afraid it's crying at night would disturb everyone. I could think of a hundred reasons why it wouldn't work, but I couldn't stop thinking about it. To my surprise, Hamp was willing to try it and see what happened.

In early April, 1974, the nun in charge of foster care brought us a beautiful, white baby girl. She was five days old. Newborn babies available for adoption often have no legal name, since their new parents will name them after they are adopted. That meant we could call her whatever we wanted. It seemed appropriate to give her a name to remind us she belonged to the Lord, so we called her Faith. The scriptural name had such a positive impact on our feelings for her we continued the practice and gave every foster baby a name from the Bible. Faith was a good baby and we all were captivated by her. The children thought she was the most wonderful baby in the whole world, while I could hardly believe we had been entrusted with such a precious treasure.

Laura with Matthew asleep on her stomach while she elevates her sprained ankle.

The first night after finally getting all four children to sleep, I sat down exhausted and lit a cigarette. I had been praying for months for the Lord to help me stop smoking, and when we applied to be foster parents, I was sure I could never take care of another baby unless I could quit smoking. Cigarettes made me feel tired and sick, and I desperately wanted to stop, but I couldn't. My parents, my husband and all my friends smoked, and I couldn't break free of it even through prayer. I prayed and tried hard to quit the whole month before we got our first baby, but without success.

Hamp was smoking too and there was an ashtray on the table between us. I took one puff on the cigarette, then watched as my hand went to the ashtray, apparently of its own accord, and put it out. I was not thinking of putting the cigarette out. I was hardly aware I had lit it, smoking was so automatic. As I watched my hand put out the cigarette, I knew in my spirit I would never pick one up again. I was surprised I felt no excitement or elation that I had experienced a touch from God. I just felt the calm assurance my addiction to cigarettes was gone. Hamp smoked for another fifteen years, and had to fight to stop, but I was healed instantly. It was the first of many miracles God was willing to do in order to provide for His babies, and it was a strong confirmation we were doing what the Lord wanted.

I had been afraid taking on another baby would be hard, and it was. Getting up during the night with a newborn is never easy, and it was a struggle to get up several times a night with Faith, then get up again at 6:00 a.m. with Hamp and my own children. Still there was something wonderful about having a tiny newborn in the house again, and after three weeks, I found myself wanting to keep her in spite of myself. I could hardly bear to think of giving her up and when we were notified her new parents were ready for her, I cried. My heart couldn't believe she had to leave. I had bonded with her in spite of my determination not to. Knowing she was not mine and absolutely had to leave made no difference at all.

If it was hard for me to face her leaving, it was no surprise the children didn't take it well either. They had all assured us they understood the baby would only be with us for a few weeks, but they all cried too, and begged me to find a way to keep her. If I'd had to decide that day if we had made a mistake in taking Faith, I would have said, "Yes, this was a terrible idea," but by the next day the Lord had calmed us down, and while there were tears when Faith left, they were not agonizingly painful, just sad and a little regretful. In a few days we were back to normal, and apparently no worse for the wear.

Faith was adopted by an excited young couple we knew would love her and take good care of her. The pain of losing her was soon forgotten in the busy activity of a family with three young children. We had no idea we had been given our first dose of the reality of serving the Lord. The first time just hurt a little, as did the second, and the third, but the time would come, when giving up a baby would be wrenchingly painful. Mercifully, the Lord had begun with small lessons, teaching us all, especially me, to trust Him step by step. I had to learn to trust Him with one of the worst pains a person can have, that of giving a loved, helpless child to total strangers.

A FEW MONTHS LATER, I GOT A CALL FROM THE SECRETARY AT Catholic Charities. This time they needed a home for a baby boy. After discussing possible length of stay in foster care, the baby's age and weight, she hesitated and said, "Oh, ah...Mrs. Singleton... did I mention, um, the baby is black?" My heart turned over. What an opportunity to show my conviction about the value of every person; and at the same time, what an opportunity to draw hostility toward my family. I felt a mixture of excitement and fear.

"I'll have to talk to my husband about this," I said. I was happy to pass this decision on to Hamp.

I prayed before I called him, reminding the Lord that Hamp was really prejudiced and it would take a work of the Holy Spirit for him to allow a little black person to come into our home. I wasn't even sure how I felt. I welcomed the opportunity to show my feelings about racial prejudice. I just hadn't expected to take a black child into my home to do it. It had never entered my mind some of the babies who needed a home would be black. The whole idea was a little scary, but we had said we wanted to serve the Lord and His baby needed a home.

| Hamp holding Grace

Hamp listened as I described the baby, including the fact that he was black, then said, "Well, I wasn't expecting a black one. I guess all babies are the same to God, though. If there is no difference to Him, there shouldn't be any difference to us. Why would we not take him?" Leave it to Hampy to settle the question with a simple why not when I had been thinking of so many pros and cons to discuss. His mind was settled by how he believed God felt. He just left the phone line silent, "Why not?" ringing in my ear.

"Ok, if that's how you feel, I'll tell them we'll take him," I said.

"See you tonight," he replied.

I called Catholic Charities and said we would take the baby. None of us were sure what to expect from our white friends and neighbors. We assumed we knew how God felt about race, and we wanted to obey Him, but while things had improved in Jackson, Mississippi, in the early 1970's there was still a lot of racial baggage in our southern culture. Hamp and I had not gone to school with black children as our children did. I also had no idea in what ways a black baby would be different from white babies. Yes, I actually thought there would be a difference!

THE NEXT DAY A SOCIAL WORKER BROUGHT US OUR NEW BABY. He was huge for a newborn, obviously a strong healthy child, and I awkwardly took him in my arms. I had never held a black baby before. We named him Joshua, the leader of Israel when they went into the Promised Land.

I soon discovered I had a big problem with Joshua. I couldn't cuddle or caress him. My maternal feelings were turned off and I couldn't seem to get them to turn back on. As I questioned myself, I realized I didn't really see him as an innocent baby. I saw him as the big black man he would grow into, and subconsciously I considered that threatening. In the south of my childhood, little white girls were warned not to leave their yards, or a "big nigger" would come and carry them away. If they forgot to lock the doors, they were warned again of the ominous big black man who would appear from no nowhere and snatch them away, never to see their mommies and daddies again. I knew there were big black men, I had seen them all my life, and had feared them until I was grown. I knew it was unfair and unreasonable, but oddly, the knowledge did not change my feelings. The fear was too deep to be overcome so easily. I reminded myself of the black men I had known, all of whom had been perfect gentlemen to me. All the black men I had ever had dealings with had been kind and gentle and thoughtful, but none of it helped a bit. I still couldn't see him as a sweet, innocent baby.

The next day a neighbor, who was very prejudiced, came by. She looked at Joshua in horror. "Are you crazy? A black baby right in your home? You are going to regret doing this! Think of your children. What will the neighbors say!" While her comments offended me, I found myself holding Joshua even more at arm's length.

A few days later while I was reading the newspaper, the Lord spoke to my mind so clearly I answered him out loud. He said, "Go get your Bible."

"Just a minute," I said, wanting to finish what I was reading and not really believing God was speaking to me.

"Go get your Bible, now!" He said again.

He spoke to me three times before I put down the paper, and went to the bedroom for my Bible. The Lord is so loving and patient with us when we are babies in Christ. Finally, I went to the bedroom and picked up the Living Bible Jimmy McGuire had suggested I read first—since I was a baby Christian. It opened at Matthew 18:10 and I began reading where my eyes fell.

It said, "See to it that you look down on none of these little children, for I tell you their angels constantly behold the face of the Father."

The scripture pierced my heart. I had no idea the Bible said such a thing and no idea that God would speak so clearly to someone like me. I cried as I read the words over and over. It was my first experience with such a powerful revelation. God loved this baby so much He came and pushed me to His Word to tell me how He felt about him.

My tears washed away all my fear and uncertainty, and for the first time I really knew what Jesus sees when He looks at every baby. He sees His creation, made in His image, a being of priceless worth, because he is human.

Now that I understood God's heart, I was free to obey Him no matter what anyone thought. I picked Joshua up and we looked into each other's eyes. His beautiful brown eyes gazed into mine with innocent trust. I saw a new child, a person full of promise, someone God had planned a life for, someone deserving of all the love I had. All the barriers between us vanished. He was a beautiful child, just like my own three beautiful children.

It was important to the Lord that I know exactly how He felt about His babies because I would be asked to explain the presence of a black baby in our family again and again. Almost everywhere I took a black baby, and the majority of our forty plus babies would be black boys, I would have an opportunity to share God's love for His babies. Literally hundreds of people have felt love for a person of another race for the first time through one of God's babies in our family.

John asleep with Jonathan

FOR THE NEXT SEVEN YEARS there was a steady procession of babies through our family. They were of both sexes, all colors, and they were all adopted except two who went back to their birth mothers. Some stand out in my memory with unusual clarity, like Sarah, the white baby girl whose temperament was so fiery. When she was angry about being put to bed, she ripped the sheet off the baby bed and threw it on the floor. There was Jonathan, a black boy with symptoms of a genetic disease, who had painful tests done in the hospital and came to us with his little face frozen in an expression of pain and terror. After several weeks he began to relax, all the tests turned out negative, and a smiling, happy Jonathan was adopted.

Some of the babies had very bad family backgrounds, and one little boy actually gave me my first "up close and personal" experience with demons. It was one of the most frightening experiences I have ever had. The incident was so bizarre I hesitate to relate it, but I want to be a faithful witness of what the Lord has shown us through His babies, so I will share it.

| Laura reading to Elizabeth

Another especially memorable baby's story involved one of the most miraculous answers to prayer we ever saw for a normal baby.

This time our prayers were for a tiny light skinned bi-racial girl we named Elizabeth, for the mother of John the Baptist. She came to us right out of the hospital on her way to adoption, but when she was only a few weeks old, her mother changed her mind, took her back, and gave her to neighbors. The mother didn't want the baby herself, but wanted her close enough to see her if she felt like it! We asked friends and our church to pray for Elizabeth and for several weeks we all prayed fervently for her, then we gradually gave her to the Lord.

About a month after Elizabeth left, we had taken a baby boy, who only stayed a few weeks before his adoption. The morning I was to take him to Catholic Charities to meet his new family, a social worker called to ask if I would take a little girl several months old who had unexpectedly come back into foster care. It was not the social worker we usually dealt with, so she didn't know about our prior connection, but as we talked about the baby, I realized she was describing our Elizabeth. She told me the neighbors to whom her mother had given her had severely neglected her, leaving her unfed and unchanged for hours at a time. The Lord had seen to it they thought she was dying and rushed her to the hospital. There the doctors reported them for neglect and called the birth mother, who had legal custody. I was surprised they had taken her to the hospital, knowing if she was dying it was their fault. But social workers told me abusers almost always panic and rush a child to the hospital when they think they have gone too far and the child might die. When her mother went to the hospital and saw what they had let happen to her baby, she immediately released Elizabeth to Catholic Charities for adoption, and this time she didn't change her mind.

Of course I gladly agreed to take Elizabeth back, and when I delivered the little boy to his new parents, I picked her up. She didn't look like the same child. She stared listlessly into space with her tongue protruding. She had stopped crying because no one ever came. I was told it took three baths before all the grime and filth came off at the hospital. When I changed her diaper, I saw that she was passing blood. In the 1970's sexual abuse never entered my mind. I assumed the blood was from an infection of some kind, but now I can't help wondering if that beautiful little girl was more than just neglected.

I took Elizabeth straight to the doctor, who said he thought she would be all right once she began receiving the attention, love and prayer she needed. He was right. She started crying the next day and a few days later she smiled. In just a couple of weeks, our Lizzie was her old self again.

The Lord showed His love and plans for Elizabeth again several months later when He brought her young Christian parents and a four-year-old brother they had recently adopted from South America. The family came to our house for their new daughter, rather than picking her up at the Catholic Charities office. We all felt she had been traumatized too much already, to be simply snatched from the only loving home she had ever known. We wanted her to have several visits with her new family so she would feel comfortable with them before they took her from us. I also wanted our children to feel good about the family Elizabeth was going to grow up with. They had been as shocked as Hampy and I when I brought her home the second time.

The day Lizzie's new parents were to arrive, we were all on edge. Our children had never actually seen a baby leave with new parents before. Usually they kissed a baby good-bye and left him at the Catholic Charities office, so this was a first for all of us.

That morning Laura came to me with tears in her eyes. "I think I'm going to be really sad when Lizzie leaves," she said. "I think I'm going to cry and cry. We never had a baby this long before, and I feel like she's my little sister."

We all felt the same. We had kept her the longest of any baby up to that time, and our protective feelings had been heightened by the neglectful treatment she received the first time she had left us.

Our concerns were completely unnecessary. Although Elizabeth's new parents were young and inexperienced as parents, they were totally devoted to the Lord. In fact they were on their way to the mission field. It was ideal for them to come to our house and spend time with us before they took their daughter, because they had no experience with babies. They didn't know how to play with Elizabeth, or show her affection in the ways she was used to. I showed them how to bathe and dress her, how to feed her, the position she liked to sleep in, what toys she especially liked, and all the things only a mother knows about a baby. It prepared the way for all of them to feel comfortable with each other right from the start.

The morning they were to leave, her mother and I spent some time alone, sharing our hearts as women and mothers. It was one of the sweetest times of fellowship I had ever had, and it was the first time I had been able to get to know the mother who would be raising one of our precious babies.

| Stacey with Rebecca

When Elizabeth and her new family drove out of sight on their way to their new life together, I felt not one twinge of regret or pain.

Laura smiled up at me, "I didn't even feel like crying; did you, Mommy?"

"Not at all, honey," I said. "Who could be sad to see a baby go to a family like that? Who could cry when they saw God provide so wonderfully for His child. All I felt was joy inexpressible and full of glory (I Peter 1:8)."

> *JOURNAL: Lord, thank You for giving me favor with Elizabeth's new mother by Your Spirit within me. She called twice before they left town the next day and told me Elizabeth never even cried her first night with them. I know You prepared her heart for them. I realize by their staying here for three days, I transferred her to them in my mind, so it felt only right that they take their baby when they left. Thank You, Lord. You knew what we all needed.*

Laura's birthday party attended by the baby of the hour.

After Elizabeth, the Lord continued to prepare us slowly and gently for the ministry we were to have later, and our photo albums are filled with the succession of our children's lives, pictured with whatever baby was with us at the time. Rachel kicks her little yellow shoes, as she watches Stacey address valentines for her second grade classmates. Tiny Matthew sleeps peacefully on Laura's stomach at age seven, as she lies on the couch with her sprained ankle resting on a pillow, and twelve-year-old John wrestles on his bed with Micah in their after-school ritual of play.

Pictures of birthday parties almost always feature a little black child in someone's lap, and Brownie and Girl Scout functions are remembered with pictures of little girls crowded around the one privileged to hold the current baby for the picture. Christmases are remembered with photos of babies under the tree or playing in the wrapping paper on Christmas morning with bows stuck to their heads. There is one picture of a baby sleeping on the clean clothes in the laundry basket so one of the children would have an excuse not to fold the clothes.

For the first time in our lives, we experienced and learned to deal with prejudice when store clerks turned away and pretended not to see us because we had a black baby with us, or when people saw me alone with a baby and frowned their disapproval assuming I was married to a black man, and the baby was mine. We learned how to function while being stared at by large numbers of people. That is very disconcerting. A particular diaper change for a shrieking black baby in a crowded store is forever burned into my memory. My hands shook, sweat poured down my face and my heart pounded as more and more people turned to see what the white lady was doing to the poor black baby. We learned by sheer repetition how to comfortably integrate babies into almost every social situation. We became so used to babies spitting up on our clean clothes, we just sponged it off and continued on our way. No need to change unless it was terrible, because it was sure to happen again. Diaper changes in every place and position conceivable became routine. We learned and became accustomed to more about babies than most parents ever know.

The babies colored all our lives with fun and love, and they kept the early years of our family's life full of opportunities for growth, but there was a much deeper purpose in it than we realized. We all became so adept at handling normal, healthy, babies, that when we began taking seriously ill and handicapped babies, the basics of care were second nature to us. Routine care was so effortless and automatic, that we were able to focus fully on the special needs each baby had.

In addition to the practical experience we received from the healthy babies, we also learned deep spiritual truths which would keep us going later. The first lesson I learned was that the Lord was willing to do miracles to accomplish His will, like healing my addiction to cigarettes. The second was how very precious to Him every child is. I will never forget His speaking to me directly about Joshua, the little boy for whom I could feel no love. The next lesson took longer, and is one many American Christians never learn. Serving the Lord has a price. The continual price of giving up beautiful babies to adoptive parents we didn't even know, was of course the hardest price, and one I never grew accustomed to, but there were others: sleepless nights, smelling like sour formula all the time instead of my favorite perfume, having to take the baby outside during the best part of Laura's band concert because he was frightened by the noise and was disturbing all the other parents. And we all felt the discomfort of being surveyed with cold disdain because one of our children was a different color from the rest of us.

We also learned something of how Satan works, and saw how he hates to see God's love magnified. We learned how to speak the Lord's truth when confronted with prejudice, ignorance or just simple curiosity. We learned that for whatever reason, the Lord had called us to His babies, and He would give us grace for whatever He asked of us.

Without fanfare, our years of preparation came to an end in 1979, when after parenting about thirty-five normal babies, we were asked to take a little black boy with severe brain damage. We had no idea when we took him we would never take a normal baby again. The easy, carefree days of school were over. It was time to go to work.

2
CALEB

*L*ate that summer we had a foster baby we called Noah. Our good friend and Catholic Charities social worker, Pat Beasley, called to ask us to pray for a little black boy who had been born with part of his brain caught outside his cranium.

"It's called an encephalocele," she said, "and it means he will be a vegetable and probably die within a few months."

Am I ever glad I already have a baby, I thought to myself. I told Pat we would pray for him (and thank God she didn't want us to take him).

Three weeks later, Noah had been placed for adoption when Pat called again.

"Do you remember the baby with the encephalocele?" she asked.

"Yeah," I said, my heart sinking.

"Well, do you think you could take him for just 6 weeks until we find an institution that will accept him?"

"Oh, Pat," I said, "I don't think we could handle a baby like that! I would be scared to death!"

"He really doesn't need anything special," she said. Then, to prove it, she described him. I was horrified to hear while he was big for his age, he would be limp, dead weight, both his parents were well over six feet tall. He was blind, deaf, had no reflexes, and responded to nothing. The only thing he could do was suck from a bottle.

"Well, I guess we could pray about him," I said reluctantly. I mean, how could I leave God out, even if I wanted to. We had seen God's hand often enough with other babies to be open to His will, but this baby sounded so frightening. In addition to our fear of trying to deal with a severely handicapped baby, we were concerned for our children. How would they feel about a baby who couldn't respond to them? Could they handle the fact that God had allowed an innocent child to be born so horribly deformed—could I?

How would it affect their faith to love a baby who couldn't do any of the things babies are supposed to do? This child would call into question all the happy things they knew about Jesus. What could I say about a baby who couldn't see the pretty mobile over his bed, or reach out to feel a teddy bear? Would they think Jesus didn't love this child to cause him to have such a body? Would it destroy their image of a loving Father God?

Because we were so totally unprepared doctrinally and intellectually for all the problems and questions which were sure to come, we all fell back on what the Lord had taught us with baby David. In uncharted waters, apply the Word and pray. We knew Jesus loved the baby, "Whoever gives a cup of water to one such little one..." (Matthew 10:42), and we knew he loved us (Romans 8:1). "There is therefore now no condemnation for those who are in Christ Jesus, who do not walk according to the flesh, but according to the Spirit." We also knew He wouldn't turn a child away. "Suffer the little children and forbid them not, for of such is the kingdom of Heaven," (Mark 10:14), and "When my father and mother forsake me, then the Lord will take me up," (Psalm 27:10). The Bible does not say to obey only if you are not afraid.

When we felt sure the Lord wanted us at least to be willing to try with this baby, I called Pat. "If we don't like him, we can bring him back, right?" I said, trying to sound casual.

"Sure," she said. "You just give the word, and I will come get him." It helped a lot to know she saw right through me and was willing to pretend to be cheerful with me.

Then she said, "You need to give him a name today, his mother has not named him." Without thinking I said, "Caleb." Then I realized it was the perfect name for him. Caleb had believed God when He told him the land was his, but he had to wait a lifetime to receive it (Joshua 14:6-11). This little boy might have to wait a lifetime for his blessing too. As the application of the name sank in, I knew the Lord had given me the name. We were to believe in God's loving mercy that one day Caleb would receive his healing from the Lord. Whether the answer would come in this life or the life to come, we had no way of knowing. Caleb in the Bible had to wait a whole lifetime to receive his inheritance because of the unbelief of others, and I worried that my lack of faith might withhold this baby's healing.

THE NEXT DAY I WENT TO CATHOLIC CHARITIES TO PICK CALEB UP. He was sleeping on his side in a bassinet. He looked like he had two noses, one on top of the other.

My breath seemed to catch in my throat. "Oh, Pat, I don't know if I can handle this," I whispered. Pat, almost always upbeat, came over and stood looking at him with me.

"I'm not doing too well with it myself," she said. "But if anybody can deal with this child, it's you and Hamp. Please, if you can, take him home and see what the Lord will do. If you see after a day or so your family just can't keep him, I'll come and get him."

Reassured I wasn't trapped, I put the strange looking little thing in the car and headed home. As I looked at him peacefully sleeping in the infant seat, I realized Caleb was just a little boy with a bump over his nose. Whatever problems he had, he was still a little boy who needed a mother and daddy, love and security, like every other little boy. By the time we got home, I was completely comfortable with Caleb and his bump.

When the children came home from school, I was standing in the yard holding Caleb and talking to a neighbor. Laura ran up to see the new baby. "Oh, poor baby!" she said, stroking his head, "He's so sweet." She wasn't put off by the bump at all. John wandered over, looked at Caleb's face, shrugged his shoulders and went into the house. Years later he said he didn't know how to show his shock and concern without upsetting me.

For the next six weeks I kept a list of things we saw wrong with Caleb. He had no startle reflex, or any other kind of reflexes. He did not react to being put on a cold counter with no clothes on, did not react with fear to being rolled gently back and forth on a hard surface, and his pupils were unequal, one being constricted and one dilated. Sometimes his eyes looked as if they were rolling free in his head—one turning down and the other looking up. Sometimes it hurt my eyes just to watch him. Once in a while his eyes looked in the same direction and I thought he could see, then he stared blindly through an object in front of him and I knew he couldn't.

I took him to the pediatric neurologist who had seen him at birth and my list confirmed her diagnosis, but I was shocked when she announced bluntly his brain was overgrowing his cranium and he would be dead in a matter of weeks! She decided he would make a good lesson for a group of medical students and ordered them all into a closet with us so they could observe his brain just about to start pushing on his cranium as she held a flashlight against his head. Tears rolled down my face as I stood in the dark holding my baby. He seemed so healthy. I had not dreamed he was in such imminet danger. She held the light against his curls. "Well, look at that! His brain looks normal. It was nowhere near his cranium. She was obviously disgruntled he had spoiled her lesson. "Maybe he won't die so soon after all," she said, snapping off her flashlight and jamming it into her pocket. The doctor was very offended with Caleb for making her look bad, and assured me there had been three babies born within one week at this hospital with the same defect and the other two had already died. The medical students were delighted though, and many of them touched and patted him as they filed out of the closet.

As the weeks passed and my love for him grew, it began to upset me I didn't know how to get God to heal Caleb. I was so young in the Lord. I had heard teaching on claiming certain scriptures and somehow conjuring up enough faith to make the Lord give you what you wanted. But in my heart I knew God was sovereign and had a plan for Caleb that might not include physical healing. I felt totally inadequate, the worst mother he could have gotten for the problems he had. He needed a spiritual giant who could march into the throne room and say the right things to God on his behalf, but I was far from that and I knew it. After much reading and praying, I had to accept the fact I could do nothing for this baby, but pray and trust God.

> *JOURNAL: Lord, please help me find Your will with Caleb. To glorify You in his unwholeness is hard. I know Exodus 4:11 says "'Who has made man's mouth? Or who makes him dumb or deaf, or seeing or blind? Is it not I, the Lord?'" But I can't believe it is Your perfect will for him to be this way. It has to hurt You to see him this way, as it does me. Lord, I feel like a little girl with a broken doll who only knows how to bring it to her Daddy and ask him to fix it. I don't know how to get the faith to believe enough to make it happen, but I know You, and I know You can have mercy on this baby and heal him. Please, Father, make him like other little boys. It hurts me so much to see him like this, Lord. Just fix him because You love him, please!*

Of course as soon as we got Caleb, we had asked the elders to pray for him and anoint him with oil. In fact, the whole church took on our concern for him, and every Sunday at least one person came over to put a hand on him and pray for healing and blessing for him.

EARLY IN NOVEMBER I NOTICED SIGNS OF SCOLIOSIS IN STACEY'S spine, but the pediatrician couldn't see her until the day before Thanksgiving. The morning of her appointment I was doing a few things ahead for Thanksgiving dinner, when I picked up a baking sheet from the stove top, not realizing the element beneath it was on. The hot metal seared into my hand. My whole left hand was so badly burned I could only tolerate the pain if I held ice in my hand, and unfortunately I am left handed. I drenched it in vitamin E oil, but the hand was useless. I couldn't even move my swollen fingers. Stacey had to dress herself, Caleb and me for her doctor's appointment. At the doctor's office I got a surgical glove full of ice for my hand, to replace my zip lock bag, and a confirmed diagnosis of scoliosis for Stacey. The rest of the day was pretty bleak as I pondered the cost and discomfort of a curved spine for my daughter, and fretted with frustration over my inability to even change Caleb's diaper, much less cook dinner for my family on Thanksgiving.

I planned to wake Hamp during the night to feed Caleb and change him, but when the baby woke me at three a.m., I was surprised to find I could use my hand. At least I could close my fingers enough to take care of him myself. By the next morning, the vitamin E had done its work and I could actually cook with a lot of help from the girls, as long as I kept that hand away from the heat. I was burned so badly the skin broke open and bled a few days later.

As it turned out, Thanksgiving was the day for a miracle. Late in the morning I was in the kitchen cooking, when Hamp called me to come and look at Caleb. As I walked toward him, I saw with amazement that Caleb was watching me approach—with both eyes.

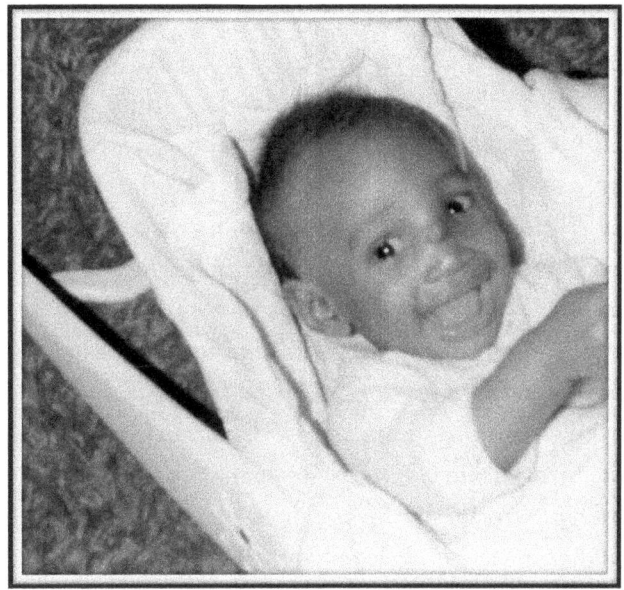

| Caleb shortly after he was healed.

"He can see, Sweet! He can see!" he said. "I noticed he seemed to be watching me, so I moved and his eyes followed me." Hampy was ecstatic. "On Thanksgiving Day too, what a wonderful Thanksgiving," he said. Caleb's eyes had come together and were working. We moved things in front of him and he watched every movement. Within two weeks his pupils were equal and they stayed equal, also within two weeks every other symptom of brain damage was gone. Caleb was totally healed. We had a normal baby on our hands, and he was a handful. From Thanksgiving Day on, he grew and developed at a phenomenal rate. Within three months he was *ahead* of his chronological age in development.

> *JOURNAL: November 30, 1979, Thank you again for healing Caleb, Lord. He watches us, he kicks and waves his arms to make the mobile move; he gurgles and smiles to get our attention. He is so beautiful and precious. Lord, please remove the bump and make the miracle complete. Every problem he had is gone except the bump. He wasn't supposed to even have a cortex, but a CAT scan, a month after his healing, revealed a complete brain, with a little flat area on the very front. It's almost as if You put Your finger on his brain and pushed it back into place. I praise You, Father, for Your love and mercy to this little one of Yours. I said if You would make him whole, I would tell everyone I could get to listen, and I have tried to do that. About eight people gathered around us today when I began telling someone in a store how You had healed Caleb. Lord, I ask you in Jesus's name, not to let Satan deceive me about this miracle. Burn into my memory how his eyes went in different directions, his left eye turning back until you could only see white. Make me remember all the rest of the symptoms he no longer has. Lord, let me always be able to see him as he was before, when I witness about Your power.*

Deuteronomy 4:9 says, "Only give heed to yourself and keep your soul diligently, lest you forget the things which your eyes have seen, lest they depart from your heart all the days of your life, but make them known to your sons and your grandsons."

As strange as it seems, I had to keep reminding myself Caleb had ever been handicapped. But I did remind myself, and the Lord reminded me and convicted me about keeping his healing ever before me and telling everyone who wanted to hear. I told people in grocery stores, department stores, Brownie meetings…everywhere I took Caleb. I tried to always be ready to tell people what God had done for him. "But sanctify Christ as Lord in your hearts, always being ready to make a defense to everyone who asks you to give an account of the hope that is in you..." (I Peter 3:15). Originally, I had prayed for the Lord to take away the bump, but I finally realized if He had removed it, I would have had fewer opportunities to tell people what the Lord had done for him. The bump called people's attention to the fact that Caleb had a birth defect. Then I could tell them about the defects he no longer had.

The Lord opened all kinds of doors for me to tell people about Caleb, and it eased me into witnessing to strangers. I didn't know then how many people would hear about God's love through His babies, and the miracles we would be privileged to see firsthand because of that love.

Before I leave the incident of Caleb's healing, I should say one more thing about my burned hand. It was the first experience we noticed of being attacked by Satan when we were about to see or receive something wonderful from the Lord. Over and over we saw sickness, financial loss, problems with the children, etc. happen before or right after a victory with the Lord. Apparently when Satan can't prevent a blessing, he tries to rob you of as much joy in it as he can. When this became a predictable pattern, we began to pray ahead of time for protection from the attacks and they eventually stopped. Once again I found that when we realized what Satan was doing, he stopped. He is truly the "father of lies" (I John 8:44).

SOMETIMES THE LORD WOULD UNEXPECTEDLY SHOW ME WHAT OUR own children were learning by the presence of God's babies in our home. One day I teasingly complained to John about all of Caleb's clutter and toys. "But Mother," he said, "we are supposed to put ourselves last and everybody else first."

"Well, that gets hard to do. Sometimes I feel like not keeping babies anymore," I said, baiting him a little. John said he guessed he would just have to move to an apartment and keep babies by himself if I decided to quit. He was ten at the time. We had put Caleb's bed in John's room when he started sleeping though the night, and I asked John if he put up with all the baby stuff in his room because of Jesus.

He smiled and said, "I guess."

As he grew, Caleb grinned and bounced his way into the hearts of everyone he met. At the grocery store white people would try to pass him by with a cold stare at us both, sure I was married to a black man. But their quick glance at Caleb's face as he sat in the infant seat was their downfall. Instantly his face would break into a big smile. His sparkling eyes and trusting look melted them every time. "Oh, well, aren't you cute? You really are a cute little boy," they would say, trying unsuccessfully to break away from his magnetic grin. Usually they were still talking to him when I stepped back to the grocery cart. Then it was time to explain who he was and how God had healed him. Time and again, people walked away from Caleb smiling, blessed by the love and mercy of God.

SEVERAL MONTHS AFTER GOD HAD HEALED HIM, CALEB'S BIRTH parents asked to see him before they decided whether to surrender him for adoption. I was devastated. "Pat, if they see this adorable child, there is no way they will let him be adopted!" I said. The mother was fourteen and the father a grown man in his late twenties. We knew he took drugs and how good the government check for Caleb every month would look to him. I fully expected his father to fight for custody so he could get Caleb's money.

"I'll send him filthy dirty and I won't feed him, and I won't let him sleep well so he will be fussy, and I'll put old clothes on him and he will be so unappealing they won't want him," I said to Hamp, frantic to protect his prospects for a happy, Christian adoptive home.

Then the Lord spoke to my heart: "Don't you dare cover up what I have done for him. You said you would always witness to what I have done for him. Now do it!"

With fear and trembling, I obeyed. I sent Caleb in his cutest clothes, well fed and clean. He looked beautiful. Sending him off that day was one of the hardest things I had ever done. I prayed fervently that somehow God would make a poor drug addict who had gotten a fourteen-year- old girl pregnant, turn down easy money and sign over his little meal ticket to be adopted. I knew in the natural (apart from God) there was no reason for him to do it.

To keep my mind off Caleb's visit with his parents, I went shopping with my friend, Sue Bruck. She and I prayed for God's protection and His perfect will for Caleb, and then I resolved to try not to think about it. Just thinking of their taking Caleb made me want to take him and run.

That afternoon Pat brought Caleb back to us with a big smile on her face. "You are not going to believe this," she said. "Well, yes, you will. God answered our prayers. When I told his parents there were people who would adopt him, Caleb's father looked at him and said, 'If he has a chance for a better life, I want him to have it. Let him be adopted.' The mother, influenced by his father also agreed and they both signed papers freeing Caleb for adoption that very day. The thing I had feared would cost Caleb his bright future, actually opened the way for him to be adopted.

I still get tears in my eyes sometimes when I think of Caleb's father. He was involved in drugs, had gotten a fourteen-year-old girl pregnant, was uneducated, probably neglected and uncared for from his earliest childhood, denied everything that should go into making a boy a man. But when he was faced with the decision of giving his little son a stable and loving home, or keeping him as a source of money for himself, he reached somewhere inside himself and found the love to give his child a future.

Caleb's father, who I never met, gave me hope for the whole human race. I know now I can never be sure someone is as bad as they seem; I can never be sure God is not working in them on some level.

Once he was freed for adoption, things moved rapidly for Caleb, and when he was seven months old, news came that a family in Oregon wanted to adopt him. I had known this was coming, but when it actually happened, I was crushed. With tears streaming down my face, I took Caleb to the porch swing, where I could be alone with him. This became a ritual with each baby when the word came their days with us were numbered.

| Caleb trying hard to master the piano by watching Stacey.

I sat in the swing holding Caleb tightly and crying. He looked up at me, puzzled. He had never seen me cry. I began to pray that somehow Jesus would communicate with his little spirit and help him understand how I could love him so much and still give him to strangers. Strangers... who were these people? Would they really love him as we did? Would they be able to deal with the deformity of his face as he grew? In their desire to see him normal would they insist on surgery our neurologist had said would be too dangerous? Oh, God, I thought, show me something, give me something to hold on to. I felt as if I had to throw my precious baby into a black hole and never know what happened to him.

My fears were soon quieted on the issue of the family when a letter arrived from Caleb's new mother, Suzy Walker. She wrote they were thanking God for their new son and were going to name him Benjamin Caleb. She sent a picture of the whole family. There were eleven children, all but three adopted. Suzy and Gary Walker's smiles beamed hope and joy to my heart as I pictured Caleb in their care. I was especially blessed they were going to keep Caleb as part of his name since it had such spiritual significance for him.

As the plans progressed for Caleb's adoption, I had two prayers. The first was that the Lord would prepare Caleb's heart to quickly love his new family. The second was that Gary and Suzy somehow would be able to leave their eleven children and come to Mississippi to get Caleb, which of course was ridiculous. If they could not come to us a social worker, or Hamp and I, would have to take him to Oregon. A social worker taking Caleb was out. I could not send my baby across the country with a stranger only to be given to more strangers at the end of the trip. One the other hand, I had never left my children for any reason, and I was not ready to start now. In the end, Hamp and I had no choice but to take him to them. I was terrified the plane would crash and our children would be left orphans.

Added to the fear of leaving my children, was my concern for the pain of separation and feeling of betrayal I knew Caleb would feel when we left him with his new family. I knew too, the pain my own children would suffer in losing the first baby who had become like a real little brother to them. This was especially true for John. He and Caleb had been sharing a room for several months, and there was always laughing and squealing and bumping coming from their room. Caleb would run up and down the baby bed laughing and throwing toys out at John, and in the mornings John woke to see Caleb grinning at him through the bars of the crib. I knew how lonely John would be when Caleb was gone. One night as we were putting Caleb to bed, John looked up at me with tears in his eyes. "I don't want Caleb to go, Mother," he said.

"I don't want him to go either, John," I said, putting my arms around him. We sat down and cried with our arms around each other, as Caleb stood in his bed solemnly watching. When I looked at him I felt even worse. He had no idea he was about to go and live with people he didn't know existed. He thought he was our baby and would be with us forever. He thought he was at home. It broke my heart to know there was no way on earth to make him understand. My mind knew I would have to walk away and leave him in another woman's arms, probably never to see him again, but my heart couldn't grasp it. It was too painful to be possible.

I SPENT A SAD, ANXIOUS AND PRAYERFUL FINAL TWO WEEKS BEFORE Hamp and I flew Caleb to his new family. I still had no idea how things would resolve themselves. I prayed for the grace and strength to do what I knew I had to do for Caleb, and at the same time tried to comfort myself and the children with the truly wonderful knowledge that the new family were strong Christians. Hamp, as usual, took everything in stride.

Three days before we were to leave for Oregon, I had to take Stacey back to the Orthopedic Surgeon we had seen in November for her scoliosis. The doctor had told me then her spine would surely be curved enough by now for her to need a brace. Business had not been good that year, and I barely had enough money to pay the doctor, much less several hundred dollars more for a brace.

"We aren't going to need a brace," Hamp said every time I tried to discuss it. "The Lord is going to heal her."

"What makes you so sure of that?" I would ask, irritated by his simplistic attitude.

"I don't know," he would say. "I just know He is going to heal Stacey's back."

"Don't you think we should have the elders pray for Stacey's back?" I asked Sunday after Sunday in church.

"No, it's already done." he would say very matter-of-factly.

Sure, I thought, "it's easy for you to believe; you didn't see her spine curving across the X-ray.

I was so tense and anxious about flying to Oregon, leaving my children and losing Caleb that I would have waited until we returned from our trip to take Stacey to the doctor if it wouldn't have taken so long to reschedule her appointment. The appointment had been made for months, and I was afraid to wait too long before I took her back. The doctor had assured me her spine would continue to curve until it was braced.

"Now you understand, Mrs. Singleton," he had said, "Stacey's back will never be straight again. Her spine will be curved for the rest of her life wherever we stop it with a brace." He had made it abundantly clear. Her spine was permanently curved.

At the doctor's office, they X-rayed Stacey's back then put us in an examining room. As the technician left the room, he put the new X-rays on the table. Stacey and I both leaned over to see how bad her back had gotten. Don't ever believe a lack of faith stops God. It may hinder the work of the Holy Spirit in certain circumstances, but the disbelief in that room could have been cut with a knife. Stacey wasn't looking forward to the brace, but since one of her close friends already had one, she knew it wasn't the end of the world either. My unbelief came from the assumption that God only moved in monumental circumstances. I thought He had healed Caleb because man could do nothing for him. Stacey's back was different. Man couldn't straighten it, but he could stop it where it was and keep it from crippling her. So, Stacey and I both stared at the X-ray in utter disbelief. "Mama!" Stacey almost screamed. "God has healed my back!" There on the X-ray was a perfectly straight spine. There was not a hint of a curve.

When the doctor came in, we sat quietly watching him examine the X-ray. He took out his little measuring instrument and turned it one way and then another. Finally he turned to us and said, "I can find absolutely no curve in this spine. I want to know what you have been doing."

"Praying." was my one-word reply.

"Well, you can't argue with success," he said. Then he climbed up on the examining table and began to discuss the benefits of a positive mental attitude, laughter, etc. on a person's health. I told him his point was scriptural, the Bible does say, "A merry heart does good like a medicine," (Proverbs 17:22). But I knew it wasn't anyone's attitude that had healed Stacey's back. God had done it for Stacey and for me as well.

As we excitedly related the good news to John and Laura, who had been in the waiting room with Caleb, I realized I was no longer afraid to leave my children and fly to Oregon. I knew in my spirit the Lord had healed Stacey to show us He was there. He knew what we needed and we could trust ourselves totally to His care. I was positive if every plane fell from the sky the day we flew to Oregon, the plane we were in would stay its course. There was no possibility of danger to any of us in connection to this trip. I knew it with all my heart, mind and spirit.

Pat Beasley stayed with our children, Catholic Charities made all the arrangements for our flight and everything was taken care of with minimal effort on my part. By the time I got on the plane, I had no worries or fears except a mild apprehension about the moment I would have to actually give Caleb to another mother.

Caleb enjoyed his first plane ride immensely. He stood on Hamp's lap and banged on the window, grinned at the passengers around us and finally went to sleep in the empty seat next to mine. He pushed his stroller around the airport in San Francisco, screamed to the airplanes going past the window and was too excited to eat his lunch while we waited for our connecting flight.

Hamp holding Caleb and his adoptive brother, Christopher, at Susie & Gary Walker's house when we took Micah to Oregon to his new family.

There were four take-offs and landings between Jackson, Mississippi, and Medford, Oregon, and by the time we arrived in Medford late in the afternoon, I felt ill from all the ups and downs. We gave the Walkers some concern by being the last people off the plane, but I felt too sick to move any faster. Never having flown so far before, I didn't know how sick landing in an airplane could make me. We arrived at their home before I felt like talking.

Gary and Suzy Walker had the largest and most diverse family I had ever seen. They had children from Korea, Mexico, Vietnam, bi-racial children, black children and white children.

We instantly recognized them as a true brother and sister in the Lord, and we all understood each other in the Spirit without any explanations.

I had dreaded the moment I would be faced with Caleb's new mother, fearing she would snatch her new son from my arms before I was ready to let him go. But Suzy understood my love for Caleb and never even held him until that night. Her children held him and played with him, but she never reached for him. She knew how hard the situation must be for me and was in no hurry to make me relinquish my place as his mother. Not feeling threatened helped me relax and by bedtime I was ready to urge her to take him.

Suzy and Gary had a biological daughter eight months old, exactly the same age as Caleb, named Carolyn. She and Caleb took to each other instantly. They were like black and white twins. She crawled around the house ahead of him, looking back invitingly as if she knew she was showing him his new home.

Soon we heard screaming and laughter coming from one of the bedrooms and went to investigate. There in one baby bed stood the two babies, bouncing and squealing at the top of their lungs as the older children stood around the bed laughing. Caleb looked as happy and at home as a child could be, and he had been there less than an hour.

That night we spent the evening with the Walkers and had much to share about the Lord. Suzy told us she had felt she would have twins when Carolyn was born. Now she believed she had been receiving Caleb in her spirit. She also said she had wished she could somehow have a black baby for their black adopted daughter, Tracey, who was having a hard time adjusting to her adoption by white parents. I was amazed by the way the Lord had fashioned Caleb for his new family and them for him.

We also talked about the names Caleb and Benjamin. Suzy and

I each felt the Lord had given us the name we gave him. I was just happy they were going to keep Caleb as his middle name, but Suzy was determined to know why the Lord had given us two different names. She was older in the Lord than I and she sensed there was significance in both names.

It had been decided we would take Caleb and spend the night with friends of the Walkers, Jim and Kathy Pearson, as there was no room for us in the Walker house. We would take Caleb back to the Walkers the next morning and leave him for a day and night so they could get acquainted without us there. We would come back the following day for one last visit before leaving for home. To keep us busy, Jim and Kathy insisted we borrow their car and drive down the coast to California. We could spend the night in Crescent City and drive back the next day for our last visit with Caleb. So we left Caleb playing happily with his new brothers and sisters and embarked on our unexpected pleasure trip.

The scenery of southern Oregon and northern California took my breath away. A Mississippi girl, I had never seen real mountains before. It seemed the Lord laughed in my spirit and said, "If you think these are something, you should see my Himalayas."

Hamp commented several times during the trip that he was acutely aware of his sins. "I can't stop repenting of things," he said. "Sins I wasn't even aware of are coming to my mind and I have an urge to be clean from them." It seemed bringing Caleb to his new family was the culmination of a warfare and now that it was accomplished, we felt literally in the presence of the Lord. The sense of God's power was overwhelming. Our minds and hearts were filled with an awareness of His presence I never knew was possible. It was like being in the eye of a hurricane. I knew the world was full of strife and trouble, but I couldn't feel it. I knew pain awaited me when I had to leave Caleb the next day, but I couldn't feel it. Where I was, there was only the Lord and His peace.

It was years before we appreciated the significance of this experience, but the passage of time confirmed the gift of prophesy (speaking forth God's truth) in Hamp. One of the signs of that gift is the strong sense of the person's own sin as he speaks God's word about a problem or sin. That is why the presence of God brought conviction of sin in him. The more of God's light he stood in, the more he saw it shining into his own heart, revealing sin. For me, the presence of the Lord manifested itself in total peace. I could totally rest in Him if only I would.

When it was time to go back to see Caleb for the last time, a feeling of panic came over me. My bond with him was so strong I didn't know if I could really leave him, even with people like Suzy and Gary. I had been his mother for eight months. He thought he was my little boy. I knew it had never entered his mind that I would leave him there. How could I just turn my back and walk away? The very thought of it made me cry as we drove back to their house.

As I got out of the car, I prayed, "Lord, please don't let him cry when he sees me. I don't think I can leave him here if he does."

We found Caleb sitting in the highchair eating a cookie. When he saw me, he looked up, smiled at me and went on munching his cookie, as if he hadn't noticed we were gone. He seemed to have a sense that he belonged here. Suzy was smiling too. "I know about the names," she said, "God gave you the name Caleb to believe for him to receive his blessing of healing. He gave me Benjamin because it means beloved son. Both names fit perfectly for the time he had them. When his time as Caleb was over and it was time to begin his life as our beloved son, God changed his name." And prepared his heart too, I thought, watching him reach for another cookie. It was scriptural and it had happened, but I was in awe that the Lord would go to so much trouble for one little boy and one grieving mother.

We tried to visit with Suzy and Gary for a while, but I couldn't enjoy conversation knowing in a little while I would have to leave without Caleb. Finally, it was time to go. I kissed Caleb and handed him to Suzy. I thought it was a poor witness of my trust in Jesus, but I couldn't control my tears. When I left the room to try to regain my composure, Caleb's new black sister Tracey, followed, watching me closely. "What's the matter?" she asked.

"I just love him so much, it's really hard for me to leave him," I said, trying to wipe the constant flow of tears from my face." Later I found out she had not been able to trust white people in the past. Her need to see my grief was more important to the Lord than my desire not to cry. She needed to see how much I loved Caleb.

> JOURNAL: Lord, thank You for showing me how important it is to be honest with my feelings. My spiritual pride made me want to look strong and in control before the Walkers. I had no way of knowing that someone might be blessed to see me cry. Help me to be sensitive to the needs of other people and open to Your place for me in them.

In the car I cried even harder as I thought about going farther and farther from Caleb. I had never made myself do anything so hard. At the same time, I was really disappointed in myself. I thought I should have been able to love Caleb with Jesus's love and not have my own fleshly love get in the way. I was still such a baby in the Lord. It was foolish to think a mother could spend eight months rocking a child to sleep, feeding, bathing, comforting him, being a mother in every way but birth and not grow to love him the way every mother loves her baby. Then the Lord spoke a strange sentence to my heart. He said, "This is a holy hurt." Then I knew He was not disappointed in me at all. The words "holy hurt" sounded awkward. I knew I would have said "godly hurt or holy pain." I knew He had put it into words I wouldn't use to assure me it was He and not an idea of my own. The idea my pain was not a sign of spiritual immaturity and fleshliness was so far removed from my thinking, I would never have thought of it.

The idea of a "holy hurt" was a new thing for me. I didn't know yet the reality of sacrificing oneself daily (Matthew 16:24) or losing one's life to find it (Matthew 16:25). I only knew a new truth: it is all right for your service to the Lord to be painful. It is all right to cry and even grieve for a loss you know is God's will. My pain was holy to the Lord because it was the result of my obedience to Him. I didn't know it then, but I would face this particular pain over and over and in much greater proportions than this. God's work for me was going to be incredibly joyful and incredibly painful, and I needed to know that pain, sorrow and a sense of loss were nothing foreign to those who serve the Lord, and I must not be deterred by them. This was a lesson God Himself had to show me. The charismatic movement was in full swing, and the idea of suffering as a Christian for any reason, was totally unacceptable to many of my Christian peers. Most of them believed Christians were supposed to be happy, healthy, and materially blessed until all fleshly needs and desires were met.

BACK AT HOME, WE FOUND TO OUR SURPRISE WE DIDN'T GRIEVE AND feel sad about Caleb. We missed him, and when I looked at his picture on the refrigerator, tears came into my eyes and a few times I sniffled for a minute or two, but the heart-rending pain and sense of loss I had felt the day we left never came back to me and never came at all to the children—not even John. I began to understand a little better about the Paraclyte, the comforting Holy Spirit. I had known He would hold my hand while I cried, but I hadn't dared to hope He would take the pain away.

Life went on and Caleb became a bright spot in our memories. We talked about him and laughed about things he had done, but we knew he was happy with the Walkers and was exactly where the Lord wanted him.

> JOURNAL: Lord, I praise You for all the ways You met my needs for Caleb's adoption. The most precious part, Lord, is that I am old enough in You to have had to go through it without Your healing Stacey and working everything out for the children to be cared for while we were gone, without Your giving Caleb such an open heart for his new family. Lord, You did so much to show Yourself in the whole placement, I still can't believe You would do all that for us. You were so wonderful to come and meet me when I was afraid to go on the plane, to heal Stacey to show me You were right with us and knew our every need.

We talked to Gary and Suzy several times on the phone that year and when Caleb had surgery to remove the "bump" there was a flurry of calls back and forth as we prayed together during the surgery for the skill of the several doctors involved in the surgery and comfort for Caleb.

During one of these calls Suzy related an interesting story about Caleb's eyes. She said when the doctors examined him to evaluate the feasibility of surgically removing the bump, they found his eyes to be out of line and said it was affecting his sight. They said they would have to take his right eye out and reset it to make it even with the left to correct his vision. When they tested his vision to see how bad the problem was, it was perfect. The doctors frowned and ran the test again, saying they must have done something wrong. He couldn't possibly see that well. Again Caleb's eyes worked together perfectly. Suzy said Gary explained that Caleb's eyes had been healed by the Lord, which must explain why they worked even though they were out of alignment. When he heard the story, Hamp said, "I guess if he had one eye in the front of his head and one in the back, if God had healed them, they would work together!"

The surgery lasted thirteen hours, but when it was done, Caleb had no bump, no scar and no ill effects from the surgery. No one seeing him today would ever guess he was born with a devastating birth defect. He is a happy, healthy, boy now, enjoying the life I once only dreamed of for him.

The bond formed with Suzy and Gary is eternal, as only brothers and sisters in Christ can have, likewise Jim and Kathy Pearson. Never expecting to see any of them again, we looked forward to the time in heaven when we could fully share all of the fullness of God together. We never dreamed five years later we would take another little boy to another family in Oregon and get to spend the night with both families. We would get to see all the children five years later and have wonderful fellowship with our brothers and sisters in Christ.

| Caleb growing with no hump!

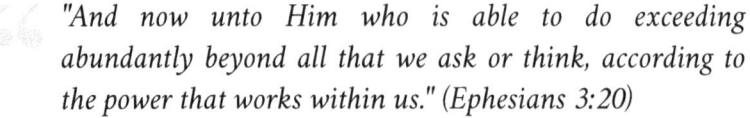

"And now unto Him who is able to do exceeding abundantly beyond all that we ask or think, according to the power that works within us." (Ephesians 3:20)

3
MATTHEW

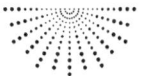

After Caleb went home to Suzy and Gary in Oregon, Hamp and I believed the Lord was calling us to a distinct ministry to His especially needy children. We felt that was confirmed at the end of summer when the next baby we were called about was sick. While we didn't know God's plans for this baby's life, we were convinced he would be a blessing to those who knew him, so we named him Matthew, which means gift from God.

Like Caleb, Matthew was brain damaged, but his symptoms were very different. Matthew had been born at twenty-six weeks, an age when children are routinely aborted and was diagnosed as deaf, blind, spastic and severely disabled intellectually—in other words, "a vegetable." He was eight months old and weighed just six pounds, nine ounces. The doctors said his size was due to failure-to-thrive syndrome, which meant he had no desire for food, and what food he did eat, didn't seem to nourish him. He could suck and swallow, but not in the coordinated manner necessary to nurse or drink from a bottle. He could only be fed with a dropper or a spoon. After a lengthy stay in the hospital following his birth, the hospital had tried to send Matthew home with first one relative, then another, but each time he was returned to the hospital in a critical state of malnutrition and dehydration. Twice he had stopped breathing and had to be resuscitated. It was obvious his family would not be able to meet his needs. He needed a foster home that would give him much more than routine care.

It was good I didn't understand the level of care Matthew would need at the beginning. If I had known, I might not have had the courage to take him. As it was when the time drew near for him to come home to us, I began to worry about the things I did understand. I knew it was a real possibility for this child to die while he was with us. What if he died and I was blamed? What if the children saw him die or found him dead and were traumatized? What if he was so demanding I couldn't take care of my own family? What if...what if...what if...Satan had an endless supply of fears. But God already "knew our frame was dust" (Psalm 103:14), and He knew one miracle baby like Caleb was only the first step on our long journey of faith.

Because He knew I was afraid, in spite of the fact that I felt called to care for Matthew, the Lord strengthened and encouraged me several times before Matthew came home. The day before I was to pick him up at the hospital, our pastor preached on Isaiah 53, which speaks of Jesus being despised and forsaken, a man of sorrows, who suffered affliction, and as I read the passage I realized God knew all about Matthew's problems and needs, and had even been similar to him for our sakes. He had entered into the bondage of a human body, which must have

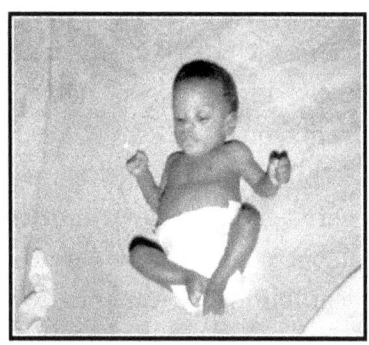

Matthew lay in this position for a year after we got him.

been as confining to Him, as being deaf, blind and spastic were to Matthew.

The next morning as I prepared to pick him up from the hospital, the news on television was reporting on the famine in Africa. As I looked at all the sick, dying children, I thought, Oh, God, what can we do, what can we do, Your poor little children? Immediately the Lord answered in my mind, "I am only asking you to take one." Then I realized there was a tiny, sick little boy just as needy as those in Africa right here, waiting for me to come and bring him home. It gave me tremendous peace to think that out of the vastness of the world's need, God had singled out one starving little child for me to care for. Surely, I thought, I can take care of *one*.

Just before I turned off the television to leave for the hospital, another news segment featured Helen Keller, and I realized if God had not sent someone to give her a chance to demonstrate her potential, she would have spent her entire life in an institution.

When I discovered how fragile Matthew really was, I was thankful the Lord's confirmations had been so strong and clear. Having the confirmations written in my journal kept me from being sure we couldn't possibly care for him.

WHEN I ARRIVED AT THE HOSPITAL, I DISCOVERED MATTHEW LOOKED exactly like the children on the news. He seemed to be no more than dry, leathery skin stretched over some little bones. His head was shaped in the telltale shape of a preemie, flat on the sides. His tiny face was so thin and his eyes so big, he looked like a little fly. His eyes stared unseeing, his arms were flexed at the elbows, hands tightly fisted, his legs were drawn up to his stomach. He was the ugliest baby I had ever seen.

The hospital staff stared at me with such curiosity and concern that only my years of being stared at with black babies kept me from being too self-conscious to think. Some of them seemed surprised a white lady was going to take a severely handicapped black child home with her and wondered why I would do it. Others were afraid I didn't know what I was getting into and I wouldn't be able to handle him. Because eating was so critical for Matthew, the nurses wanted me to feed him before I took him home, to be sure I could do it. When I agreed, they brought me a dish of scrambled eggs and a big soup spoon from the hospital cafeteria.

"My goodness, don't you have a baby spoon?" I asked. No, this was all they had. I quickly saw a "big" part of Matthew's feeding problem. He had a tiny, bird-like mouth, just big enough for the tip of the spoon. He had to try to suck the eggs off and work them to the back of his throat and then swallow. It was too much trouble for someone who wasn't hungry any way. I remembered what Bob Thompson, our pediatrician, had often told me when I was having trouble with a baby. Look for a simple solution first. "Most unhappy babies don't need medicine," he had said. "They need something changed in their routine of care." The hospital staff was so concerned with the calories in his food and his trouble swallowing, they overlooked the necessity of using a tiny spoon for his tiny mouth. The next time we went to the hospital for a routine visit, I took them two baby spoons. How typical of our high-tech society, to have computers to monitor every bodily function, but no baby spoons for little mouths. Needless to say, I proved as capable of feeding him with a soup spoon as anyone else, so they sent us off with assurances of their availability by phone if I needed any help.

As we settled in for the first night at home, Matthew's breathing began to sound congested, but my efforts to suction him with a baby bulb syringe accomplished nothing. Now I know Matthew desperately needed a hospital type suction machine, but at that time medical machinery in the home was unheard of. When I called the nurses at the hospital they said the congestion was from lung damage due to his long months on the respirator. I suppose he was so clear when I picked him up at the hospital because the Lord didn't want the congestion to frighten me. I tried to sleep in the bedroom with Hamp and Matthew, but Matthew's breathing kept me awake. I tried to sleep on the couch in the den so I wouldn't hear him, but I was afraid he would choke to death if I couldn't hear him, so I went back to the bedroom and lay awake most of the night listening to his labored gurgling, breathing.

Like many of the babies, Matthew spent a lot of time in our bed. It calmed them and made them feel safe. Here he and Hamp are fast asleep.

It was almost a year before I could really sleep in the room with Matthew and not be acutely aware of his noisy breathing. Fortunately, Hamp could sleep beside a busy railroad track, so he never heard the noise. The next morning I felt tired and defeated. Matthew cried when I tried to hold him. I couldn't give him any relief with his breathing and I couldn't get him to drink. I picked up my Bible, wondering if in spite of all the confirmations I had thought I had, it had been a mistake to take this baby. He seemed so far beyond my range of expertise. When I opened the Bible, it fell open to Isaiah 51:3. It said, "Arise, don't be defeated, I am He who comforts you." It seemed as if the Lord had written it especially for me, and I thanked Him for stooping to encourage me, and thought how frustrated He must get with me. I was so quick to receive a spirit of fear. In a little while, I got Matthew to lie down with me and take some water and pasteurized honey from a dropper, and we both got a much needed nap.

I SOON REALIZED IF WE HAD NOT SEEN THE MIRACLES WITH CALEB, we would never have had the faith to keep going with Matthew. He had suffered so much in his short life he seemed to have blocked out the world. He was literally covered with scars from I.V. cut downs and monitors and machines, and he seemed to associate human touch with pain. He screamed when we took him out of his infant seat to hold him. It would be a year before he would positively respond to human contact.

My first order of business after bringing Matthew home was to have our pediatrician, Bob Thompson, take a look at him. "There's nobody in there," he said, shaking his head sadly. "The most you can hope for from a baby like this is for him to cooperate more with your handling than someone else, but don't look for any real development. This isn't Caleb." While this was discouraging to hear, I had the benefit of having seen Caleb healed, and I knew man's scientific diagnosis could only speak to what appeared to be wrong now, nothing more.

> *JOURNAL: Sin causes me to doubt because sin causes guilt. My guilt causes me to feel that God won't work miracles for me or answer my prayers because of my sin therefore I can't have faith. "Whatever is not from faith is sin" (Romans 14:23). Whatever is sin is a lack of faith.*

While I had not even realized Matthew had extensive lung damage when I brought him home, it proved to be one of his worst problems. His lungs filled with mucous continuously, especially at night, as they rebuilt themselves. The doctors felt his lungs would eventually function normally, but it would take several years.

> *JOURNAL: God's purpose for us is the same as it was for Adam and Eve. He still wants to fellowship with us. He doesn't want us to work for Him, but to pray and spend time communing with Him and praising Him. Then He will cause things to happen in our life which will bless Him and others. As we pray, and commune quietly with Him, His hands are moving things in our life and the lives of those we pray for so we never have to rush and struggle to try to make the desired things happen for God. He does it all. All we have to do is fellowship with Him in His word, with praise, and prayer. It seems unreasonable. But so was the cross.*

Because of the mucous build-up during the night, I spent several hours each morning just holding Matthew as he coughed and gagged up huge amounts of clear mucous. By the time he had gotten the night's worth of mucous up, there was a pile of ten or fifteen cloth diapers for the wash and Matthew was so exhausted, he was ready to go back to sleep.

I agonized over all the energy he expended every morning, using up the precious calories he had managed to keep down just trying to clear his lungs so he could breathe. This terrible drain of energy was compounded by his failure- to-thrive syndrome, which also involved continuous vomiting. Matthew vomited up over half of everything he ate. His insides seemed dedicated to ridding themselves of anything they found inside him.

The spitting up and vomiting continued for almost the entire two years Matthew was with us, and for the first eighteen months there was no improvement, in fact it got worse. The vomiting was so constant I never moved without a handful of cloth diapers. If I went to the store with Matthew, I took diapers. If we went for a walk in the yard, I took diapers. Matthew threw up at the children's school, at Girl Scout meetings, in stores, at church, literally everywhere he went. It was especially embarrassing at the grocery store. People buying food really don't want to see or hear someone vomiting. I became fairly adept at using a cotton baby blanket at the grocery, holding Matthew face down on one arm and the blanket bunched loosely under his face. They could hear muffled sounds, but at least they didn't have to watch.

> JOURNAL: *Lord, show me how to walk with my feet upon the earth and my hands ministering in the reality of the needs of the flesh and the natural, with my spirit and my heart in communion and fellowship with You.*

I had talked to nutritionists and doctors about what to feed Matthew so he would gain weight and grow, but we weren't making any progress. I had been reading and studying about nutrition and giving my own family vitamin supplements since the children were little, so I thought vitamins might help Matthew at least to nourish what brain and nerve development he did have.

I found some enzymatically pre-digested liquid brewer's yeast at the health food store, which had all the B vitamins and enzymes necessary for absorption. As I always tasted anything I gave a baby (Not all "especially for children" medications taste even remotely pleasant as advertised), I made a very important discovery. Matthew couldn't taste! I knew this when I tasted the brewer's yeast and then put some on his tongue. It tasted and smelled like distilled dead cats and Matthew accepted it without complaint. When I knew taste made no difference to him, I began mixing a concoction of cereal, high calorie formula, fruit, meat, vegetables and vitamins that would turn a normal child into superman. When

I told the doctor at the high-risk clinic at the hospital about the vitamins I was giving him, she became very upset and sure I had overdosed him on something. She tested his blood for the imbalance she was certain must be there and found to her amazement the vitamins in his blood were exactly right for his size and weight. They wouldn't have been if not for the vitamins I was giving him.

I read a lack of zinc could cause him to fail to grow, taste or have an appetite, but I couldn't find a doctor who felt comfortable prescribing it for him. It is hard to determine a proper dosage for zinc, although they all agreed it might help him. I called several researchers doing zinc therapy experiments with mentally disabled children in other states and finally found one who would tell me how much he was giving the children in his study, who were all much larger than Matthew. I cut it by ¾ and gave it to him once a day, praying each time I wouldn't harm him. In about a month Matthew began to show a preference for vanilla pudding and would actually cry for more if I stopped feeding him before he was ready. I was elated because I thought being able to taste would make him eat more and gain weight. But it didn't. He still couldn't keep down but about 1/3 of what he ate. When he was three years old Matthew only weighed fifteen pounds.

JOURNAL: Lord, help me obey Your word implicitly, not being deterred if I don't see immediate results.

For over a year Matthew lay in the same position unless we moved him. He never acknowledged anyone or anything. So we moved him, propped him, talked to him and kept him in the middle of the family's activity to try to stimulate his brain. The children and I talked to him, carried him around the house and took him everywhere we went. When Hamp came home at night he would sit with Matthew in his lap, stroking and rubbing his arms and legs and playing with him, even though Matthew never responded. I also took him to Kim Cooper, the physical therapist who helped me with nearly all the handicapped babies, and got exercises to do with him to help him learn to control his body and gain strength.

One night in December, when Matthew was nearly a year old, Hamp was rubbing and exercising him when he suddenly called me excitedly.

"Watch Matthew's eyes when I move this light!" he said when I came to the door. Hamp took his cigarette lighter and moved the flame laterally in front of Matthew. Matthew's eyes followed the light.

"He sees it! He is following it with his eyes." Matthew wouldn't turn his head to follow it and he didn't look at all excited about it, but the child was definitely looking at the pretty gold light. We called for the children to come and see, but Matthew wouldn't look at the light again. The next day he still wouldn't look at anything. We were confused. We knew we had seen him track the light. A few days later, now constantly subjected to having things put in front of his face to look at, Matthew fixed his eyes on a toy and followed it. The tracking came and went, but the next time I took him to the hospital for a high-risk baby follow-up, I told the nurses who had cared for him that he could see. Of course he wouldn't perform for them, and I could see the sadness in their faces as they thought, "Bless her heart, she doesn't understand he couldn't see now anyway. His retinas would be too damaged by the oxygen we had to give him to keep him alive. How sweet for her to care so much, just like his real mother would." They patted my shoulder and said maybe the next time he would do it for them. I fussed at Matthew all the way home for making me look so foolish, but the next month when we went back, I silently dangled my keys in front of him and he followed them immediately. Soon people were coming from all over the hospital to see Matthew watching the keys. Doctors who had cared for him were summoned over the PA system to view the miracle. It was a miracle and they all knew it. Then one of the doctors leaned down to me and said very gently, "Get him to a retina specialist immediately. This ability might not be permanent." They gave me the name of a retina specialist and told me not to be too optimistic, because his retinas had to be damaged; they just had to be. Much less oxygen had blinded other babies. A few days later I took him to a retina specialist. When he finished his examination, with Matthew screaming bloody murder, I knew he hadn't missed anything. He had all but taken Matthew's eyes out of his head. I was still a bit lightheaded from watching something so awful, but I could hear just fine. "His retinas are perfect," he said, "There is no damage at all. There should be, but there's not."

Even though he could see now, Matthew still only lay passively watching the world go by. It seemed the Lord had only touched his eyes and had left his brain as it was. He never moved or reached out to touch anything, and often when I looked at him Bob Thompson's words echoed in my mind. "This isn't Caleb." Still I felt compelled to do all I could for him, and slowly an understanding of "my part" began to clarify in my mind.

I knew I couldn't heal the baby; that was up to God. I knew there were a great many things about his condition I couldn't do anything about, so they had to be left to God too. I had no idea if the Lord was ever going to totally heal Matthew, but I saw that He had called me to "a part" in His plan for Matthew's life. Jesus had called me to hold, love, cuddle, kiss, feed, talk, pray, stimulate, protect, and do anything else a mother *could* do. It was "my part" to do everything I could to bless Matthew and help him develop to his full potential, and that was all the Lord asked of me.

Getting this straight in my own heart kept me from crushing frustration as month after month, we did everything we could think of to help Matthew develop and nothing seemed to change. Every servant of God needs to know he is not always called to win, but he is always called to fight, and we fought hard for Matthew. We put him on a quilt on the floor with toys around him and put John's parakeet on the floor beside him in his cage. To make him lift his head, Hamp made walls of white poster board to stand on each side of his head. We put him on his stomach with toys in front of him so he had to raise his head to see anything more than white poster board. I rolled him for hours on a big beach ball to strengthen his neck and back. We turned him from back to front and front to back, over and over, doing the exercises the therapist had recommended.

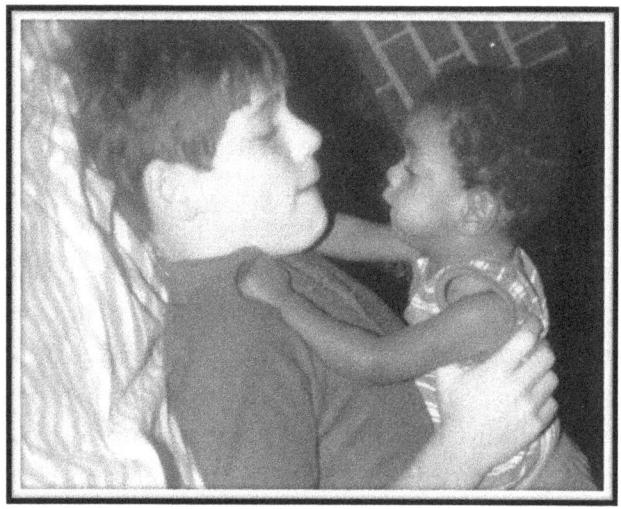

Matthew about two years, pushing up on John and trying to make the face John is making.

I sat with him seated between my legs, holding him firmly at the waist to make him learn to sit up and give him a more normal view of the world than he had lying down. He fought this so hard I thought he would dig up the carpet with his heels. We pulled his hands to midline over and over. We put toys in his hands and clapped his hands. We splashed his hands in water and rubbed different textures, ice cubes and anything else we could think of on his skin, to get his brain's attention.

 JOURNAL: Jesus will bless me and grow me where I am with the tools at hand in my life. He rooted me here. He

can accomplish His total will for me here. I don't have to struggle to get where He wants or needs me to be before He can bless me or use me.

One day after putting Matthew on a quilt with toys within easy reach, just in case he decided today was the day to begin to reach out to the world, it happened. As I walked down the hall out of sight, I heard the Happy Apple jingle. I ran back to look at Matthew. He had quickly resumed his fetal position and was staring at the ceiling. I was sure I had heard the toy, so I went down the hall again, but this time I hid and watched. Matthew lay motionless for a moment, then slowly turned his head and looked at the bright red apple with the smiling face. Slowly he moved his arm and bumped it to make it jingle. He pushed it again, and again it jingled. Matthew was playing with a toy! He was eighteen months old, and for the first time in his life he was playing. I ran to him and snatched him up.

"I saw you! I saw you!" I told him. "Why didn't you want me to know you were playing? Don't you know I put all of this here for you to touch and play with?" If he could only understand I love him and want to help him...then I thought, this must be how Jesus feels about us. He loved us, grieved for us, knew what we needed and provided it, and still the world sat, cold and rejecting of the very thing it needed, refusing to respond to all He offered. I stood holding Matthew as I thought about the striking parallel. He hung limply in my arms, staring over my shoulder as I kissed and congratulated him for taking such a big step. I could see so much and he so little. He had no idea of the significance of what he had done. Only I knew he had taken a step into a new dimension. How like a new Christian! He knows he has received Christ, but has no idea how it is going to change his life. Matthew had stepped from a living death into life and he had no idea of the changes it would bring him.

I called Bob Thompson with the news about Matthew's

progress and he was delighted. How different from the neurologist who was angry that Caleb was healed because it made her look bad.

> *JOURNAL: "See now that I, I am He, and there is no God besides me. It is I who put to death and give life. I have wounded and it is I who heal..." (Deuteronomy 32:39).*

After almost eighteen months of doing absolutely nothing, Matthew's progress from that day on was impressive, at least to us. It was slow and inconsistent, but as the months passed, he mastered task after task. He learned to reach out for toys and transferred them from one hand to the other. He finally learned to sit alone and to scoot around in a walker. He responded to "No, no" and knew his name. When he was about two, I put him into the high chair propped with baby blankets and showed him how to feed himself with a spoon. 1 expected months of repetition before he got the idea, but he threw the spoon twice and then began putting it into his mouth. In a month he was feeding himself. It wasn't pretty, but he was feeding himself. We finally got him a "corner chair" which provides more support for sitting alone for handicapped children and he learned to feed himself with very little help.

The only drawback to Matthew beginning to develop came when he realized he existed in relationship to other people. He became terrified of strangers and would not let anyone hold him but me. He felt safe enough for the family to hold him at home, but anything new or different put him into a state of panic. If anyone outside the family tried to hold him for me, his heart-breaking sobs and torrents of tears brought him quickly back to the safety of my arms.

As if one intellectually challenged baby was not enough for us to deal with, Laura appeared late one afternoon with another. This one was black and furry and even smaller than Matthew. Laura had rescued a puppy from a toddler a few streets away, who was carrying it with his hands around its neck. The puppy was filthy and covered with fleas. The owners had inherited the puppy's mother and didn't want her or her puppies. "Oh, no, honey," I said to the pleading look on Laura's face as she stood silently holding the puppy in the middle of the kitchen.

"You know we can't have a dog with fleas and dog hairs around the babies." We already had birds, hamsters, gerbils and gold fish to make up for not having a dog.

"But Mommy, look at him; you can see how miserable he is." There was no denying it was a very unhappy puppy. He had not moved or made a sound. Fleas were crawling all over his face.

"Well, we could give him a bath to make him feel better," I said, "but then he has to go home."

It took two baths to make an acceptable reduction in the fleas and still the puppy didn't even wag his tail. Worse yet, somehow in the course of the two baths, I found myself agreeing to a foster puppy. There was just too much precedent for foster babies in the family to turn one away just because it was a baby dog instead of a baby person. There were only three problems with this foster care arrangement: First, he was a she. Did ever a child bring home an orphaned male anything? Second, of course she had not been wormed or had any of her shots. Third, no one we knew wanted her.

Hamp backed me up, "No dog!" But after two weeks, it was I who whispered so the children wouldn't hear, "Couldn't we keep her? She is so cute; I am really attached to her." Hampy looked at me in disbelief and then caved in.

He shook his head with his, "I might have known," look; but since I wanted her, he agreed.

That night at the dinner table, we tried to name the puppy. Lots of good doggie names were suggested and voted down. The children couldn't agree on a name. Finally Hamp decided to settle the issue once and for all.

"Name her in one minute or she goes to the animal shelter." The children looked at each other in panic, "Beth!" John shouted.

"Yes!" the girls chorused instantly. "Beth?" Hamp and I looked at each other.

"Elizabeth." Stacey whispered to Laura.

Now I had two babies to care for, neither of whom were potty trained and both of whom slept more during the day than at night. Beth ran between my feet while I was carrying Matthew and swung on the phone cord while I tried to talk. She whined all night and slept half the day, but she loved Matthew. At first he was bigger than she, but she quickly outgrew him. By the time she was six months old she seemed to regard him as her puppy. She would lie on the floor by his infant seat and lick his feet. When he was on the floor in the den, she would lie beside him, allowing him to pull her long black fur and dig his toes into her side. If he got too rough, she would move just out of reach. She never just got up and left the area, but always stayed as close to him as she comfortably could.

THE FIRST SPRING WE HAD MATTHEW WAS AN EVENTFUL TIME. In addition to adding Beth to the family, my father's cataracts became bad enough to require surgery, which made it necessary for him to move in with us for several months.

Daddy was in his fifties and had lived alone since my mother's death in 1975. He was an architectural supervisor and spent most of his time outside on construction sites which had contributed to his development of cataracts at a relatively early age. Being naturally independent, he waited until he could no longer find the food in his cabinets before he agreed to move in with us and have the surgery. Daddy didn't want to move in with us for several reasons, not the least of which being his strange living habits. He had model trains in his living room and a pistol target on his kitchen door. When the children went to visit, they would play with the trains for a while, then sit in the den with Daddy and shoot pellet guns through the den into the kitchen at the target on the back of the door. It didn't bother Daddy at all if they missed the target and shot the pellet into the door. He was a grandfather most children only dream of. He also took and developed wonderful pictures, grew tiny things to view under his microscope and was too busy exploring the world and working at his job to stop and have surgery on his eyes.

When Daddy finally gave in and came to stay in John's room, we were all excited, especially John. There was no one he enjoyed more than his grandfather. John and Daddy had been extremely close since John was a baby. They had a spiritual bond, an empathy with each other, much as Daddy and I did. Since John's room was in the center of the house, Daddy was literally in the middle of the family, but it was never a problem. He was so sweet and agreeable it was a joy having him with us for three months.

Smoking for almost forty years had given Daddy emphysema and he had to have five days of intensive oxygen therapy before he could be put to sleep for the eye surgery. He could have easily died during surgery and I thanked God again both of my parents had become Christians before Mother died.

WITH DADDY ACCOMPANYING US, MATTHEW AND I BECAME EVEN more conspicuous than usual when we went out in public. This was especially true when Daddy's eye surgeries required him to wear a black patch over first one eye, then the other. I caught a glimpse of the three of us in a mirror at the grocery store one day as I was wondering why people were staring at us more than usual.

The mirror reflected a silver haired man dressed all in black, with a black patch over one eye, rather like an aging pirate, a middle aged white woman and an emaciated black child. No wonder people were staring at us. They must have been dying to ask us how on earth we came to be together. Daddy and I laughed about it, but it was a good picture of how God's love brings diverse people together in the family of God. Only Jesus could have brought three such unlikely people to live together in a love relationship.

When his eyes had healed sufficiently, Daddy went back home, but his time with us had been so enjoyable for all of us, we knew we wanted to add an apartment for him on to our house so he could be with us all the time. It would take a lot of work to get his house ready for sale and there was even more to do to ours to add him an apartment, so everyone pitched in and we spent Saturday after Saturday at Daddy's house cleaning and scrubbing and painting.

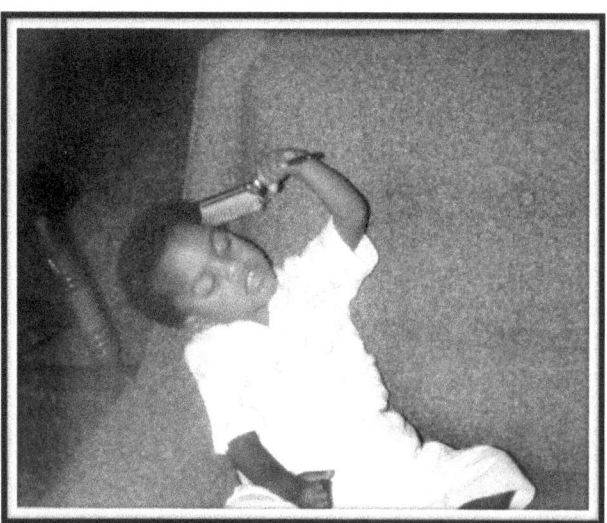

At age three, Matthew liked to try to brush his hair by himself.

By the time Matthew had been with us for two years, he had changed miraculously. He could see, sit alone and scoot around the house in a walker. He played with toys and people, family only of course, fed himself, obeyed simple commands and tried to brush his hair. He was still very disabled intellectually and always would be unless God intervened, but he was a lovable little boy and ready to be adopted.

After several months of advertising his availability, a couple looking for a special needs child was found in upstate New York. They were older than we had expected, and they were white. They had several grown children and felt they had love for one more child. They had added a room onto their house for a new baby, and had searched through dozens of books cataloging special needs children before picking Matthew.

We spoke to them on the phone several times telling them about his needs, his care, and his fear of strangers. We invited them to come and stay with us for several days to let Matthew get to know them before they tried to leave with him. It would also let them learn how to do things that would feel familiar to Matthew to help ease him into their family.

As soon as we knew this family really wanted Matthew, we all began to pray diligently about his move. We were happy for Matthew, but worried about the trauma of separation for him. He was still so attached to me he screamed if a stranger even tried to hold him.

It had been hard enough to leave Caleb with the Walkers and he hadn't cried for me, at least not while I was there. I knew I would not be able to turn my back on Matthew's tears and frantic screams. I could barely stand to think of my poor baby being taken away from the only people he had ever loved and trusted, with no possibility of explanation. There was no way to make him understand what was going to happen to him. The impossibility of avoiding the pain and fear I knew he would feel made me frantic, but there was nothing I could do.

After fostering children for twenty-seven years, this is still the thing that reduces me to tears. There is no pain to compare with looking into the loving, trusting eyes of a little child who knows nothing but your love, and foreseeing the fear and abandonment he will feel when you do the best, indeed the only thing you can do for him. It is what women fear who say they could never be a foster mother. They are right to fear it; but for the comfort and grace of the Lord, no mother could stand it twice.

I had prayed harder for a family for Matthew than for anything in my life, and it was confusing now to find myself afraid of the answer to my prayer. I could see in the natural there was no hope of his outgrowing his attachment to me in a matter of weeks. I was so unable to see how it would all work out I hardly knew what to pray. I only knew for him to receive them and not be afraid of them would require a touch from God.

I prayed diligently for this touch and one morning before his new parents came to get him, the Holy Spirit let me know Matthew would have the touch from God he needed. As I prayed, I saw a picture in my mind of Andrew and John walking with John the Baptist, and I remembered the Bible says that when Jesus passed by, John the Baptist had pointed Him out to them. He said, "Behold, the Lamb of God." (John 1:36). He is the one you are looking for. I had to come first, but I am not the ultimate you seek. The scripture says they immediately turned from John the Baptist and followed Jesus. I felt the Lord was showing me when Matthew's time with me was over, God would turn his heart to his new parents. The picture was so clear in my mind, and so far removed from what I had been thinking and praying, I felt it had to be the Lord, at least I hoped so with all my heart.

Before Matthew left for his new home, he learned one more thing. He learned how to laugh. It didn't look like laughter, or even sound like laughter, but one night when he was almost three years old, John did something Matthew thought was so funny he had to try to laugh. He was lying on the floor watching John try to stand on his hands. I noticed every time John tried, Matthew made a strange noise. I went over for a closer look. I told John to do it again as I watched Matthew's face. John stood on his hands again and Matthew's face twisted into a wry expression I had never seen, and he made the sound again. His face didn't look happy or amused, and the noise didn't sound like laughter, but he was certainly doing it in response to John's efforts. His body didn't seem to know how to respond to the amusement he felt, but there could be no doubt Matthew was trying to laugh at John.

I wasn't surprised it was John who first made Matthew laugh. We had noticed in the pictures we took of the babies, it was most often John who was asleep on the couch with a sleeping baby in his arms, or changing a diaper, or making a baby smile for the camera. He had a special rapport with babies and they all responded to him. As he got older, we would see his gift for comforting babies in some very profound ways.

Those last few weeks Matthew and I sat in the swing often, while I held him and cried as I prayed somehow the Lord would speak to his little heart and comfort him when I was no longer there. I worried about his new parents' ability to deal with the reality of his problems. Unlike the Walkers, they had never adopted a handicapped child before and had no real idea what it was like to care for him. Matthew demanded much more attention than a normal baby. He didn't sleep all night, he still vomited often and had no desire for food. This family seemed very unprepared for him. I had no choice but to trust the Lord they were the family He had chosen for Matthew.

WHEN THE NEW PARENTS ARRIVED, I KNEW THEY WERE EXCITED about finally getting to see their new son, and I committed myself to be as much of a blessing to them as I could.

We had explained Matthew's fear of strangers on the telephone, and asked them not to try to hold him right away. But his new mother didn't have that kind of self- control. Ten minutes after they arrived, she reached out and picked Matthew up and sat him gently on her lap. We all caught our breath, as he looked solemnly up into her face, but didn't cry. She talked to him and stroked his cheek, and he still didn't cry. Matthew didn't lean toward me and cry for me to take him until the next day. He looked very serious and would not smile or laugh, but he was not afraid of them. The Lord had done exactly what He had said. He had turned Matthew's heart to them.

The next four days were uncomfortable for me as I tried to help people I didn't know and whom my heart didn't totally receive, form a bond with "my child." It is hard for an ex-mother to know what to do with herself. In a matter of minutes I went from being the mother, to someone who no longer belonged in the picture. If I didn't hold Matthew and cuddle and talk to him as usual I felt cruel, as if I were rejecting him. If I treated him as if he still belonged to me, I felt as if I was deliberately deceiving him into believing everything was all right. It was a very tense, very emotional situation for me.

Matthew had been an integral part of our family for two years. Our friends were used to him always being with me when they saw me. The children and their friends loved him and considered him as part of the family. We all did. Even the clerks at the grocery store knew him by name. Matthew was known to so many people in the community, *The Clarion Ledger* newspaper did an article with a picture of him about his adoption. I literally could not picture our family without him.

I could hardly function.

The second day Matthew's new parents were with us, I was praying to be able to live through the separation from Matthew and not make it harder for the children by being unable to control my grief. I was crying in the bathroom when I felt the Lord prod me to face the pain. He impressed me to turn around and look at what I feared and acknowledge it. I literally turned around. It was then that I realized it was the fear of pain I was running from, not the pain itself. When I realized the pain couldn't possibly be worse than the fear, I immediately calmed down. I realized my part now was to suffer the inevitable pain of losing Matthew.

> JOURNAL: Lord, Your word says in Joshua 1:7 that we are not to look anxiously about us to the right or to the left, but to know the Lord our God is with us. Help me to remember You and I are alone in my heart, and all of life outside is important only as You and I relate to it together.

There was nothing left to do but to do it, as Hamp often said. I still had to excuse myself, go into the bathroom, bury my face in a towel and cry three or four times a day. But now when I cried, there was no knife of anxiety in my heart, only sorrow. The sorrow was a necessary consequence of what the Lord had ordained, and it no longer controlled me. When I had done all I could to prepare Matthew's new parents to care for him and make him happy, it was time for them to take their child and go home. We took pictures, went to the airport and took more pictures. The beautiful, young, black social worker who had just taken Matthew's case at Catholic Charities, Dolly Hambrick, was there. So was Patty Jones, from Health and Human Services, who had actually handled the adoption.

I knew the children would deal with Matthew's final good-bye well if I did, and I tried to look calm and happy for them and for Matthew. But when his new parents boarded the plane with him and he disappeared from sight, solemnly looking at us over his new father's shoulder, I had to sit down and weep. When I finally glanced up, Dolly and Patty were both crying too. It was so comforting to have two other mothers there who understood how I felt. The children took the separation amazingly well with just a few minutes of tears as Matthew disappeared into the plane. I think they were trying to be strong for me since I was such a failure at being strong for them.

Because the situation was so emotional for all of us, Hamp had decided the family should stay together for the day. He didn't go to the shop, and we kept the children out of school. We tried to make the day as much a celebration for Matthew as possible. We went out to lunch and then went swimming at Hamp's parents' apartment. While we were at the pool, I noticed John kept looking anxiously at me, sometimes leaning around a corner to look at me if I was quiet. Finally I said, "John, what's the matter? You look like you think I am going to explode or something."

"I do," he said, quite seriously.

"I'm ok, really, I'm ok. We wanted Matthew to have a family who would love him and take care of him forever, and that is what he has. I know God has other babies for us and we couldn't take them if we had kept Matthew. This is what the Lord wanted. I am all right, really," I said.

John knew his mother. The next day I exploded. A few weeks before Matthew's new parents had come for him, I had a professional picture taken of him. I thought it wouldn't come until at least a month after he was gone, but it came the next day. When I took out the 8 x 10 picture and looked at his now beautiful little face, I began to cry. I cried so hard I couldn't breathe. I cried for two hours, until almost time for the children to come home from school. I didn't want them to see me so upset. I couldn't even talk to tell them what was wrong.

I managed to call Hamp and make him understand I couldn't stop crying. He immediately came home to be there before the children. I cried for hours.

I COULD NOT GET CONTROL OF IT. IT WAS AS IF GOD HAD TURNED ME upside down and was shaking out all the pain and grief I had been trying to ignore. After four hours, it began to taper off and was finally over.

> 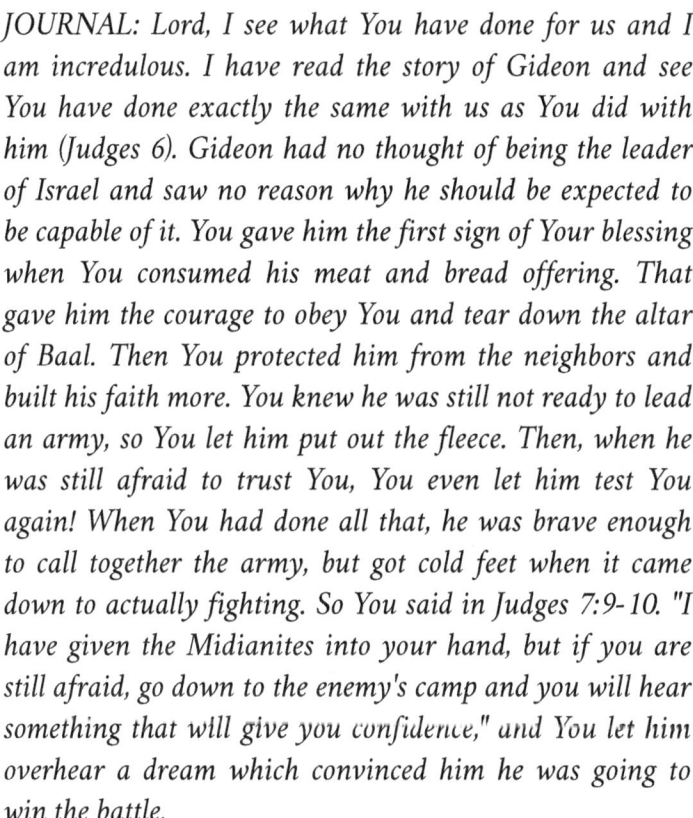JOURNAL: Lord, I see what You have done for us and I am incredulous. I have read the story of Gideon and see You have done exactly the same with us as You did with him (Judges 6). Gideon had no thought of being the leader of Israel and saw no reason why he should be expected to be capable of it. You gave him the first sign of Your blessing when You consumed his meat and bread offering. That gave him the courage to obey You and tear down the altar of Baal. Then You protected him from the neighbors and built his faith more. You knew he was still not ready to lead an army, so You let him put out the fleece. Then, when he was still afraid to trust You, You even let him test You again! When You had done all that, he was brave enough to call together the army, but got cold feet when it came down to actually fighting. So You said in Judges 7:9-10, "I have given the Midianites into your hand, but if you are still afraid, go down to the enemy's camp and you will hear something that will give you confidence," and You let him overhear a dream which convinced him he was going to win the battle.
>
> Lord, how longsuffering You are! How patiently You put up with us! You held Gideon's hand and gently showed him sign after sign that his fear made him need. You healed me from smoking so I could have the energy to mother Your babies. You gave us baby after normal baby to give us enough confidence to take sick ones. You healed Caleb and gave us the faith to take Matthew. You healed Matthew to show Your loving kindness and Your constant presence with us. I never dreamed Your Father's heart was so gentle and loving. You met us all right where we were and led us

to where You wanted us to be, encouraging and strengthening us a step at a time.

> JOURNAL: In Exodus 33:13, Moses says to God, "Let me know Thy ways, that I may know Thee, so I may find favor in Thy sight." God's answer to Moses's desire to know Him was, "My presence shall go with you and I will give you rest." God's rest is Sabbath rest that He speaks of in Isaiah 58. It is in not seeking your own way or pleasure and not speaking your own words, but God's."

I believe Satan deceives Christians into believing our "acts" are service to God. That our power comes from forcing ourselves to obey His word, when really our loving communion with our Redeemer-Husband will transform us into what He wants us to be. I think the Word is for our minds, to enable us to follow the Holy Spirit and not be ignorant and therefore a hindrance to His desire for us.

Our first step away from the Lord is the loss of our first love (Revelations 2). Then we react to that loss by going into empty works.

> JOURNAL: He alone is worthy, because He alone gave up His absolute essence for His love. He gave up everything to come here and give up everything.
>
> Lord, show me how to give up everything to Jesus. I don't comprehend it. Show me how to bear fruit born of sacrifice; I don't know how.

4
MICAH

*A*fter Matthew was placed in New York, I was sure the Lord was going to give me a nice long rest. I thought I had cared for the hardest baby He ever made, and I deserved to relax for a while. Little did I know within a month I would learn a great spiritual truth: When the Bible speaks of showing yourself to be trustworthy with a little so God will trust you with a lot, it isn't referring to earthly wealth. It is referring to responsibility. While I thought I had earned a good rest, God thought I had earned Micah.

The call came for Micah at the end of a wonderful day. I had been buying clothes for some needy children at the school our children attended. All day I had felt a deep sense of gratitude to the Lord for the privilege of serving Him. I had thought about the babies we had parented and the things we had learned and seen because of them. The presence of the Lord seemed to enfold me like a cloud. All day I was filled with a powerful awareness of the Holy Spirit.

That afternoon the call came from a social worker in the

northern part of the state. A little black boy needed a foster home. He was eleven months old and had only half of his brain. He was spastic, quadriplegic, blind, couldn't eat, had breathing problems and would probably die soon. I couldn't believe it. I wanted to sit down on the kitchen floor and cry. As I stood there listening to her describe the poor child I was thinking, "No, please, Lord, not another one so hard! Not so soon. Oh, Lord, I don't want to, I don't want to." I stalled her by saying I would have to pray about it and talk to my husband.

"The mother wants him put to sleep to put him out of his misery, and we don't feel we can guarantee his safety beyond this weekend when relatives will be with her. Please let us know something Monday," she said.

Micah asleep is worthy of a picture itself. Here, Laura dressed him in the clothes of her Charlie McCarthy puppet.

As I hung up the phone, the dread of this child weighed on my heart like a huge stone. The social worker had given me the name of the doctor who had been treating the baby, and a nurse at the local hospital who had cared for him. I called the nurse first, knowing by experience she probably would know more about his daily needs than a doctor. She said he had breathing problems, was blind, spastic, disabled intellectually and had seizures. She painted a picture of a child who needed heroic care, but as disheartening as the situation sounded, I heard myself telling her about Matthew and Caleb. "No one can know what God might do for this baby," I said. I knew that was true not withstanding my great desire not to take him.

"I don't know what you look like," she said, "but you are a beautiful person."

I knew the Lord was letting me know He had shone through me to touch the nurse's heart. It was an assurance He was in the midst of what was happening.

I talked to Hampy, when he got home. "I think we should take him. I think if we have been asked to take him, we should assume it's God's will," he said.

I talked to each child separately. On hearing his dire situation, they all wanted us to rescue him. The family was divided on whether to keep his birth name Samuel, as our name for him. There was concern we would call him Sammy, which none of us cared for. We decided on Micah. Samuel was his birth name, and already scriptural, but no one was put off by Micah.

That night the clanking of the dog's collar woke me. I was instantly wide awake and wanted to pray. Knowing I have never had the discipline to do without sleep to seek the Lord, I knew God must want to tell me something. I began to pray for confirmation about this baby and to entreat the Lord not to let us take such a hard child if it was not His perfect will. I thought about the name Samuel. Someone had given it to him, and the names Caleb and Benjamin had such significance I was prepared for his name to be important. Samuel had left his mother at a very early age and gone to live with a priest. There was a parallel there, all believers being priests.

Then the Lord told me why He had awakened me: "If you begin to pick and choose babies, it will no longer be My ministry, but yours."

Of course, how simple; I wanted to do what Christians so often do. I wanted to take the part of God's will which suited me and reject the part which was hard and required real faith. I also realized why God had wrapped me in His Spirit all day. It was because He knew the call was coming and He knew it would be hard for me to take this baby so soon after Matthew. So He came close enough for me to feel Him and know He was with me.

"THAT BABY WILL DIE ON YOU. YOU WOULD BE CRAZY TO TAKE THAT child into your home! He can't eat, he is spastic, he has seizures, he cries all the time. Not only that, he has apnea and is only alive now because we had him on an apnea monitor in the hospital and could revive him every time he stopped breathing," the doctor told me the next morning when I called him. I was glad I had called the nurse first. The doctor, who had spent minutes with the baby was making pronouncements which the nurse, who had spent days with him, knew were not true.

When I told our social worker we would take Micah, she gave me the reassuring news the social worker in Micah's county was going to bring him to Jackson with a nurse and a highway patrol escort. They were afraid he would die before they could get him off their hands and out of their county and into mine. I laughed when I told Hamp. I was sure he wouldn't die before he got to me. The Lord had gone to too much trouble preparing me to take him.

That night we got our final confirmation Micah was for us. I mentioned some details of his legal situation to Hamp at the dinner table and he flew into a rage.

"We aren't going to babysit with him! We aren't going to take a baby like this without more assurance of his safety and release from his family than that!"

I didn't know what to do. I had already said we would take him, but Hamp seemed totally unwilling now. Then I realized I didn't have to do anything. Nothing had changed as far as God was concerned. I knew from the other confirmations this was our baby, no matter what Hamp was saying at the moment. So I said nothing. In a few minutes, as we all silently ate, Hamp said, "I'm doing exactly what I said I wouldn't do again. When Matthew was placed, I said we should just take the next baby and not worry about the details and that's what the Lord wants us to do. This is just an attack from the enemy to try to keep us from taking him." We had finally both grown enough to know any time something is going to bear fruit for the Lord, Satan hits really hard. It never failed year after year, baby after baby; every time there was a major victory coming, Satan did his best to stop it, or at least rob us of as much joy in it as possible.

JOURNAL: Out walking and praying, I said to the Lord, "I have tried to become a strong warrior for You, Father, but I have to come back to You yet again and say, "I am not nearly ready to fight for You. I am just a child, too young to even wear Your armor." (Ephesians 6:11-17). As I was drooping dejectedly across a street, I heard the Lord laugh gently, "Oh, you mean like David, when he killed Goliath." I stopped in my tracks. Fortunately there were no cars coming. David didn't let his age or size keep him from doing what he could, I thought. He tried on Saul's armor, but it was so big, he said he couldn't even walk in it. He was too small for the men's weapons, so he took the sling he knew he could kill lions and bears with, picked up some rocks, and ran toward Goliath trusting that God was with him. And He was. David had received the anointing of the

Holy Spirit from Samuel when he anointed him to be king over all Israel. And he had communed with God sitting out on the hillsides guarding his father's sheep, killing predators with strength from God and practice. He had learned to obey and trust God. The "doctrine of the anointed rock" formed in my mind at that moment. I might not be able to wield a sword, and carry the full armor of God because of my youth, or pain, or some other weakness, but we can all throw an anointed rock. An anointed rock, thrown in faith, can often accomplish what the "big, strong, mature men" can't. The men the armor fit in the Hebrew army were all hiding; including the king, who was unusually tall for a Hebrew. And he had one of the few swords in the army. But he wasn't sure God was with him. Not a man on the field would have believed the giant could be brought down by a rock. How many times since then have I thrown an anointed rock as hard as I could and trusted the Lord to honor my effort, weak though it seemed.

Micah sounded so intimidating, I was afraid to pick him up alone, so Hamp went with me. He was a beautiful little boy with a cherubic face, big brown eyes and tight black curls. But his body was so stiff we could have put him between two chairs and used his tummy for a table. His hands were tightly fisted and his arms pulled back against his body like little wings. He began screaming almost the moment we took him. Hoping he was hungry, we rushed home to feed him. I was glad Hamp was there to drive us because I could hardly hold onto him. He was so stiff he rode standing on my lap with his back arched away from me, try though I might to bend him in the middle and sit him down.

At home, Micah wanted no food and continued to scream. Finally, exhausted with trying to hold and comfort him, I put him in the crib. He arched his back until his head and heels were the only parts of him touching the bed. He screamed until he had to stop and gasp for air, then screamed again. I had never seen anyone scream like that. The muscular contortions of his back arching so abnormally seemed to indicate seizure activity and the pediatrician gave him seizure medication, but we were never sure it was actually seizures that caused it. We tried everything we knew about babies, but nothing fazed Micah. It was a real mercy we couldn't see into the future. I would never have had the courage to begin if I had known what was to be required of me with Micah.

 JOURNAL: Micah cried and screamed for hours. After staying up with him for hours, I finally woke Hampy to come and agree with me in prayer for peace for the baby. I don't know if he wore himself out, or if the Lord answered our prayers. The next morning, he was screaming constantly, and I had to go the grocery store. I told the Lord in the car I was almost convinced we were not supposed to have Micah, because He didn't seem to be blessing our efforts to help him. I told the Lord I really needed to know if we were out of His will. As I was saying this, I drove into the drive-through at the bank, where the teller stopped me to say our witness with the babies had touched her heart, and she had cried when she read in the newspaper Matthew had been adopted. Moments later a song came on the car radio about Shadrach, Meshach and Abednego. It spoke of the Son of Man being in the fire with them, and I remembered they were so content in His presence, the king had to command them to come out of the fire. I knew the Lord was telling me it was better to be in the fire with Jesus, than outside it without Him. I was definitely in the fire with Micah, but the Lord was there with me, and I felt a surge of strength just knowing that.

A few days after Micah came, Hamp decided to call Matthew's new parents to see how he was doing. I thought it would encourage us to hear Matthew was doing well. When he had finished talking to Matthew's new father, Hamp came back into the den where I was trying to quiet a screaming Micah.

"You aren't going to believe this," he said. "They are going to bring Matthew back."

"Hampy! You can't mean that!" I said, tears welling up in my eyes.

"They say he whimpers all the time and it's driving them crazy," he said.

"Whimpers? He whimpers all the time? Because he misses his family and is afraid?" I was shouting over Micah's screams and fury was taking me over.

"We told them he would cry for us! We talked about his grieving for us before they took him! Ask them if they want to swap babies!" I screamed, holding Micah out to him. "I could stand a little whimpering right now!" Angry tears were running down my face. I couldn't believe what I was hearing. Micah was making me deaf shrieking in my ears, and they were going to send a precious little boy back because he whimpered and it bothered them.

"Maybe you should call his mother..." Hamp began. "No! I'm not going to call her! Let them bring him back!

I don't want him in a home where they can't stand a little whimpering!" I shouted.

I gave Micah to Hampy and called the social worker who had placed Matthew with his adoptive family. I found they had not even notified her they didn't want Matthew. Apparently Hamp's call had made them face the fact they had made a mistake. I was devastated. How could this have happened? I had prayed for Matthew and the family God would send him more than I had ever prayed for anything in my life. And what about the way he had received them? How could that not have been a confirmation they were God's family for him? How could it have turned out like this? How could he be so far away from us with people who didn't want him?

We did the only thing we could with Matthew so far away. We prayed and asked the Lord to protect him and send angels to comfort him.

> *JOURNAL: When the Jews were in the wilderness, the people panicked every time something appeared to go wrong because they only knew about God. They had not had personal contact with Him as Moses had. Moses knew he could trust God because he had experienced contact with Him. There is no excuse for me to ever turn away from the Lord in panic, fear or anger, because I know Him more intimately than Moses did. I am His child, bought with the blood of His Son.*

The next day work began to bring Matthew back to Jackson. Hamp and I wanted to take him back, but we had made a commitment to Micah. I tried to convince myself I could take care of both babies and my own family, but in the end I had to acknowledge there was a limit to what I could do. I couldn't take Matthew back unless I sent Micah away. Strangely, I found I had a resolve not to take him back. I sensed if we did, he might never bond with another family. He might feel if he just whimpered long enough, he would get back to us again. And I didn't want that for him. As painful as it was, we felt it was better for Matthew not to come back to our family unless we were going to adopt him. There were a lot of prayers and tears for several days as we sorted out the situation. We felt called to be foster parents to sick babies. We already had our next baby and there had been abundant confirmation for him. Also, white parents weren't allowed to adopt black children in Mississippi at that time. We finally decided since Micah had already come to us, there must be a family somewhere for

Matthew, and it wasn't ours. It was not possible God didn't care about Matthew. We had to trust Him to place him where He wanted him.

The next step was to find God's family for Matthew, and in the meantime a new foster home in Jackson. Our friends Susan and Jeff Wilson had always had a special love for him. They had lost their own little Matthew to Sudden Infant Death Syndrome when he was a tiny baby. They had a daughter, and were a loving, Spirit-filled couple who were willing to obey the Lord with no questions asked. To our great relief, they immediately agreed to take Matthew when he came back.

It made no sense to me that the Lord allowed the adoptive family to disrupt, and then provided another temporary home for Matthew. But I was encouraged to see the Lord continuing to provide for him in the midst of what was total confusion to me. It wasn't long however, before I learned that while I was confused by the events in Matthew's life, the Lord was operating in extraordinary order.

The day before Matthew's New York father brought him back to Jackson, I received a call from Catholic Charities. A lovely black couple had called them and asked about adopting a little boy. They hadn't thought of a handicapped child, but were open to hearing about Matthew. I went to the office with pictures of him and told them all about him. Later Hamp and I both met with them. They were a wonderful couple. The husband was a pastor and they had teenage children of their own. Matthew began visiting their home as soon as he came back to Jackson. Within a few months he moved from Susan and Jeff's home to theirs and became their son permanently. They changed his name to Kevin and loved him as their own. Their children took him everywhere they went and he was very happy with them. They even lived close enough for us to see him again when enough time had passed for him not to remember us.

After all these years of walking with the Lord, I still don't really understand the relationship between God's will and our prayers. But I do think God convicted so many of us to pray diligently for Matthew's adoption, because the timing would be so critical and the placement so complicated. I knew timing and prayer had always been important in Matthew's life. He had been sent home from the hospital three times, and brought back just in time to save his life. In the hospital, his Christian doctor, Sue Campbell, prayed fervently for him. He left us after two years, during which we had prayed constantly for his healing and a permanent family for him. One month before Micah would have to be taken from his home to protect his life, Matthew went to live with the family in New York. After we had made the difficult commitment to Micah, the father in New York brought him back. Two days before, God's family for him appeared at Catholic Charities asking to adopt a little black boy. Susan and Jeff were called in for the interim between New York and his permanent family. When I considered all of this, it finally became clear to me how strong God's hand had been to bring a family for Matthew, and at the same time deliver Micah from his mother. Rather than a reason to question the Lord's love Matthew's broken adoption was really proof of God's love and perfect timing. Only Jesus could have worked such a situation out for the protection and provision for both babies.

WHILE IT WAS A RELIEF TO WATCH GOD SETTLE MATTHEW'S FUTURE, every day during those weeks we realized how complicated Micah's brain damage was. The hardest to deal with was his almost complete inability to sleep.

I quickly got into the habit of going to bed at night as soon after Micah was asleep as possible. I would have long enough to sink into an exhausted sleep, when he awoke screaming. It was cold, and I was miserable leaving my warm bed, holding and rocking Micah until he stopped screaming. I would get back into bed just long enough to get warm, only to repeat the whole procedure a few minutes later. I tried letting him sleep on top of me, which always calmed other babies, but it didn't calm Micah. I tried letting him sleep between Hamp and me, but still he screamed. Nothing I tried made Micah sleep. For almost a year Micah required me to get up from seventy to eighty times a night. Yeah, I did the math. I didn't do it then, I didn't want to know, but I did eventually. I finally stopped going to bed at all. I slept, or catnapped, on top of the covers in my gown and robe with an afghan over me to avoid the terrible sensation of leaving the warm bed every few minutes. When the weather got warmer I didn't have the cold to add to my discomfort, but I can't honestly say it was any easier getting up and down all night on summer nights. By summer I had stopped going into a deep sleep. I would remain unable to sleep deeply until twenty plus years later, when I got medication for it. Micah also had another problem which added to my lack of sleep. He breathed with a loud rasping noise medically referred to as stridor. It was caused by having had a tube carelessly or improperly put down into his trachea during one of his many hospital stays. This made him breathe so hard I had to buy his shirts two sizes too large because his stomach ballooned out with every breath, and made his shirt work its way up to his chest.

> *JOURNAL: If I can walk, see, think, and comprehend to a small degree the love of my Lord, if I can use my hands to hold what I desire, if I can get up and walk away from pain or dislike, can I worship that? Can I worship those abilities and indulge myself to use them selfishly? Or did Jesus give me those capabilities to be His hands, feet and eyes on earth, to care for those who lack these abilities? Would Jesus turn His back on self-denial to preserve His own pleasure?*
>
> *If I had one year to live, would I not concentrate on*

bearing the most fruit for Him that I could? Lord, help me commit myself totally to Your will.

When we had had Micah about a month, we decided to spend all day one Saturday at Daddy's house, cleaning and painting, getting the house ready to sell. I would have to pack up all of Micah's food, diapers, meds, etc., food for the family, cleaning supplies, and paint, and be able to work all day and take care of screaming Micah at the same time. I was positive I could not do it without a good night's sleep first. Instead I got a miracle. I was so tired from getting so little sleep at night, I felt I had an especially legitimate need for sleep that night.

"Lord," I said before I went to bed, "I have to go tomorrow and work all day to help my daddy, and I just can't do it if I don't get some sleep. Please let Micah sleep tonight." I felt I really deserved a little rest. I had been faithful to get up with him night after night, and now in order to help my father, I had to have some sleep. It seemed reasonable to me. I had not yet realized God is not reasonable. He is God.

I put Micah to bed with hope the Lord would make him sleep more than usual, but as soon as I had fallen asleep, he woke up screaming. I awoke feeling angry. I had a splitting headache, my back ached terribly, my eyes were so dry and scratchy they hurt and I was so sleepy I could barely force my body out of bed and to his crib. I leaned wearily on the side of the crib to pat his back.

"Lord," I said, "Please let this child go to sleep. I have just got to have some rest."

As soon as I said this, I perceived a deep, masculine voice over my left shoulder saying, "This is pure gold to you. This child is not awake because I can't make him go to sleep. This child is awake for you to have the privilege of staying up with him all night."

I did not hear the voice with my ears, but seemed to receive it as if he spoke directly to the hearing center of my brain. I heard it as a deep man's voice and I could locate the sound of it. When he began speaking, I froze, afraid to move, fearing I would miss something. But I felt no fear. It felt perfectly natural to be addressed by an angel (which I assume it was). In a few seconds I straightened up and turned around. I saw no one, but could feel the presence now in front of me, in the same place. As I was about to ask if we could change the part about staying up all night that particular night, I felt a warm sensation beginning at the top of my head and proceeding downward. I had heard of this healing warmth, but never expected to feel it myself. It went slowly enough for me to wonder how far down it would go. Would it stop with my head and back, or go all the way to my feet? It dissipated around my knees. My head no longer ached, my eyes felt fine, as did my neck and back. I was no longer angry, but wanted nothing more than to stay up with Micah all night. I felt as if I had not missed any sleep in months.

My visitor said no more and was felt no more. That seemed natural too. I understood what he had come to tell me and he had touched my body to care for Micah. I picked him up and went to the den. He was awake until six o'clock the next morning. I slept for an hour, went to Daddy's house and worked and scrubbed and took care of Micah and fed Hamp and the children and did all I needed to do without feeling unduly tired.

That night I put Micah to bed and although he had screamed most of the day, he slept his usual few minutes and awoke screaming. Nothing had changed in our physical circumstances, but my understanding of it and my anointing for it had. When the Lord sent His angel to touch me with His warmth that night, He anointed me with strength to withstand all the trials of caring for His child, Micah. I did share this a few weeks later in women's group at church, but probably not like I should have. We received too much praise for the babies as it was. I couldn't bring myself to say, "Well, God sent me an angel and healed my pain and exhaustion," when there were many women all around me who suffered differently for the Lord, and they got no angels. Maybe he came to me because so many people were watching, and Jesus knew how weak I was. If He let me fail, it would have cut off a flow of grace which He wanted everyone who was watching to continue to see.

As we struggled to understand and meet Micah's needs, one of the hardest things we had to deal with was the questioning of other believers about our lack of progress with him. Some people thought we must be out of the Lord's will in some area of our life, or have some un- confessed sin in our lives for the Lord to allow such painful circumstances to continue. We were serving Him after all. Surely He would make it easier if He was pleased with us.

>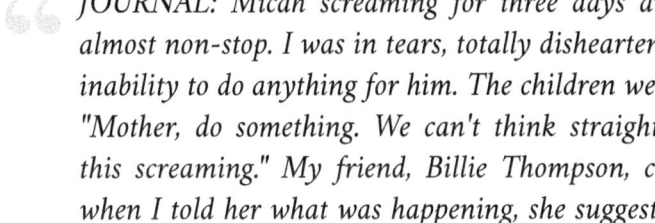
> *JOURNAL: Micah screaming for three days and nights almost non-stop. I was in tears, totally disheartened by my inability to do anything for him. The children were saying, "Mother, do something. We can't think straight with all this screaming." My friend, Billie Thompson, called and when I told her what was happening, she suggested I fix a cup of tea and sit down with the Bible, and let the Lord refresh me. I opened the Bible to look for a place to read and the first words I saw were, "Anyone who receives one such little one receives Me (Matthew 18:5)." Thank you, Lord. I never thought about how well You know the Bible.*

I had repeatedly told people my experiences with other babies had taught me serving the Lord was not all miracles and exuberant joy. I had learned well with Caleb and Matthew that pain could be very much a part of Godly ministry, but as I sought the Lord for Micah's relief and ours in prayer, I also searched the scriptures for insight to help me understand why the Lord was allowing Micah to suffer so much, and allowing our ministry to him to be so difficult.

I had already believed it was a privilege to serve the Lord in a hard place before we took Micah, because I knew I was supposed to be growing into the likeness of Christ. How could I become what the Father wanted without suffering if Jesus didn't? Hebrews 5:8 says, "Although He was a son, He learned obedience from the things He suffered; and having been made perfect, He became to all those who obey Him the source of eternal salvation." What would make me grow spiritually if the Lord always made everything easy for me? Isaiah 53:3 also says Jesus was a man of sorrows acquainted with grief; and Hebrews 2:17- 18, describing Jesus, says clearly that He had to become like his brothers in every respect so He could become their merciful and faithful high priest. I knew according to I Peter 2:5, we are priests too, for the offering up to God of spiritual sacrifices through Jesus, and Romans 8:17 says we are joint-heirs with Christ if we suffer with Him. This all gave me an expectation of suffering, to be molded, sometimes painfully into the image of Jesus (Romans 8:29). Also, if my obedience to God never brought me pain, what would I have to say to people who were suffering? How could I be a priest to them if I had no idea what their suffering felt like?

The touch the Lord gave me that night permanently dispelled any doubt He was right there with me, and confirmed that our willingness to suffer with His baby was pleasing to Him. It *was* a privilege to stay up all night with Micah, to be chosen to be his mother for the Lord. David said, "I will not offer a sacrifice that costs me nothing." (I Chronicles 21:24). I could certainly say the sacrifices I offered with Micah cost me, and the Lord had sent a messenger to say He was pleased. After that we were sure the Lord had a purpose for Micah's being as he was, and the situation became much easier to accept. As we kept trying to be a blessing to him, we gradually learned things which helped him and made his life more comfortable and enjoyable.

As I got to know Micah and the Lord gave me a motherly sensitivity to him, I realized much of his pain was coming from his muscles. His biceps and calf muscles were so overdeveloped and rigid from spasticity they were as hard as rock. I took him to Kim Cooper for an evaluation and learned some exercises to help him relax. But Kim also confirmed the diagnosis of every doctor who had seen him. He was neurologically devastated and there was little reason to hope anyone could do much for him. The exercises Kim recommended didn't seem to be much help at first, because he was in so much pain he just couldn't relax.

Finally, after two months of Micah's screaming night and day I called Bob and asked for medication. I had been determined not to drug Micah because I wanted him to be alert in order to learn, but the baby was suffering and I knew he couldn't learn if he was distracted by pain. Bob prescribed a tiny dose of valium and it worked. Micah actually relaxed a little. He even slept as long as three or four hours at a time once in a while.

> *JOURNAL: We sold Daddy's house and he has moved in with us until his apartment is finished above the new garage. We have hung a bedspread between the den and dining room and put Daddy's bedroom furniture in the dining room. Lord, I am so glad he has made this move now, before he feels forced to do it because he can no longer take care of himself. He goes to work every day as always, but when he comes home we are all here, and the children can get on his bed with him and talk and watch TV. I am so glad they are having this time with him. He is a wonderful grandfather.*

One of the most painful conditions Micah suffered with, which also contributed to his sleeplessness, didn't come to light for months. It had been apparent for several days that something worse than usual was wrong, so I took him to Bob Thompson to see if he could track it down. I suspected an ear infection because Micah's respiratory passages were abnormally small due to his microcephaly (small brain and head,) but his ears were fine. Bob looked in his throat, no problem there. Then he mashed on his stomach. "Oh Micah," he said, "I know what's wrong with you. You have a tummy ache."

Bob took my hand and pressed it against Micah's abdomen. I could feel something small and hard inside.

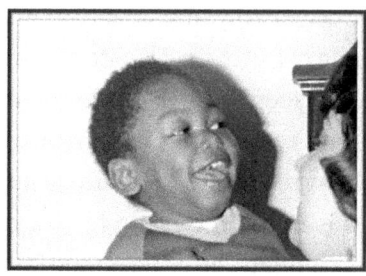

Micah holding his head up and laughing.

"His gut is not working," Bob said.

"But he has a bowel movement every day or so," I argued.

"I know, but the gut isn't working like it should because of his brain damage and his immobility. The softer material is passing around the little rocks forming in there. It isn't uncommon with a child like Micah because they don't move around like other children. It's also possibly because of weak or improper signals from his brain. It's hard to detect until they show evidence of distress," he said.

The blockages in his intestines were causing gas pockets to form behind them and the gas pains were contributing to his inability to sleep. We had discovered another important piece in Micah's puzzle of pain.

Now that we knew this was a problem for him, we incorporated dealing with his colon with his exercises to relax. At night when he awoke screaming in pain, instead of putting him on my shoulder and patting his back, I bent him into a little ball and rolled him around on my lap to relieve the gas pains. Pulling his legs up and rotating him at the waist, in addition to helping him relax, helped his intestines work a little better too. We also looked for a stool softener that would help. We worked our way down from the best tasting to the most disgusting. The fourth one which tasted awful, worked. Unfortunately for this situation, Micah could taste, and wouldn't touch it. I tried drink after drink to disguise the taste. Nothing could get that medicine into Micah until one night I was pouring Daddy a glass of his favorite root beer and thought it might be unusual enough to cover the medicine. I poured some root beer into a bottle, added the medicine and approached Micah in my sweetest voice. He guzzled it down. After that our root beer bill went up. I had to have plenty on hand for our two root beer lovers. Every little human thing like this made Micah easier to relate to as a little boy instead of a blind, spastic quadriplegic, microcephalic.

> *JOURNAL: Hampy and Daddy have designed an addition to our new bedroom that will be under Daddy's apartment. They have made an alcove between the bedroom and the bathroom, with room for a baby bed, a small table, and floor to ceiling cabinets for baby things. I am more excited about that than the new bedroom. At last, the baby will not be eighteen inches from our bed, disturbed every time we turn over, and I will have a place to put all the clothes, toys, diapers, etc.*

> *JOURNAL: "Desist from your own ways, seeking your own pleasure, speaking your own words, then you will take delight in the Lord and I will make you ride on the heights of the earth" (Isaiah 58:13). Lord, my will is to speak Your words today and not my own. This is how I can fulfill my prayer of walking upon the earth with my hands in the reality of the needs of the flesh and the natural, and my spirit and heart in communion and fellowship with You. Thank You, Lord, I am aware of an increasing ability to remember the Word and quote it. I believe You are*

beginning to accomplish the answer to my prayer about my memory of scripture.

JOURNAL: The Lord gave David the zeal to say in I Samuel 17:26, "Who is this uncircumcised Philistine, that he should taunt the armies of the living God?" Then David ran out to attack Goliath, trusting God to deliver, shouting, "You come to me with a sword, a spear and a javelin, but I come to you in the name of the Lord of Hosts, the God of the armies of Israel, whom you have taunted." (I Samuel 17:45) "...and that all this assembly may know that the Lord does not deliver by sword or by spear; for the battle is the Lord's and He will give you into our hand." (I Samuel 17:47). Lord, put Your sword in my hand (Ephesians 6:17) and teach me to swing it even when my enemy has dealt me a stunning blow. Let me not take off my armor and lay down my weapon because I am tired or hot or discouraged. Make me a seasoned warrior. In addition to the full armor of God in Ephesians 6, Isaiah 59:17 says, "He wrapped Himself with zeal, as with a mantle." Lord, wrap your mantle of zeal around me.

As if one baby on seizure medication was not enough, when Beth was less than a year old, we made an interesting discovery about her. One morning after Hamp had taken her outside, he said, "This is the second time this week Beth has started shaking and then vomited."

"I know, she must be finding magic markers under one of the children's beds and eating them, or something," I said. "I have looked for what she might be getting into that is making her sick, but I can't find anything. If it happens again, I am going to take her to the vet." The next day Beth got sick again, and John and I hurried to get her to the vet while she was still shaking. Of course, by the time Dr. Kyle saw her she was fine. "I don't have to see her do it," he said. "From your description, I know she is having seizures. Lots of dogs have them."

I stared at him in disbelief. "Seizures!" I said. "You are kidding! Tell me you are kidding!"

"Nope, I'm not kidding," he said, laughing. "We can give her some Phenobarbital and it will probably control them just fine." Beth got a prescription for the same strength Phenobarbital tablets Micah took crushed up in his food for his seizures. I had two babies with seizures taking the same medicine, only one of them was a dog. When Micah ran out of his pills, I just gave him one of the dog's until I could get to the drugstore, and vice versa.

MANY PEOPLE HAD ASKED ME WHY ON EARTH HAMP AND I WERE willing to burden our family with children who had little or no potential, but they really loaded their guns with Micah. "Why do you keep doing this to yourself? What are you trying to prove? Call them and tell them to come and get him. You are not able to take care of your own family when you are so tired," they would say.

"God brought him to us and we love him," we would reply. "We don't know why he is so hard to take care of, but we know the Lord brought him to us, and we wouldn't be happier without him."

One day while visiting my good friend, Kathy Sones, (who had two birth children and four adopted, and had experienced her own sleepless nights and endless days in the name of love) Micah began to scream. I knew he was probably hungry, but we were deep in a discussion about our children, and I wasn't quite ready to go. I picked him up and tried to comfort him as we went on talking. He had reached nineteen pounds and was hard to hold because his spasticity bowed his back away from me and it took two hands to just hold on to him. I shifted him from one arm to the other, then back again, trying to ease the pain in my neck I seemed to have had almost constantly since we had gotten him. As we talked, I kissed him and rocked him back and forth, telling him one more minute and then we would go. After about fifteen minutes of this, we finally got to the front door. By this time, Micah was frantic. "I have to take this poor baby home and feed him," I told Kathy reluctantly ending the conversation.

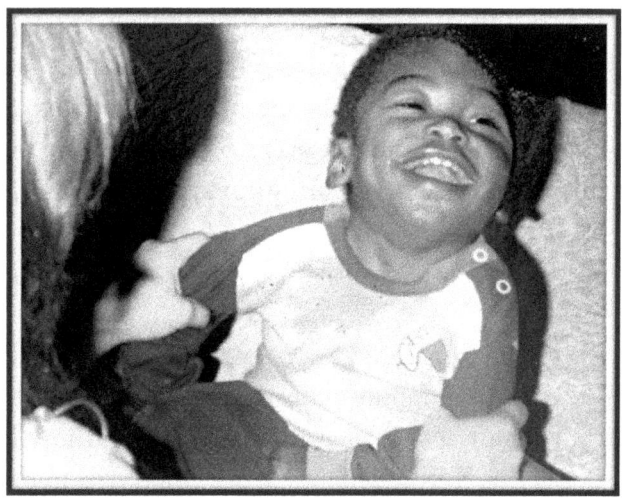

Micah enjoyed being shaken from side to side in a playful manner.

As I went out the door, Kathy said, "You know, your patience with him is incredible. I couldn't stand the screaming and the fighting just to hold him, and the frustration of never being able to satisfy him no matter what you do. I just couldn't handle it."

"But he can't help it," I said.

"I know, but I still couldn't do it, even knowing that," she said. "I know it's the Lord in you, giving you that love and empathy for him. Nobody could deal with him day after day the way you do without getting angry and frustrated with him unless it was Jesus in them doing it."

Not long before that, Hamp had said something very similar. He had said he had never seen such an anointing of love as the one I had for Micah. "If we all loved Micah like Mommy does, he would probably get better," he had commented to the children one night. I had heard similar words from Bob Thompson and several other people. I couldn't see what they saw. My feelings and actions seemed perfectly reasonable and ordinary to me. Obviously Jesus was using me in a way that I was unaware of. His grace felt so natural to me I didn't realize He was showing other people something supernatural. Years later I came to realize it was the anointing the angel gave me that night beside Micah's crib.

As I pondered this, I began to see one reason why God doesn't always heal the way we want. It's because when people see a supernatural miracle of healing, they see it, but their minds can't relate it to their life. Eyes which stare vacantly for months suddenly see. It is a miracle. At first, you acknowledge it with awe, but now that the eyes see, you begin to smile at the baby and move things for him to look at, and in literally seconds he has become a sighted child, something you are used to, something you understand. It is hard to remember how he looked before. It's hard to take in the miraculous change which has occurred. It doesn't change you, except that now you know God still does miracles unless or until you talk yourself out of it. But when the miracle is love and grace, that is a different thing. People understand that. Everyone can imagine how they would react if a baby screamed at them for hours and resisted everything they tried to do for him. Everyone can relate to being exhausted but faced with the need to go on. When people see someone who can love the unlovable, when they see someone standing, when in the natural, it is impossible for them not to fall, everyone seems to be able to relate to that. And they know they couldn't possibly do it on their own, and neither could we. Thus, the miracle of supernatural love and grace is often more beneficial to God's people as they seek to be like Jesus than seeing supernatural healing. It also gives a witness to unbelievers they can relate to. They can't explain it away or say they don't believe it.

> *JOURNAL: I saw the doctor for the pain in my neck and shoulders. He called it fibromyalgia and said they weren't sure what caused it but tension and stress make it worse. And it turns out, sleep deprivation. He prescribed some medication I don't want to take, but I suppose I will have to try it. The pain is really bad. Lord, I have prayed, been prayed for by the elders and my husband. If You will, I ask You to deliver me from this pain that I might serve You better.*

As our ministry to Micah continued to be so hard, I began to see the Lord wanted to show His love to the people around us through our relationship with him. People watched me wipe bloody vomit off of Micah and his clothes, and me and my clothes, and proceed on to wherever we were going without getting upset. They watched us rock him and kiss him and give him his medicine. They saw us leave the worship service at church to slip back to the baby room to check on him. They watched our children holding Micah and playing with him, so obviously loving him as a little brother. They were putting themselves in our places, thinking, "I could never love that child like that; how can they? Surely the Lord has given them supernatural grace." I came to realize one reason Jesus had given us such a hard child to care for was to get people's attention. To make them ask these questions so he could answer them and draw them down their path of sanctification as He was us.

Another reason and maybe the best reason the Lord gave us Micah was to show us ourselves. People continually asked me "Who in the world would want to adopt a baby like Micah?" One day the answer hit me in a flash of enlightenment—God would! I realized I was just like Micah! I was a blind, crippled, hyperactive baby with severe learning disabilities compared to my elder brother Jesus, and the Father's response was to adopt me. If Jehovah God had adopted me with all my defects, what should my response be to this innocent little child who bore no fault for his condition? Indeed, what should my response be to every other person God had made? This realization transformed my mind. I began to see who and what we actually are. We think we do so much for the Lord. We consider ourselves so intelligent and capable, but that is only because we compare ourselves with other people, who don't know any more than we do. When I compared myself to Micah, I saw dimly how Jesus probably feels when He looks at me. No wonder He looked on the people with such compassion. How much love He must have for us to adopt so many of us—to be willing to adopt us all!

> *JOURNAL: Lord, I am glad you gave us so much experience before you brought us Micah. Raising our own three children, owning a small business and having my father living with us is enough to keep us busy and tense, but no one could do all that and deal with Micah too if we didn't have Your grace, and the practical experience You have given all of us in dealing with babies. Micah is so hard to care for and so disruptive with his screaming, if we didn't have some spiritual maturity Hamp and I would probably be having problems in our marriage. A screaming baby eighteen inches from your bed every night isn't conducive to much relaxed communication.*

I Corinthians 10:13 speaks of God providing a way of escape from temptation, and while the Lord does not always provide relief the way we think we need it, He did actually provide us a few peaceful nights of sleep, to give us strength to keep going with Micah. Our friend Gay Lee, did respite for handicapped children full time. She took Micah overnight several times so we could sleep. Those three for four nights without Micah gave Hamp and me the only time we had during Micah's fifteen-month stay with us to be alone together and sleep all night without interruption. It was a tremendous blessing. People who don't have handicapped children have no idea what a few quiet hours or a good night's sleep can mean to people who never have them.

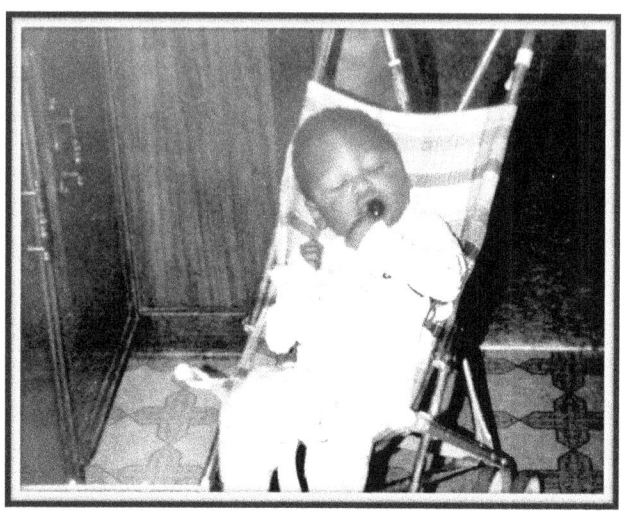

Look closely. He's holding a string-handle lollipop in his hand.

While we had Micah, we discovered how alone parents of handicapped children are. Most people seem to be afraid of handicapped children. They focus so on their abnormalities they fail to see them as children. Our sin nature also seems to make us turn away from anyone who is weak, or doesn't look like everyone else. It occurred to me when the children of Israel came out of Egypt, they all came. God's people all left Egypt. The cripples, the elderly and the babies all came too. Those who couldn't walk were carried, in someone's arms if necessary. I think this is God's intention for the church. Anyone born to us, or brought to us, should be enfolded in our collective arms and cared for as family. It wouldn't be so hard for a few of us if the others were willing to share the burden. Galatians 6:2 says, "Bear one another's burdens and thus fulfill the law of Christ." It is truly a terrible deficiency in the Church that the Christian mother whose child is born handicapped does not have the comfort of brothers and sisters in the Lord who will help her bear the burden of a special child. She will be verbally sympathized with and encouraged, but very few fellow believers will actually reach out to help her carry that child.

Special children are sent to bring us a special message from the Lord, to teach us singular lessons about His love. They should be treated as such by the family of God, and not like organic refuse to be destroyed or neglected because it is "less than perfect" in the eyes of man.

> JOURNAL: When a person is holy before God, other people will be drawn to them for the source of what they have. Lord, please make me a person who shines Your love and light to the people around me.

> JOURNAL: Everything I do should accomplish first a witness to the love and truth of Christ, and second, a job well done. The spiritual dimension of a job is much more important than the earthly dimension.

As part of our struggle to relate to Micah as a baby and not an enemy trying to drive us crazy, we gave him nicknames. Hamp called him Micah Mouser, and I started calling him Mousie, but John's boyish exuberance saw him as The Great Mouserini. I loved it. It seemed to give him all sorts of great potential and abilities as yet undiscovered and soon I was calling him Mouserini too.

John had a gift of seeing beyond the disabilities to the little child inside. And when Micah had started on the valium and relaxed a little, John began to play with him as he knew the little boy in Micah wanted to play. When he came home from school he would shout "Pookey Bear Knot!" at Micah, who would instantly smile with anticipation. John would quickly snatch him up, take him to his room and throw him onto his bed. He would wrestle and roll him around until he finally wadded Micah into a "Pookey Bear Knot," a gentle kind of tangling arms and legs called an Indian knot. Other times John wrapped himself and Micah in a sheet, holding Micah on top of him and rolling all over the carpet, with Micah grinning from ear to ear. But Micah's very favorite game was being held by the shoulders and shaken from side to side. He would laugh out loud for as long as someone was willing to shake him. I often worried it couldn't be good for his little brain to be shaken so much, but he loved it more than anything, so we thought it was worth the risk. After all, the Bible says, "A merry heart does good like a medicine," (Proverbs 17:22). Another occasion for laughter was Hamp's arrival every evening. As soon as he heard Hamp's voice, Micah would squeal with pleasure.

He even eventually learned to enjoy riding in the car and going out in the stroller. For months the motion frightened him, but as he learned to trust us, he relaxed enough to enjoy riding. He also loved sitting outside in warm weather and he would smile when put outside in his infant seat in the shade of a tree or on the back porch. The singing of the birds and the breeze on his face were as sweet a pleasure to Micah as to anyone else, especially since he couldn't see or open his hands to play, or even touch anything without help.

AS I GOT TO KNOW HIM BETTER AS A LITTLE PERSON, I REALIZED I had reacted to Micah at first as if he were only the sum total of his medical problems. I had thought, how much of a person could a twelve-month-old baby be who had no brain in the left side of his head and nothing but disordered electrical activity on the right side? I didn't realize those problems with his brain did not affect the little human being inside. His spirit was not handicapped; it just lived in a body that was. When he had come to us he was tense and terrified as any child would be under the circumstances. Only, tense for Micah meant more painful impulses from his brain to his muscles than usual. He would never be able to tolerate crowds or noisy stores with loud speaker systems, because they overwhelmed and frightened him. He lacked brain capacity to sort out stimulations.

In our home he heard voices he didn't recognize, he couldn't see where he was, or even open his tightly fisted hands to feel around him. No wonder he had been terrified and shrieked in panic. His mother apparently had not had the ability to offer him any comfort, so he had no former sense of security to fall back on —no hope in some corner of his awareness that there were good, loving people in his world who would try to make him feel better. He was so frightened and vulnerable for the first month with us that just taking him down from my shoulder and laying him beside me on the couch made him scream with fear. Now I understood he could feel himself falling backward and didn't know he could trust me not to let him fall. No wonder he had been so out of control. I had thought it was all just related to his brain damage, but now I realized the little boy inside had been terrified and his brain damage had rendered him unable to express it in ways we could understand. Micah had wanted to run hide under a bed and whimper for home, or at least something familiar, but he couldn't do that, so he screamed.

Slowly, slowly, the person inside Micah's spastic, malfunctioning, little body showed himself. Quite by accident I noticed he sometimes became still and attentive when he heard music playing, so I bought him a stuffed puppy dog with a radio in its stomach and put it in his bed.

When I wanted him to go to sleep or just try to relax, after I had tried everything else, I would put him in bed with his dog radio and close the door on his screaming. Not always, but often, he would calm down as he listened to the music and would relax and sometimes even go to sleep for a little while. A therapist confirmed that music often helps brain damaged children calm down because they begin to breathe in synch with the beat of the music.

As Micah grew, his spasticity pulled him to one side, causing his spine to curve. Kim's recommendation was for us to have him fitted for a special chair which held his back straight and prevented his spine from curving any more. While he was in his chair I would sometimes pull his fingers open and put a lollipop in his fist. His hands were so spastic he couldn't open his fingers to drop it. There was actually something good about Micah's brain damage. He could hold a lollipop because he couldn't open his hand to drop it. I had to help him get the lollipop up, and his head down, to get it into his mouth the first few times, but once he tasted it, he worked hard to get it back into his mouth. Watching him work to get his hand up and his head down to get the candy into his mouth reminded us again there really was a little boy inside.

> JOURNAL: Lord, the medicine for my neck stops the pain but has such side effects I just can't take it. Please heal me. I promise to give You all the glory.

> JOURNAL: Lord, Micah can hold a lollipop because his hands are so tightly closed. Help me to remember Micah's lollipops when I think there is nothing positive in a situation.

Because Hamp worked hard all day and the children were well, children, I felt responsible for the lion's share of caring for the babies. I had not really thought about the Lord wanting to teach them how to be servants, or to give them the experience of being useful to the Lord. But one night when Micah and I were both sick with a virus, the Lord showed me I was not the only one He wanted to use to minister to the babies. When I tried to put Micah to bed that night, he skipped his usual thirty-minute nap and went immediately to his crying. I knew he felt bad, but so did I, and I was so tired I didn't see how I could physically stay up with him. As I stood by the crib holding him, trying to decide what to do, Laura came in. "You go to bed, Mommy. I'll take care of Micah for you," she said.

"Oh, Laura, you are sweet to offer, but I can't let you stay up so late. He might cry all night," I said.

"Tomorrow is Saturday and I'll sleep on the couch," she said, taking him out of my arms. I reminded myself though she looked about eight, Laura was really eleven and with all of her previous experience with babies, she was quite capable of caring for Micah all night. The thought of relief was so inviting, I said maybe I could get some sleep and then take over later if she needed me to. I fixed Micah some Tylenol and a bottle and got Laura settled with him in the den. I told her to check his temperature every few hours and call me if it went higher. I got up once during the night to check on them and found her rocking him while she watched the late movie. I didn't wake again until morning and went straight to the den. Micah was sound asleep sitting straight up in his infant seat with a bright yellow washcloth draped over his head like a little washerwoman (a cool cloth to make him feel better), and Laura was asleep on the edge of the couch, lying on her stomach with one hand on the infant seat she had been gently shaking to soothe him to sleep. I stood for several minutes just looking at them. The little black boy who suffered so much from so many things—pain, fear, abandonment—was now safe and comfortable in the care of a little white girl with long strawberry blond hair, in her nightgown, children who had been lovingly prepared by the Lord for just such a night. How the Lord seems to delight in blending the improbable and incongruous, I thought. His love removes all the silly boundaries men put up. When I took Micah's temperature, it was about

100. Laura reported she had given him Tylenol every four hours and had dropped water in his mouth every thirty minutes with an eyedropper so he wouldn't get dehydrated when he refused to take his bottle. I couldn't have done any more if I had stayed up with him myself. After that night it was easier to let the children make sacrifices for the babies because I realized Hamp and I were not the only believers in the family who had been called to their ministry.

> JOURNAL: I must desire each day to enter into the delight of the holy day God has given me. Today is a special, holy day. Every day should be like a special holiday, a day to particularly do God's will and exalt Him (Isaiah 58:13).

> JOURNAL: Walking and praying today I was thinking about going back to school and getting a degree in special education or social work so I could help more than just one baby at a time. As I prayed, two trees with fruit like oranges on them appeared in my mind. A fruit fell from the tree on the right and it burst open on the ground. There was nothing in it but dust. There was no life in it, no seeds to perpetuate its life. I knew this was symbolic of fruit I would produce by my own effort. It looked good, but it would only last a short time and had no eternal value. It would turn to dust and disappear. Then a fruit fell from the other tree, and when it broke open it was full of juice and pulp and seeds. It had all it needed to perpetuate life. I knew this was fruit produced by the Holy Spirit in my life and what I did in obedience to God had eternal value.

Micah's spastic muscles had been somewhat relieved and his intestines were working fairly well, when he developed a new problem which threatened his life. Having left him with the children while I went to the grocery store, I was startled to hear myself paged over the public address system. It was Laura, calling to tell me Micah had spit up blood. I went straight home, looked at the color and amount of blood on the sheet, and thought he had probably broken a blood vessel in his throat screaming. I called Bob and he agreed, but told me if it continued, we would have to put a tube down into his stomach and look for the source of the blood. A few days later he did it again, but it was just a little and it was fresh blood, so I put off taking him to the doctor. Micah had blood drawn every few weeks to keep a check on his fluctuating Dilantin level and with his fragile little veins it was a painful ordeal for him. I hated to put him through an unpleasant procedure if it could be avoided. I was also avoiding it for myself, because I always stayed with a baby having a painful procedure done. I dreaded holding Micah down while Bob put the tube in. Unfortunately, about two weeks after the first episode, Micah and I were in the car when he suddenly started vomiting old blood, lots of it. It looked like he had drunk a whole Coke and vomited it back up. It wasn't the consistency of Coke, though, and it was everywhere. He was soaked, the seat of the car was soaked, it was on the floor, and of course by the time I had changed him into clothes from his diaper bag and wiped up what I could, it was all over me. I had no choice but to take him in to let Bob put a tube into his stomach and see if he had an ulcer.

Having a tube put through your nose into your stomach is no fun for anyone, and it terrified Micah. He gagged and cried as I held him down while Bob inserted the tube. Bob aspirated a little blood, but not enough to be sure Micah actually had an ulcer in his stomach. As soon as it was over, I picked Micah up, still gagging and coughing and cuddled him in my arms. How I hate doing things to my children they think are mean, but are really for their good, I thought. Even if Micah was a completely normal baby, he still would feel vulnerable and betrayed by my having let someone do this to him.

> **JOURNAL:** *Agape means unconquerable benevolence. I will do you good, whether you reciprocate or reject it. It doesn't matter what the other person's response is. No matter how my children fight me, my benevolence toward them will be unconquerable.*

> **JOURNAL:** *Lord, I keep facing situations which require me to be hard on my own children and Micah for their good. I guess I am too sensitive to their feelings, but I want so much for them to believe I am motivated by my love for them. It breaks my heart when they think I am being vindictive. Do You feel this way when You make me go through something so I will grow and become a stronger Christian? Is this why You say over and over in Your Word, "The just shall live by faith" (Habakkuk 2:4, Romans 1:17 Galatians 3:11, Hebrews 10:38)? By putting me in Your place are You showing me when things are hard or seem unnecessary, I have to choose whether to believe You are motivated by Your love for me (exercise my faith) or think You are unloving or just don't care?*

Bob decided Micah had either esophageal reflux or a stress ulcer caused by his brain damage. He explained the body reacts to the stress of improper brain function the same way it does to other kinds of stress, and it was not uncommon for people who suffer brain damage in accidents to immediately develop stomach ulcers from the stress. Further tests would be dangerous because of Micah's seizure disorder so we decided to treat him with general ulcer medication and pray. Now Micah was taking medications for a bleeding ulcer, gas pains, spasticity, two medications for seizures and medication for thrush, which he seemed to have continuously. It felt as if I spent half of my time giving him medicine.

A week on the medication brought no change and I called Bob again. After we talked briefly and I brought him up-to-date on the vomiting, Bob said, "I hate to say this..." I knew what he was going to say and tried to brace myself to hear it. After a long silence he reluctantly finished his sentence. "This could be the thing that does Micah in." How I appreciated his understanding that I loved Micah. Most doctors assumed I had a totally clinical attitude about my babies and blurted out terrible opinions they would never have sprung so abruptly on a birth mother.

"I know," I said on the verge of tears, "and I want it understood I don't want Micah to end up in the hospital on life support we can't stop. If the Lord is not going to heal this I want him to stay right here with me until he goes home to Jesus. He has suffered too much in his short life for us to make it worse by inflicting useless technology on him."

When we hung up, I felt relieved to have expressed my feelings about continuing to fight to keep Micah alive if it became obvious it was time to let him go. The thought of the great Mouserini hooked up to machines with needles and tubes that wouldn't let him go home to Jesus made me feel literally sick. I had been his mother through so many months of pain, a bond had formed between us I had never felt with any other foster baby. Somehow, even though he couldn't see me or understand my words, I knew he knew me and I knew him. I felt my love had to protect him from further suffering if I possibly could. That also included preventing adoption if he was going to die soon. I didn't want him put through the trauma of separation from us only to die among strangers. I was sure it would be easy to give him back to the Lord in death, knowing he finally would be healthy and happy.

It was hard to even think in terms of Micah dying, because I had prayed so hard for him to be healed. I had knelt by his crib again and again, entreating the Lord to heal him and allow him the freedom and pleasures other children took for granted. I pictured him in a Cub Scout uniform, running and playing with other little boys. Oh, how I wanted that for him! I wanted so much for him to be healed as Caleb had been—completely. I knew it was possible; I had seen it. But I also knew the Lord had plans and an agenda I was not privy to.

While I tried to see what the Lord was doing in Micah's life as he was now, I kept hearing in my mind, "Who has made man's mouth? Or who makes him dumb or deaf, or seeing or blind? Is it not I, the Lord," (Exodus 4:11)? I knew in the over-all providence of God's will in a sinful world, He had allowed Micah to be handicapped, but that was true for Caleb too, and He had healed him.

As I saw that Micah was not healed, I fell back on what I did know. I knew I was to obey the Lord, whether I saw the healing I wanted or not. My responsibility to Micah was love, compassion and service, no matter how long or short his life. I tried to obey what I knew the Lord wanted from me, and Micah gradually recovered from his bleeding. It stopped and never recurred.

JOURNAL: Lord, thank you for Daddy's presence with us. He adds so much to the family. Now that two of the children are teenagers, there is much more tension around here than when he lived with us for his eye surgery. When we get into a dispute with one of the children, Daddy just quietly disappears into his room. He never complains about Micah's screaming, but I know it drives him as crazy as it does us. I never dreamed he would be so much help. He can fix anything, and knows so much about so many things. He helped Laura make an active volcano for a school project and is a much better cook than I. He fixes supper when I am late because of Girl Scout meetings or Micah's doctor appointments and is a wonderful blessing to have around.

When we had had Micah close to a year, he began to regress. He had been making some real progress, but now was acting almost as he had at first. We asked for prayer for him one Wednesday at prayer service even though we were unable to attend that night. As the church prayed, a man we hardly knew told the group he felt Micah was being oppressed by demonic activity. When the pastor told Hamp, we thought it sounded a little farfetched although he certainly acted like someone being tormented by demons. About a week later, Jeff Wilson, the foster father who had taken Matthew when he was brought back from New York, called the *700 Club* to ask for prayer for something. As he was explaining his prayer request to the counselor on the phone, she interrupted him and said, "Excuse me, but do you know someone named Mickey or Mecca or something like that?"

"I know someone named Micah," he said.

"Well, I believe the Lord is telling me he is under demonic attack," she said. Jeff called us immediately with this amazing information and we decided to have Micah prayed for. We gathered with the pastor and several others and prayed for deliverance for Micah, if indeed he was being oppressed by a demon spirit.

Not being experienced in the area of deliverance, I can only report what I saw. Micah started coughing as we prayed, and he coughed until we were almost through. Apparently, this can be a symptom of a demon leaving a body. He did settle down immediately and grew calmer and happier and started sleeping better. We never saw that extreme, hysterical type of behavior from him again. Why he would have been suddenly attacked by a demon, and why the Lord would have told people who didn't even know Micah, I have no idea.

Even though there were days I thought it would be a relief when Micah was adopted, when the call actually came, I was devastated. The social worker, Nancy Grenfell, was so elated when she called to tell me there was a family who wanted Micah it took her by surprise when I choked up and couldn't speak. It took me a little by surprise too. I don't think I had realized, myself, how deeply I had come to love him.

 JOURNAL: Lord, I remind You of my prayers about

Micah's adoption. I don't want him to leave me only to die among strangers. If this adoption actually happens I will assume he is going to live for at least several more years.

We were extremely happy to learn the family who wanted him lived in Oregon. That wonderful place was going to receive another of our little ones. The family was Mormon and had five birth children and seventeen adopted. They actually sounded qualified to parent Micah. Their adopted children had just about every birth defect I had heard of and some I hadn't. They wanted Micah very much and were anxious to get him as soon as possible.

"Wonderful," I sniffed tearfully to Micah as I picked him up. "Just when you start to sleep all night once in a while, you go and get adopted."

We went to the swing, and as I hugged his chubby little body while the swing gently rocked us, I thought surely this time the pain would be too much for Jesus to soften. How could I ever give my little Mouserini to someone else. How could I ever tell them all of his needs; how he acts when this is wrong, or that is wrong. It had taken me fifteen hard months to understand him so well, how could I ever prepare them to take care of him the way I did? Of course the answer was that I couldn't. But I could do "my part" and I began to make a mental list of the things I could do to make things easier for him. I could make a notebook detailing his care. I could have someone with a video camera come and make a tape of Micah when he felt good, showing what he could do, etc. so when he got to them, they would know the difference between a happy Micah and an unhappy Micah. If you didn't know him, sometimes it was hard to tell the difference. I wanted so much to avoid his having to suffer with them as he had with us for the first months because we didn't understand his problems. I made his new mother a notebook covering all the information about Micah I could think of. I explained sleep, medication, play, exercise, fun, everything I knew about Micah went into that book. I mailed it to her as soon as I could. I talked to his new mother on the phone often, and Hamp had some friends make a videotape of Micah, and we sent that too.

Having done all we could think of to prepare the way for Micah to become part of their family, there was no more to do but trust the Lord to make it all work. I discovered that this time, I really had faith He would do what Micah needed because I had seen it before. Each baby had built on my store of knowledge about the Lord. There were things I didn't really have to hope for (Hebrews 11:1). I knew they would be there, because I knew the Lord and I knew how much He loved Micah.

One thing bothered all of us. The family was Mormon. They were obviously wonderful people; we knew that from our conversations on the phone, but we always prayed the Lord would bring Christian parents for our babies, and Mormon doctrines do not adhere to the Lordship of Christ. We prayed about this and got peace so fast we questioned if it really was from the Lord. How could He give us peace about Micah going to a Mormon family without much prayer and revelations? But the peace was from Jesus, as we would see later.

When I expressed my pain at letting Micah go to Nancy, she suggested it might be a good time for me to see Matthew again. He had adjusted to his new family and enough time had elapsed for him not to remember me.

I met Matthew and his adoptive parents at Catholic Charities and it was a blessing and encouragement to see him. He was obviously relaxed and happy with his new parents and was very important part of their family. It was good to see the provision of God for Matthew and it reinforced my confidence that His arrangements for Micah would be just as complete.

WHEN THE DAY CAME TO FLY TO THE WEST COAST WITH MICAH, I

wasn't afraid at all. I knew everything was in God's hands. Hamp and I planned to rent a car and drive to San Francisco, stopping overnight to see Caleb and his family in Portland, where they were living now. The anticipation of seeing Caleb and his family gave me something to look forward to after we left Micah and I was grateful the Lord allowed us such a wonderful treat. I had never expected to see Caleb again, unless he looked us up after he was grown. When we had flown to the west coast the first time with Caleb, I had been bothered by air sickness every time we landed. There were four landings scheduled for this trip and I was a little apprehensive. On the first trip the nausea had gotten progressively worse with each landing, and seemed to be related to how tired I was and how much my neck hurt. I took the medication the doctor recommended and had plenty of gum to chew, but it had no effect. After landing to change planes in Dallas, I was only a little nauseated, but my headache got worse when we boarded the biggest plane I had ever seen. We were assigned two seats on the side, and would have to hold Micah in our laps. My head ached and my neck hurt terribly from the contour of the airplane seats. "I can't believe we have to sit like this all the way to San Francisco," I moaned to Hamp.

After we took off, He asked a stewardess if we could move to the rear of the plane where there were several rows of empty seats. She agreed, and we moved back to the cool, dark area in the back of the plane and gave Micah some valium so he could go to sleep. It was a great relief to be able to lay him in a seat between us after hours of holding him.

Because everyone on our side of the plane passed us on their way to the restroom we spent most of the flight answering one person's questions after another about Micah and our other babies and what the Lord had done for them. White parents with a black baby attracted questions, especially when they heard our southern accent.

I had eaten what they brought me for lunch in the hope food

would help combat the nausea I feared when we landed in San Francisco, but when it was time to land, I found it had not helped at all. As the plane began to descend and the cabin air changed, I broke out in a cold sweat, I was overcome with nausea and my ears started to ring. Oh no, I thought, I'm going to throw up and then faint! The more frightened I became, the worse I felt. In a matter of seconds, I was completely panicked. Hamp was looking at me with concern, "Are you ok?" he asked anxiously. I slowly turned and looked at him, my face a deathly white. "Oh, no," he said. "What can I do?"

"Pray," I managed to whisper. This doesn't have to happen, I told myself. I don't have to do this, I don't have to faint, I don't have to be sick. I looked out the window across the aisle from me. The sky was blue and beautiful. Lord, I silently prayed, You can stop this. You can do anything, please, Lord, don't let me throw up. As I frantically begged the Lord to help me, I sensed the Father in the Spirit, and He was laughing! The instant I became aware of His laughter, He reached out and touched my left shoulder and I began to laugh too. I laughed so hard tears were running down my face and I couldn't get my breath. My fear of being sick had become the funniest thing in the world. I laughed so hard for three or four minutes, I was unable to talk. Hamp was looking at me with real alarm. He probably thought my mind had snapped. "Are you laughing? What are you doing!?" he demanded.

"I'll tell you in a minute," I managed to gasp as I laughed. Finally, I got control of myself enough to try to tell him what had happened. Then we were both laughing at how wonderful the Lord was and what a sense of humor He had. I never would have expected Him to heal someone of intense nausea and dizziness by making them laugh, but that is exactly what He did. I was healed by a sovereign act of love by my heavenly Father, when I was too sick to even think coherently. No one could laugh that hard when they felt as sick and frightened as I did, except by a touch from the Lord. It is utterly impossible to laugh when you know you are about to vomit. I had nothing to do with what He did. Of all the loving and merciful experiences the Lord has given me, this one more than any other, burned into my spirit, the reality of His love and the closeness of His presence. He is Jehovah Shammah, the God who is there. I don't know that He would have done this for me if I had been flying to Hawaii to lie on the beach and spend money on things I didn't need, but I do know what He will do when you are about His business and find yourself in desperate need of supernatural help.

We still had to land and take off several more times before we reached Eugene, Oregon, our final destination. The next time we landed Hamp looked at me, "Are you okay?"

"I am great, no problem." I said. In fact, I have not been sick on a plane since.

At the airport in Oregon, we had to walk across the cold, windy airstrip to the terminal. I was trying to hold my jacket around Micah and didn't even see the glass doors until we reached them. On the other side we were surprised to hear cheering from several dozen people waiting for us inside. When we opened the doors they began to clap. They were adoptive families and social workers there to help his new family welcome Micah. His new mother whisked him out of my arms and I let him go. I didn't hold him again until that night when they put him to bed.

Micah's new family is a book in itself, only his mother, who died of a brain tumor a couple of years later, never got a chance to write one. The house was full of children from every part of the country. There were little boys who were deaf, with learning disabilities, and were hyperactive, a little girl with Downs, a set of teenage twins who had cerebral palsy and were mentally disabled. The girl was blind and the boy couldn't walk. There was a daughter who had no arms and only one leg whose birth mother had taken drugs laced with thalidomide. While all of the children begged to hold Micah, I realized one of the reasons God had sent him there. There were twenty-two laps for him, not including the parents. He would always have someone to hold him and carry him around. He would never be left alone, even for one minute. They were a wonderful family for him. On the refrigerator was a chore list for the children, much like ours at home except theirs took up the whole front of the refrigerator. Each child had work to do, and was expected to do it, no matter what their handicap. The last little name at the bottom of the list was the tiny two-year-old girl with Downs. Her job was to smile. I passed through the kitchen the next day, and saw one of the twins sitting on a couch with piles and piles of laundry around him. I could hardly see him among the clothes. His sight was poor, but unlike his sister, he could see a little. I watched as he carefully picked up piece after piece of laundry and folded it. Some things didn't look any different when he put them in the folded pile, but that wasn't the point. The point was he was doing his chore, carrying his share of the load, and he was clearly proud of that.

As the parents told us how they had acquired their children, I started to grasp an astounding truth. Each child born on the earth is infinitely valuable to his Creator. He cares for each one of them. They are all made in His image and their exterior has nothing whatever to do with their worth to Him. I thought again about the scripture in Exodus 4, "Who has made man's mouth? Or who makes him dumb or deaf, or seeing or blind? Is it not I, the Lord?" How can we begin to fathom God's designs for each life, especially based on how they look to us on the outside? I looked around the room at all these beautiful children, and had a glimpse, for an instant, of what He sees when He looks at them. "In as much as you have done to the least of these my brethren, you have done it unto Me," (Matthew 25:40) rose in my spirit. These were Jesus's little brothers and sisters. Many of them would never know right from wrong or be able to make a moral decision, but they were already written in the Lamb's Book of Life and were here for a reason. To show Him to us, to show His pure, innocent love, to allow us to serve them and care for them in His name, as if we were serving and caring for Jesus Himself. A scripture that had been coming to my mind all the time I had Micah, now burst into bloom in my mind. (I Corinthians 1:27) "But God has chosen the foolish things of the world to shame the wise, and God has chosen the weak things of the world and the despised, God has chosen the things that are not, that He might nullify the things that are, that no man should boast before God." I saw for the first time how man tends to look up, up to the heights he desires to attain, up to scan the horizon to see his future, up to see what he will achieve for himself, much as Satan said, "I will ascend to heaven..." (Isaiah 14:13). And all the while God has been saying, "Look down, child. Look down and see what I am doing at your feet. Look around you and see the need. Look down to the weak and the needy who are afraid to ask you for your attention, you who are so capable and strong. Stoop down to the little ones like Matthew and Micah, who can't learn to speak your language so they can tell you what they need. They can only cry and drive you crazy with their crying, pushing you away when they want you to come close and love them."

The next day we drove away from Micah's new home and I never saw him again. I cried most of that day, but by the next, the Lord had comforted me more than I would have thought possible in so short a time. I was actually able to look forward to seeing Caleb (now called Ben) and the Walkers.

When we turned into the Walker's driveway in Portland, Caleb, now five, was watching for us from the window. When we went inside and greeted his mother and brothers and sisters, he hung back and wouldn't speak to us. "That's all right," I said, "We can talk later," and I went into the kitchen with Suzy. She laughed as she told us he had been kneeling on the couch all day watching out the window for us, then when we came, he was too shy to talk to us. He gradually relaxed and opened up to us and it was a blessing to see him so happy and healthy. When I held him in my arms again and read him a story before he went to bed, I was conscious the whole time of never having dreamed this could happen. I hoped to be able to see Micah like this one day. We had a wonderful visit with the Walkers. Caleb and his sister Carolyn were still like twins. They shared a room and raced around the house playing, just as they had that first day when we brought him to them. Caleb told his mother before we left, that his foster parents were nice people and he liked us a lot. What a strange relationship foster parents have with foster children. Even though we had loved him like our own and had given him much of his ability to trust people, and a sense of worth and security that remained deep in his subconscious, he had no conscious memory of us. It made me think what unique relationships God will give us when we follow Him in obedience, not measuring what is happening by the world's standards.

> *JOURNAL: Mothering Micah was the hardest, most consistently taxing thing I ever did. There was little about him that was easy or came naturally, and there were more days than I can count when I thought I could not bear with him one more hour. If ever I was in over my head, it was with Micah.*
>
> *I remember Daddy taking me swimming in the summer when I was little. I loved for him to walk out into the deep water, carrying me in his arms. I never had a twinge of fear while I was in my daddy's arms. It didn't matter how deep the water was, I knew he would hold me up. When Peter said, "Lord, if it's really You, tell me to come to You on the water" (Matt. 14:28), Peter believed intellectually that Jesus could make him walk on water; but to know it experientially required stepping out of the boat when Jesus said, "Come."*

Before Micah, I had heard the report Jesus would keep me from sinking, but now I have experienced it. It is the difference between believing and knowing. Without the experience of Micah in my life, I would have intellectualized about the faithfulness of Christ, and learned all the correct things to say about it, but I never would have known He would uphold me and carry me in His arms like a Father carries his son, (Deuteronomy 1:31) through the deepest water I had ever come through.

5
NATHAN

Three months after Micah was adopted, another little black boy was ready to leave the hospital. He was three months old and had never left intensive care. Born with a chamber missing from his heart and an obstruction in his intestines, he had already been through two major surgeries. The surgeries combined with his badly deformed heart, had left him small and frail for his age. Prior to his birth, his teenage mother had made arrangements for him to be surrendered for adoption, but now she was prepared to forego college and take him home if a family could not be found for him.

When Catholic Charities called, I went through the motions of asking for time to pray and talk to Hamp, but I knew unless the Lord clearly told us not to, we would take the baby. The children were ready for a baby as evidenced by John's remark a few days before: "We need another baby around here!" My arms felt empty too, and while I still felt very much connected to Micah in my heart, I was ready for the next baby.

The baby was to be released from the hospital the following Tuesday, so Hamp and I began our visits to Pediatric ICU the next day. The baby was weak, but he smiled sometimes with a forlorn expression that made me want to take him home and take care of him. This baby, we called Nathan, was covered with scars much like Matthew. There was a big scar from his breastbone around the right side of his body (his heart was on the wrong side) to his spine from heart surgery. Another scar tracked across his abdomen from surgery to correct an intestinal defect he also had. In addition, he had all the routine scars from I.V. cut downs. The scars and the dark circles under his eyes left no doubt he had already suffered too much for one so young.

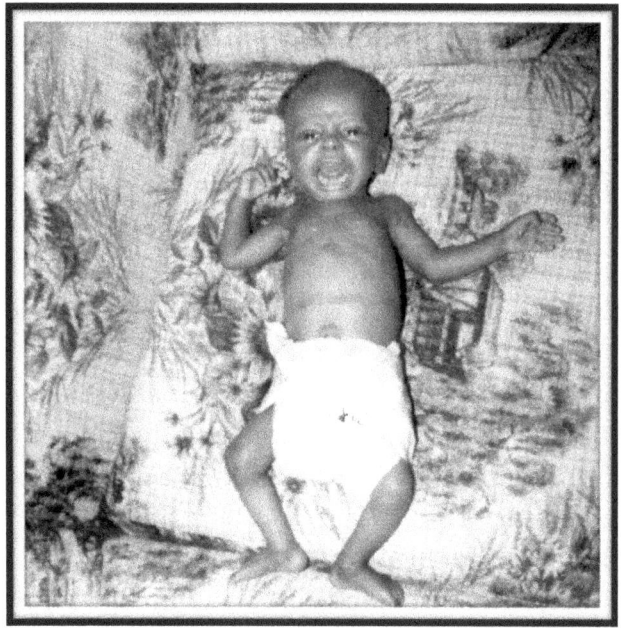

Nathan when we got him. He's wearing a newborn diaper.

His doctors explained that his condition was extremely serious and his life expectancy was short. In addition to missing a whole chamber in his heart, he had deformed blood vessels which had been surgically rerouted. It was hoped the rerouted vessels would serve him adequately for several years. Then they would have to be altered because of his growth. His condition was complex, but the care he needed from us was simple. We were to carefully watch his fingernails and lips for a bluish tinge that would alert us to oxygen deprivation and we were to monitor his heart rate with a stethoscope. If his heart, which beat much faster than a normal baby's, was beating faster than the doctor wanted, we were to give him his heart medicine. The hardest part of his care for me was his need to eat every two hours around the clock. His heart worked so hard to make up for the missing chamber he quickly burned up the nourishment in his high calorie formula and he was so small his tiny stomach could only hold three or four ounces of formula at a time. We were told nothing we could do would help Nathan if his heart started failing. He would have to be rushed to the hospital immediately. Even then, there was no guarantee they would be able to save him. This was a completely new type of situation for us. Caleb, Matthew and Micah had serious conditions, but this baby had a bad heart. He could die on us any minute. I knew the Lord had moved us into a new dimension.

> *JOURNAL: I am impressed by the power of God to sustain life under the most awful circumstances. The life force He gives is so powerful. It is hard to believe Nathan is still alive after what he has been through. He is so tiny and frail, but he clings successfully to life. There is a beautiful white flowering tree growing out of the bank of the lake near where I walk and pray. It is*
>
> *literally parallel with the water. The right side of the tree trunk and the top of the tree are almost in the water. Half of the roots are exposed in the bank. It must be terribly stressful for the tree to live in a horizontal position hanging out over the water instead of upright as it is supposed to be. I first saw it in winter and was sure it was dead. I thought it would be impossible to sustain life in such a position, but in the spring it burst into full bloom. It*

> *must have a long taproot which anchors it so securely and deeply, that in spite of the position in which it has to grow, it has everything it needs (Jeremiah 17:8 and Colossians 2:7).*
>
> *When I think sometimes I am pressed too hard to keep going, I think of that tree and encourage myself to push my roots deeper into Jesus.*

On Monday of the following week, one day before Nathan was to come home with us, Catholic Charities called. The social worker had called intensive care to check on him and been told his orders showed he would be released that very day. This was news to everyone. The nurses had no idea why a doctor had written the release order for Monday instead of Tuesday, the original release date. The social worker was on her way to the hospital to sign the papers releasing him to me and I needed to be there to pick him up. Laura and I quickly threw our car seat, some tiny diapers and baby blankets into the car and headed for the hospital.

There was a party atmosphere in ICU that day as we gathered up the toys and clothes nurses had brought him during his stay, and we made the rounds to say goodbye to all the nurses who had cared for him. Nathan had been a patient all his life and everyone was happy that at last he was going to get to be a little boy with a home and a family.

Walking across the parking lot, I stepped into the sunlight and as he blinked and looked up at the light, I realized he had never seen the sun before. The only time he had ever left the hospital was to be shuttled into an ambulance for a trip to another hospital for heart surgery, and even that was done under a sheltered portico. I smiled as I realized the privilege God had given me. It is no small thing to show a child sunshine for the first time.

We had been home for about an hour and I was rocking Nathan in the rocker in our bedroom, giving him a bottle. The phone on the night table rang. It was Hamp. He said, "Nancy Grenfell, from Catholic Charities, was just here."

"At the shop? What for?" I asked.

"Well," he said, "she thought she should come tell one of us in person, and she couldn't reach you."

I was totally unprepared for what came next. "Sweet, Micah has gone Home to the Lord. He died in his sleep one night last week."

My little angel was gone. I would never see him again until I joined him in heaven. My weeping brought the children. They cried too, but being children, they reminded each other they would see him in heaven, and besides, they couldn't play with him any more in Oregon, anyway. After a few sad minutes, especially for John, who had loved Micah almost as much as I had, they were ready to go back to their play, but I had to mourn for my baby. I felt as if he had never left me, as if I had lost a baby, not his adoptive mother. Hamp said his new mother was devastated when she went to get him up one morning and he was gone. I could imagine how she must feel, and I prayed for her. I hugged Nathan as I cried. It was comforting to have my next baby in my arms to hug and rock as I cried for Micah.

I knew I would have felt much worse without Nathan to hold, and as I pressed my cheek against his head, Hampy's words sank in. He said Micah had died almost a week before, that the family had tried to reach us, or Catholic Charities or Human Services but couldn't reach anyone to let us know what had happened. The funeral was already over. I wondered why they couldn't reach someone. We had been home all week; both agencies had been open all week; there was no reason for them not to be able to notify someone of Micah's death. Then it hit me why the doctors had released Nathan a day early. The Lord had known how I would feel when I heard my Mouserini had died only three months after we had taken him to strangers. God knew I had begged Him not to take Micah away to die, and He wanted me to have the comfort of Nathan in my arms before I found out. It amazed me the Lord would care about something so insignificant as when I found out Micah had died. I was comforted by the Lord's concern for my feelings, but I was heartbroken He had taken Micah away to die. I felt He hadn't cared that I wanted Micah with me when he died. I told myself the Lord had reasons for allowing Micah's adoption just three months before his death and I tried to let go of it, but deep inside I was hurt. I had wanted so badly to keep Micah with us if he wasn't going to live. I couldn't help feeling the Lord just didn't care.

It should have been obvious to me if He had gone to so much trouble to protect me from the pain of knowing Micah had died until I had Nathan in my arms, He must have had a good reason for taking Micah away to die, but I didn't see it.

AFTER JUST A FEW DAYS AT HOME WITH THREE CHILDREN TO PLAY with, Nathan perked up considerably, but there was a distinct sadness about him which lingered. I noticed he had strange ridges in his nails, and when I took him to Bob, I asked about them.

Bob looked at the floor and said, "That is caused by stress."

"You mean pain," I said. "Yes."

A picture someone took of Nathan sitting in the lap of a lady in the nursery at church caught the essence of what he had endured. I didn't see him clearly until I saw this picture. He looked like a weak, worn out, old man. I hadn't known a baby could look so tired and sad.

OVER THE NEXT COUPLE OF MONTHS, NATHAN BECAME A DIFFERENT child, or rather, he became a child for the first time. He went to the grocery store, played in the church nursery and went with us to visit friends. He played with the children, went for rides in the stroller and discovered life outside a hospital. Because he was so small, he had to wear a little knit cap to help keep him warm. It made him look like a little French dock worker, and Kathy Sones greeted him with "*Bon jour, mon ami,*" whenever she saw him.

Like many of the babies, Nathan had a special love for John. The rest of us called him "Scooter-pie," but John dubbed him "Sonny-boy." Whenever Nathan heard "Sonny-boy" his whole face lit up. Stacey and Laura enjoyed him immensely and carried him around like a little doll. He was responsive enough for them to play with and small enough to cuddle. I had prayed the baby after Micah would be fun for the children because he had been so hard for the whole family. I thanked the Lord for the treat of a happy, responsive baby. The only real drawback to living with Nathan was the feedings every two hours. I had quickly gotten used to sleeping all night over the summer and it was hard, having to drag myself up and feed him so often. But Micah had been good training and I knew every two hours was a luxury I would have been anxious for just months before, so I tried not to whine too much.

> *JOURNAL: Lord, I believe our power comes directly from our obedience to the Holy Spirit within us. Hebrews 5:8-9 says Jesus learned obedience and became perfect. Was it not His obedience which gave Him the perfect power to win the terrible struggle in the garden which resulted in His sweating blood?*

When I took Nathan to the heart specialist who had done his surgery, his eyes were sparkling and he was almost chubby. The doctor was so pleased with his progress he said he thought Nathan might live much longer than originally thought.

I had high hopes for an adoptive home for him when I began to sense "something coming" in my spirit. There is no other way to explain it. I felt something. I didn't know if the Lord was going to heal Nathan, or maybe even take him home to Heaven. But I felt something coming. About the same time I began to have this feeling, I started seeing flashes in my mind of me sitting in a rocking chair with Nathan dying in my arms. I instantly rejected the images as soon as they presented themselves. I thought they were just my negative personality trying to keep me from getting too optimistic about his progress.

With Thanksgiving growing near, Hamp began hoping the "something" I felt was healing for Nathan. God had healed Caleb on Thanksgiving, so there was precedent. When the day came, Nathan was unusually fussy all morning, so when John rocked him and finally got him to sleep, he put him in his crib in our bedroom for a nap. When the children were helping me get the food on the table for dinner, we suddenly heard a scream from Nathan like nothing we had ever heard before. We all froze and looked at each other. I thought if Nathan had a heart attack he would black out and not be able to scream. It reassured me he was screaming so energetically. I ran to the bedroom and picked him up, but he kept screaming. I talked to him and patted him, walking back and forth, but he kept screaming and seemed strangely unaware of me. The bedroom was dimly lit.

"I can't see his nail beds or his lips," I told Hampy as Nathan continued to scream.

He said, "Take him to the kitchen so we can see under the fluorescent light." I was running down the hall with him, when his screams suddenly stopped and he went limp. In the bright fluorescent light, I could see his lips were black and his nail beds were dark blue.

"Call an ambulance!" I screamed. Angry in my anxiety, with Nathan lying draped over my arm like a rag doll. I snatched up the phone myself and dialed the number for the rescue unit and screamed at them too. "Hurry up!" I shouted, "He's dying!" I was frantic that I couldn't do anything. We all were. We stood rooted in our places, unable to move. We all stood watching Nathan breathe while he lay unconscious in my arms, at least not in pain, and totally unaware of us. Although his breathing was labored, he was breathing on his own, and I was glad I didn't have to try to do CPR on a ten-pound baby.

Even though they were only five minutes away, it seemed an eternity before we heard the siren in the street. Daddy, who had not been called to dinner yet, was up in his apartment napping when he heard the siren of the rescue unit. He could hear it was at our house and came rushing down his outside stairs to see what had happened. Much later we learned all the neighbors had rushed outside to see which one of their friends needed an ambulance and were naturally discussing how sad my father had suffered some life threatening event on Thanksgiving. They were all speechless when they saw the object of their concern come running down his stairs and into the house. No one had thought of Nathan.

I rushed past Daddy and into the ambulance with Nathan. Hamp told the children and Daddy to eat without us and he followed in the van. What a blessing Daddy is here, I thought. I couldn't bear to leave the children alone on Thanksgiving without someone they love to comfort them and keep them busy while they wait for word about Nathan. We had no idea when we would be back, or if Nathan would be alive when we came back.

As I climbed up into the ambulance I could only think of one thing: This was my fault. I should have prayed for him more. Why didn't I pray more? I knew something like this could happen. I have not been worthy of the trust the Lord put in me, I thought over and over. I knew Nathan was dying, and it was all my fault. I watched him take loud, heaving breaths every five or six seconds and thought surely each one would be his last. There was a malfunction of the oxygen equipment and they couldn't even help him breathe. As soon as we reached the hospital and Nathan was finally able to receive oxygen, the change was incredible. He brightened up and began to look around him and play with the tubing on the oxygen mask. He was looking perfectly normal when the heart specialist arrived. I turned to the nurse, feeling as if I were in the Twilight Zone.

"Am I crazy, or was this child in crisis when we got here?" I asked her.

"Oh, he was in distress all right," she said. "I thought he wasn't going to make it when you came in."

The cardiologist looked and listened. They drew blood. Finally, he said, "I think he is breathing a little faster than the last time I saw him. I'd like to keep him a few days to monitor him." What followed was a nightmare for Nathan and me as he was admitted into the ICU.

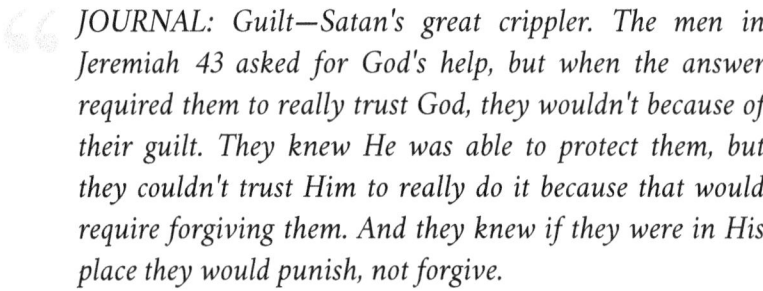

> *JOURNAL: Guilt—Satan's great crippler. The men in Jeremiah 43 asked for God's help, but when the answer required them to really trust God, they wouldn't because of their guilt. They knew He was able to protect them, but they couldn't trust Him to really do it because that would require forgiving them. And they knew if they were in His place they would punish, not forgive.*

When he found himself in another ICU, Nathan lost hope. This was not the same ICU he had spent his early months in and he felt the difference. On top of that, we could only see him for fifteen minutes every four hours. I would not have believed a six month old baby could be depressed, but each time I went in to see him, it was obvious that he was deeply depressed. He lay facing the wall, turning away from the people and activity just the opposite of a normal baby's response to being in a hospital. He had a needle in his arm and an oxygen mask taped to his face. The tape made raw sores on his skin and drove him crazy. He hated the mask and I counted the days for him until he no longer needed it. He was so sad he didn't seem to care whether I gathered up all of his tubes and monitor wires and held him for a few minutes or not. About the third day, it occurred to me if he would respond to anything, it would be seeing John.

That afternoon I took John to see him after school, and I had been right. When we got there, Nathan was lying with his face to the wall. But when John leaned over him and said, "Hey, Sonnyboy!" he whirled around and grinned up at John. He smiled and played with John a little that day, but it was the only time he ever smiled while he was in ICU.

To be fair, it was a large overworked ICU in a teaching hospital, caring for some desperately sick children, but Nathan did not get the care he needed there. With every new shift there was new staff, often people who had never seen Nathan before. I muttered to myself that I should make a tape to be played for each new shift about Nathan's needs, but I knew they wouldn't take the time to listen. I could never convince the staff of the hour that even though he weighed only ten pounds, he was almost six months old and he needed to eat more than a couple of ounces of milk every four to six hours. He had progressed to cereal and fruit at home and he needed to eat all he could. They would not feed him solids no matter what I said, and I got far beyond angry. I talked and talked to each new resident and was assured over and over they would take care of adding the fruit and cereal, but no one ever did. All they had to do was write it on the chart!

> JOURNAL: *The prophet Daniel did not stop serving God because he met with trials. He kept on going. He did not say, "Well, God can't expect me to go on this way, under these conditions." God did not keep Shadrach, Meshach and Abednego from the fire, but was in it with them. They had to face the furnace and even be thrown in. <u>Then they saw Jesus, but not before.</u>*

Finally, after days on no food but a newborn measure of

formula and no solid food, Nathan had lost a pound and I was livid. I called the cardiologist and asked if Nathan was stable enough to be moved into the special care area, where families could be with their children. He agreed and Nathan and I both felt better. At least I could be with him long enough to feed him some of his meals myself. When they moved him from intensive care, they tried to decrease his oxygen, but he immediately turned blue. Nathan was no closer to getting off the oxygen than the day we brought him in. In addition, they had ordered meat and vegetables he had never eaten before to feed him. The complete inability to obtain the care I thought necessary for my baby was shredding my nerves. I was used to talking to my pediatrician, and carrying out his instructions myself. I knew it would take only one more thing for me to explode at some member of the hospital staff.

The next morning after I got the children off to school, I tried to calm down and pray before going to the hospital, but I was too angry. I opened my Bible randomly and began to try to read. I read Luke chapter 6, "Be merciful as your Father is merciful," and, "do not pass judgment; can the blind lead the blind?" And especially verse 46, "Why do you call me Lord, Lord and do not do as I say?" Everything I read exhorted me to godliness and warned me not to ruin my witness by venting my frustration on whomever I could get my hands on first. I began to hear in my mind, "Weapons for the right hand and the left..." (II Corinthians 6:7) over and over. I didn't know exactly where it was, but I recognized it as scripture. When I found it, it also said, "Behold the acceptable time is now. " (II Corinthians 6:2).

When I saw those words a chill went through me. "No, I don't receive this," I said out loud. "I don't believe You are going to take that baby Home. He has done so well." Fearing this was the Lord's way of telling me He was indeed going to take Nathan home, I remembered the picture I had continued to see in my mind, of Nathan dying in my arms in the rocking chair. I can't receive his death just based on this scripture, I told myself. This is not sufficient reason to think the Lord is going to take him Home. As I said this, my eyes fell on the opposite page. "For indeed in this house we groan, longing to be clothed with our dwelling from heaven." Then, "It is better to be at home with Jesus and absent from the body." Everything seemed very specific. Nathan longed to be free from his broken little dwelling and it was time for him to go home. Tears ran down my face. I just didn't want to believe it.

Restless and still unable to pray, I flipped through Matthew, stopping at Peter's discussion with Jesus in Matthew 16:21, in which Jesus says He will suffer and die, to which Peter replies, "God forbid it, Lord, this shall never happen to you."

And Jesus's answer: "Get thee behind me, Satan, you are setting your mind on man's interests, not God's," made my heart sink. I was setting my mind on my human interest and not God's. It was my natural desire for Nathan to live but it could be in God's interest to take Nathan home. Flipping through my prayer journal I read, "Don't call to mind the former things, or ponder things of the past, behold, I will do something new. Now it will spring forth: will you not be aware of it?" (Isaiah 43:18-19).

I thought of the picture in my mind of Nathan dying in my arms in the rocking chair and quickly pushed it away. Death just couldn't be the new thing Nathan was going to have.

I soon gave up trying to pray and got dressed. I had become frantic to get to Nathan. I was also still upset and angry, but the Lord was clearly telling me to keep my mouth closed unless I could be godly. I knew I shouldn't go to the hospital without arming myself with prayer, but I just couldn't pray. I paced back and forth in the house talking to myself. I picked up my Bible to put it away and a piece of paper I had tucked between the pages during the last week's sermon fell out. It said, "It is a sin not to pray and seek God." That did it. I knew the Lord was calling me to pray. Almost as soon as I knelt down, I began to cry. I just wept before the Lord. I had no words. I didn't even know why I was crying. I never got out a word to the Lord, I just cried. I thought maybe the

Holy Spirit was interceding for Nathan through my crying, since the Scriptures say He, "intercedes with groanings too deep for words" (Romans 8:26). Afterwards I thought maybe the Spirit was crying out to the Father for me to have His peace and feel His presence, because when I stopped weeping I felt the Lord's presence all around me. Whatever God was doing, I was calm and I knew He was there. When I looked at the clock two and a half hours had passed. It had seemed like twenty minutes.

When I finally got to the hospital that day, I asked for a meeting with the cardiologist, who promised he would personally go and change Nathan's chart to note the feedings I wanted him to have. He also told me he wanted to do a heart catheterization the next day and if it showed nothing he could fix, he planned to send Nathan home on oxygen the following day.

I SPENT THE DAY OF NATHAN'S HEART CATHETERIZATION AT THE hospital. Sitting in the rocking chair beside his crib, I read my Bible and prayed scriptures over him such as "those who wait upon the Lord will gain new strength...they will run and not grow tired..." (Isaiah 40:31). Some of the nurses talked about the Bible and asked questions when they saw me reading it. Several were already Christians and I told them about some of our experiences with healing as the others listened. I soon realized that being a white Christian woman who had a sick black baby living with me had given me credibility I would otherwise not have had. Then I knew why the Lord had been so determined I not lose my temper about Nathan's care. He wanted to give me favor with them so they would receive my witness about Him. Driving home, I thought about what the Lord had done and I remembered James 1:17, "the anger of man does not achieve the righteousness of God." I was thankful He had not allowed me to act in my flesh and destroy my witness.

The heart catheterization showed that Nathan was only getting oxygen to one lung, which explained why he needed the oxygen so badly, and why he turned blue when it was decreased even slightly. It was depressing to think of him having the plastic tube he hated so much taped to his face for the rest of his life, but at least he was going to get to come home. I encouraged myself he would be much happier with us than in the hospital.

I had bought him several new toys after he went to the hospital and only taken one for him to play with, at the nurses' recommendation. He will have his new toys to play with and the children to entertain him, I thought. We can make him happy for whatever time he has left. Knowing he would be on oxygen for the rest of his life seemed to confirm he might well die in my arms as I rocked him at home. I had peace about that now, especially with the prospect of his being tied to an oxygen tank and not feeling well. I also thought it would surely be easier to give a child back to the Lord than to strangers. My main concern now was that he not suffer any more medical procedures which couldn't help him.

That night after a quick supper, Hamp, John and I went back to the hospital. After we stopped to get John some notebook paper for school, a desperation came over me. "We have to get to Nathan," I said as I started running back to the car. When I reached his bedside he was asleep. I automatically checked his nails, even though he was receiving oxygen. They were deep blue! I turned his head so I could see his lips. They too were blue-black. "He is blue!" I called to the nurse. Then wanting to stimulate him to breathe, I shook him and called his name. After a few seconds he awoke and began to cry. Then he started to scream as he had on Thanksgiving. He seemed to be in pain, but I thought it was a reaction to the anesthesia or pain at the site of the catheterization. "Hurry, get a doctor!" I said picking him up. "This is what he did at home." The nurse was dialing the phone as I sat down in the rocking chair by Nathan's bed. Suddenly he began to gasp for air. "He is in trouble!" I said to no one in particular. We could all hear him. I sat him upright trying to help him. Nathan's eyes were wide with fear as he struggled to breathe. He gasped three more times, and fell back dead in my arms. His eyes were still wide with fear, but the gasping for breath had stopped, leaving a hollow silence. The nurse dropped the phone and ran for Nathan. Throwing him onto the bed, she told us to leave and began CPR. A minute later we heard the call for emergency help come over the PA system. It seemed forever before doctors and nurses came running from surrounding areas to help.

| Nathan at four months, the month he died.

I watched through a tiny opening in the blinds over Nathan's bed as they did all the expected protocol for a baby in cardiac arrest. I wasn't crying yet. I was upset, but the Lord had prepared me for this. I was almost certain they wouldn't be able to revive him. As Hampy and John and I stood in the darkened hallway waiting to see if Nathan's short life was over, I remembered the picture I had been pushing from my mind for the last month. Nathan had just died in my arms in a rocking chair. I had always assumed it was my rocking chair at home. Nevertheless, it was a rocking chair and when it happened, I had peace. I knew Jesus was there. A child had died, but how merciful Jesus had been quietly sending a gentle picture of death to my mind; showing me over and over, as I rejected it, strongly at first. Then continuing to make me look at the reality of what would happen, until He brought me to the point of knowing as I stood in that hospital corridor all was well.

As the time dragged by and they did more and more to him, I started to cry. I didn't want Nathan to have to go through this. If he was going Home I wanted him to go quickly and not have to suffer. The cardiologist had been called and as he came down the hall, he looked at me with great sadness in his face. He silently spread his hands in a gesture of sorrow and resignation and went in to see what he could do.

Hampy went to find me some coffee, John went to call his sisters, and I found myself alone. The hall was empty and quiet. In the surrounding rooms the world was continuing on as if nothing had happened. I walked up and down, wiping tears and waiting.

"To this have I been called, to walk hospital corridors alone, and cry for children who are not my own," ran through my mind.

I didn't realize it rhymed until the next day. But it struck me as a kind of confirmation that I was in God's will. Even though waiting in a hospital corridor to be told if a six- month-old baby's life is over, was an uncomfortable place to be. It seemed to say I was supposed to be there and cry for that little boy who had no one else to cry for him. I was called to weep over him because every child deserves to have a mother weep when he dies. The Lord wanted someone here and I got the job. I was the mother the Lord had chosen to love Nathan and care for him, and cry when He took him Home. I couldn't help crying, but deep in my spirit, there was a kind of peace that I was the one standing outside the door, crying for God's little child.

The doctor came out and said they had been unable to save Nathan. He apologized for not having been able to foresee his death, but said it was impossible to anticipate death sometimes. He felt very sorry for us, but Hampy and I assured him we were happy to have the privilege of being Nathan's parents, even at that sad moment. Then he asked if we wanted to see Nathan. Hampy didn't feel a need to, but I couldn't leave him without saying good-bye. John wasn't sure how he felt but I took him in with me, so he wouldn't regret later he had not held or touched Nathan one last time. In the confusion, as the nurses tried to give John and me time alone with Nathan we somehow ended up almost in the middle of the large room full of sick babies, in full view of all of the doctors and nurses who had come to try to save him. At the time, I was so intent on Nathan and John, I was unaware of the others in the room. John and I sat down and the nurse laid Nathan in my arms. He looked as if he were sleeping. I talked to him softly, commiserating about the little heart which just wouldn't work and telling him how good it would be now, to be out of that weak little body that had held him back. Now he could run and play and be free. John stroked his curls as I talked and kissed him. Then John leaned down and kissed his cheek and said good-bye. There was no more to do...no more to say. Nathan was no longer in that little body and there was nothing to keep us there. As I laid his body back on his bed, the tide of grief I had been able to put off until that final moment began to rise in me and I wanted Hampy. I practically ran past the nurse's station and out the door. As I passed, I saw a large group of doctors and nurses standing silently watching us, and there were tears on many of their faces. At the time, the scene did not even register in my mind, but the next day I remembered all those people. My first thought was how sweet they were to feel such sympathy for us. Then I realized what they had been looking at. A white mother and her teenage son tearfully holding and kissing a dead black baby, deeply grieved by his death. My eyes filled with tears. Could it be the Lord had used our pain to show His love? Could spiritual lessons have to cost so much?

John had phoned the girls to tell them Nathan wasn't breathing, and I knew they were anxious to hear if he was all right. I called

Kathy Sones and asked her to go over and tell the girls Nathan had died and be with them until we could get there. When we got home she was there and they were all crying.

After Kathy left, I walked back to our bedroom and looked at Nathan's crib, the new toys he would never play with, his medicine and his clothes. It was after midnight but I began packing them away. I told Hamp I couldn't face waking up in the morning and seeing them there, silent reminders that Nathan was gone. While he started taking the crib apart, I took Nathan's heart medicine to the bathroom to pour it out and as I watched the medicine which had helped him live pour down the drain, I started to cry again. Hampy put down what he was doing and came to hold me.

Then it hit me! I thought, "Oh Lord, how could I have lived if I had had to do this with all of Micah's medicine! How could I have stood the pain of coming home to Micah's bed, his clothes and everything that had been his and having to do this?" It had never *once* occurred to me how I would have felt if Micah had died with me. I had only thought of how much easier it would be for him.

"I don't think I could ever have taken another sick baby if I had had to do this after losing Micah," I sobbed to Hampy.

I had never thought of the affect Micah's death would have had on me, but the Lord had. The Lord had protected me from what I didn't know to fear. He had known what it would have done to me, and He had known the pain would have been so great I would have been too afraid of losing another sick baby to take any more.

I sat down as the lesson of the Spirit flowed over me. It hurt to lose Nathan, but I had only had him three months. I loved him and I would miss him terribly, but it was nothing compared to what I would have felt if it had been Micah. Micah had been the most precious foster baby I ever had, and I had had him for fifteen months. Sparing me Micah's death was one of the most loving things the Lord ever did for me, and I had been hurt and angry about it. I learned that night for the first of many times, not to question the Lord when He doesn't do things my way. I learned to trust Him with purposes I can't see. Now I know how altogether faithful He is, and I have come to believe when we feel He has betrayed us the most, He has probably actually blessed us the most, and we are too ignorant to realize it.

 JOURNAL: Before Nathan died, I had felt God was saying He was doing a "new thing" but I didn't accept the possibility that it meant a baby would die with me. Now I am thankful He showed me, even though I rejected it. I know now His plan had always been for this child not to stay long on the earth. Because of the reality of sin and the corruption of the creation, there have to be babies like Nathan, but that doesn't mean God doesn't oversee the formation of each one. When He sends them to live with His own children, they become beautiful channels of His love and wisdom, and recipients of His mercy. I don't know why the Lord sent Nathan to earth or why He took him back so soon. I do know He had good reasons, and I can trust Him with them.

I notified Catholic Charities Nathan had died. They called his birth mother in another part of the state and arrangements were made to take him back to her hometown for burial. When the children heard there would be no funeral in Jackson, they were very upset. Stacey and Laura seemed to need an official leave taking, a chance to say goodbye as John had done. They also wanted to express Nathan's value by giving him what they knew people were supposed to have when they died.

"He needs a beautiful little box, Mommy," Laura said, "and flowers; he *has* to have flowers."

Realizing the children's emotional stake in all of the babies' lives, Catholic Charities arranged a little funeral at a local funeral home. Catholic Charities provided the little satin covered casket, not much bigger than a shoe box, and we bought a blanket of pink roses with the card saying, "Jesus loves (his real name)." Father Sunds from Catholic Charities officiated, and of course the social workers who had worked on his case were there. The service had to be held on Sunday afternoon immediately after church because of arrangements to take Nathan's body back to his mother's hometown for burial. It was interesting to see the particular people who left their own church services and drove across town, some with small children, to attend Nathan's little funeral: our youth director and his wife, Rusty and Kim Rawson and their small son, who were so close to our children, Hamp's business partner, Dewayne Miller, who had only seen Nathan once, an older lady from our church who had cared for Nathan once in the nursery, and a young couple with a toddler, also from our church, that we didn't even know very well at the time. They were all people who had been touched by the love of Christ through Nathan and I had not expected any of them to come.

I got a little more uncomfortable when I was told Nathan's birth mother was coming to the funeral. I had never met one of my babies' birth mothers, and I didn't know how she would feel about me under the circumstances. The children scanned each black woman who came through the door, discussing if she could be Nathan's mother, but the moment she came in we all knew her immediately. She looked just like Nathan. She also had his sweet disposition, and expressed her gratitude to us for all we had done for her baby. We had taken some beautiful pictures of Nathan the week before he got sick, and I gave her several so she could see he had been happy with us.

As a final note about Nathan, I should point out the children handled his death well. We had told them from the beginning he might die suddenly, and they took their cues from their parents. We were always honest with the children about our feelings about the babies, and I think that gave them a sense of security and confidence even when one died. When I came home from the hospital the night Nathan passed away, my eyes were red and swollen from crying. They understood and we all cried together. When they heard me laugh softly the next day, they knew the sadness and sense of loss did not have to take us over. It seems if you are honest about your feelings, you may have to apologize sometimes for not feeling as godly as you should, but people will know they can depend on you to be truthful with them and they can trust your spirit.

It was hard to say goodbye to Nathan and know we would not see him again until we got to Heaven, and I thought of a song I had heard some years before which said, "I've got more to go to Heaven for than I had yesterday." That was increasingly true for me. I had my mother, my beloved grandmother, Micah and Nathan all waiting for me now in Heaven. In the weeks that followed, I grieved for Nathan in a way I had not grieved for babies placed for adoption. There was a finality in losing him I had not experienced before.

Shortly after Nathan's death, I received a call from a social worker at the hospital where he had died. A little black boy there with severe brain damage and a tracheostomy was ready for discharge. I had passed this baby every time I went to see Nathan, and had even picked him up and talked to him several times. He was older than Nathan and much harder to handle. He was a big, stiff, spastic baby much like Micah, except because of his tracheostomy, he couldn't cry. He could only make a soft little noise caused by air rushing through the plastic tube in his throat. I told the social worker we would pray about taking him, but I was scared. I didn't feel ready for another severely damaged baby, but I knew from our experience with Micah that my emotional reaction was not a dependable gauge. The issue was whether or not this child was our next ministry for the Lord. I went to the hospital to see him several times, still praying for the confirmation that would give me the courage to take him home. On one of my visits, a nurse offered to show me how to suction his tracheostomy tube. I watched in horror as she stuck the plastic tube into the tiny opening in his throat that allowed him to breathe. In order to clear the breathing tube of mucous, it was necessary to also suction the air out, and for a few seconds the baby was unable to breathe. As he waved his arms and struggled for air, I broke out in a cold sweat my ears started ringing and I felt faint. The suctioning only took a few seconds, but it seemed much longer to the baby and me. I groped for a chair and closed my eyes. No air meant death, my mishandling his air supply meant death— the baby felt death when he couldn't breathe while his trach was being suctioned. I would have to suction him many times every day if I took him home. Now that the death of a baby had become a reality to me, the thought of caring for a baby like this one terrified me. I went home and prayed and talked to Hampy. He only said to be careful not to let fear keep me from God's will. As gentle and intuitive as Hampy was, he was still a man, not possessed of a mother's heart.

Neither he nor anyone else ever really understood what mothering the babies took from me, except other foster mothers. He knew the Lord would give me confirmation if this was our baby, because I was the one who was afraid and I would have the responsibility of his care.

> 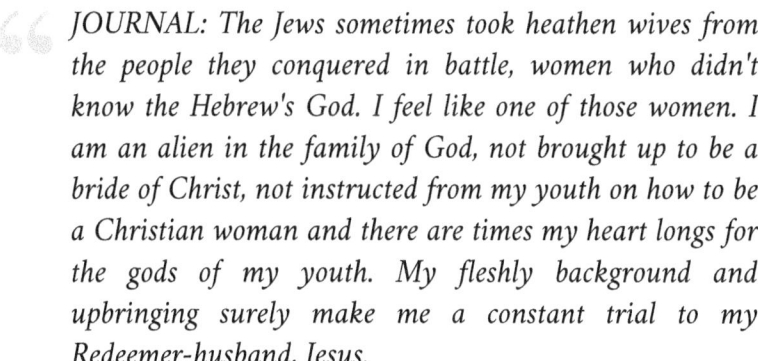 *JOURNAL: The Jews sometimes took heathen wives from the people they conquered in battle, women who didn't know the Hebrew's God. I feel like one of those women. I am an alien in the family of God, not brought up to be a bride of Christ, not instructed from my youth on how to be a Christian woman and there are times my heart longs for the gods of my youth. My fleshly background and upbringing surely make me a constant trial to my Redeemer-husband, Jesus.*

Right before Christmas, I tried to see the baby several times, but he was always asleep or the social worker wasn't there. I finally steeled myself to go and tell her if he still had no place to go, we would take him. I had not received the confirmation I wanted to have, but I kept thinking of the scriptures that say, "bring the homeless poor into your house," (Isaiah 58:7) and, "inasmuch as you have done to the least of these my brothers, you have done it to Me." (Matthew 25:40). I thought surely one can't always expect to hear straight from the Throne about his obedience to the Lord. But before I could arrange a meeting with her, she called to tell me the baby's grandmother was going to take him to live with her. I was both relieved and happy. Now he would stay with his own family and not have to get used to us and an adoptive family. I thanked God for His goodness to the baby and to us. This time we could all have what we wanted.

Most of Nathan's pictures were given to his birth mother. The two shown in this chapter show the dramatic change in him during the short time he was with us and his brief, but beautiful, life.

6
AARON

On December 10, 1984, I was praying and fasting in preparation for a healing service at our church. Among those needing healing was a good friend who was confined to a wheelchair. She was a devoted Christian and had been prayed for many times. Several friends and I were praying together especially for her. I had fasted that morning and been deep in prayer for about two hours.

After my prayer time, I dressed, straightened up the house and with my mind on my errands, headed for town. The roads between our home and Jackson were not often crowded in those days. I was on a beautiful stretch across the spillway road over the lake when the picture of a huge piece of crystal invaded my thoughts. A laser beam of light coming from heaven tried to shine through it, but it was diffused and deflected by the flaws and layers in the crystal. Beneath the crystal were people looking up, hoping the light would come through to heal them. As I saw this, I knew the crystal represented individual Christians. The light was the power of God, and the flaws in the crystal were sins which diffuse and deflect God's power in us. In one place there was a flat "ceiling" in the crystal over the Christians' heads, and the light spread out and covered it like a liquid. These people could see the light and feel it's warmth, but it was not strong enough to heal them. These were the people who say, "I felt the presence of the Lord," or, "I feel better," but are not healed. The deflected power was strong enough to be seen and even felt, but not strong enough to heal. I understood the surface meaning, but didn't begin to grasp the full meaning of it. As I looked at the crystal, the scripture, "Whatever is not of faith is sin," (Romans 13:23) ran through my mind.

I shared my vision with the Wednesday night group at church, and thought about it for several weeks, then forgot about it. Fortunately, I had recorded it in my prayer journal. I knew it was important or the Lord would not have shown it to me in such a startling way. (My friend did not receive physical healing as we had hoped). We had no foster baby at this time.

> JOURNAL: When I became anxious for another baby I said, "Lord, You have prepared me so. You have given me experience, a support base. I know doctors and therapists all over town; surely You won't let all this go to waste." In essence, "Lord, You need to use me with Your babies." He laughed and said, "I don't need you. I can make sons of Abraham out of stones! (Matthew 3:9) I don't need anything you have. I could use an illiterate teenager to do what you do. You don't minister to my babies because you are good at it. You do it because it pleases Me to work through you."

> JOURNAL: Lord, it is so hard for me to see my children pulling away from the purity and protection of their faith. I know children and teenagers have to test their parents' beliefs and take them or reject them for themselves, but it is so painful. I believe You have given me the desire of my heart to see my children walking with You in strength and

power, but I know I have to wait for Your perfect time to see it fulfilled. My enemy presses hard on every side. I am trying to "take every thought captive to the Lordship of Christ" (II Corinthians 10:5,) and I am facing the pain I feel and trying not to run from it. I believe this is what Jesus did in the garden of Gethsemane the night before He was crucified. He overcame the fear and dread His flesh felt

(Luke 22:42 and Hebrews 5:7) when He faced the pain of obedience. There is much scriptural precedence for waiting for You, and I take comfort in that. Joshua had to wait seven days before Jericho. The 120 had to wait in the upper room for ten days for Pentecost, and David knew he was anointed king, but had to wait for years before he was finally king over all of Israel. Lord, help me wait for You with patience, and trust my children to Your care.

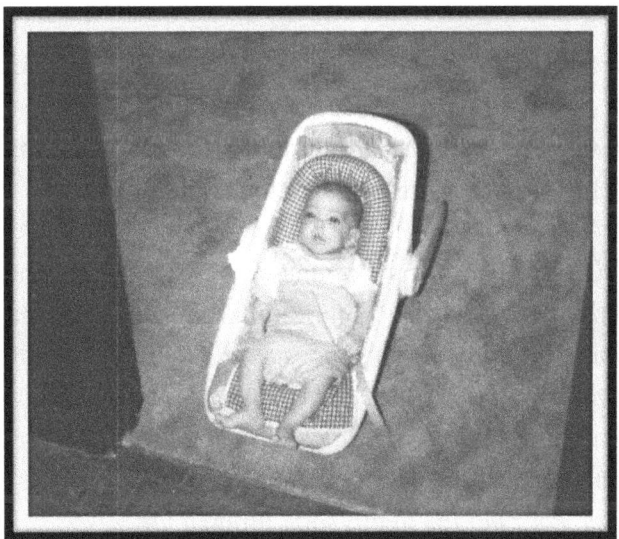

| Baby Aaron.

On May 8, 1985, Catholic Charities called me about a little

white boy with cystic fibrosis. This was a baby who would probably spend time in the hospital, and the little rhyme which came to me while I was waiting to see if Nathan's life was over, came back to me. "To this have I been called, to walk hospital corridors alone, and cry for children who are not my own." This baby not only had cystic fibrosis, but the worst form of it, and had been in the hospital the entire five months of his life. He was born in January, a month after I had seen the laser and the crystal. Cystic fibrosis killed. I knew something about it because our neighbor's daughter had it. Her name was Anne Marie Henderson. She also had cystic fibrosis in the worst form. It clogged the ducts of her endocrine glands so she had to take enzymes to digest her food and she lived in constant danger of lung infections, which eventually scarred her lungs so badly she died. Anne Marie died in July of 1991, after fighting her disease for seventeen years. I knew this little boy would require more medical care than I had ever had to give. He was five months old, but was very small for his age and frail, like Nathan.

After talking to the children, Hamp and I felt we should take the baby, simply because he needed a home and family.

We had been told his grandmother might take him and we prayed if he was not for us, she would take him.

> *JOURNAL: I confess I cannot bless this baby in any way. Only the Holy Spirit coming to him through us can bless him. I confess I have no special skills or abilities to minister to him which I do not receive fresh daily from You, Lord. I reject intellectual pride and the desire to make men think I am wise and capable. Make me truly wise, Lord. Pour out life to this child through us.*

> *JOURNAL: I have experienced the most incredible loss of contact with the Lord since we got word about the baby. I am amazed how easily I have fallen back into my self-*

indulgent patterns, but I won't give in to them. I will spend my time in prayer. I believe Psalm 119:25, "My soul cleaves to the dust; revive me according to Thy word," and verse 32, "I shall run the way of Thy commandments, for Thou wilt enlarge my heart."

> JOURNAL: I will not imagine how bad things could be with this baby if Jesus does not supply help and strength. He will. I will not let other people's attitudes and fears exalt themselves against my knowledge of Jesus and His desire. I will take every thought about this baby captive to the obedience of Christ (II Corinthians 10:5).

> JOURNAL: Lord, we have decided to name the baby Aaron after Moses's brother, the first high priest of Israel. I praise You for the witness of Your love that You plan for him to be.

Stacey suggested the name and I like it. I had never thought of naming one of the babies Aaron. As it turned out, God had given Stacey a name which would have extremely powerful implications for me. The day Aaron was to arrive, I was very unsettled. His grandmother had to bring him to Jackson and I knew she could change her mind at any time and decide to keep him. I didn't know if I wanted that or not. I was vacillating wildly between confidence and fear. One minute I was certain if she actually brought him to me, I was supposed to have him and the Lord would make me able to meet his needs. The next minute I was afraid she was going to keep him and I was disappointed. Late in the afternoon Aaron arrived at Catholic Charities and we were called to pick him up.

By the time I finally saw Aaron, I was anxious to meet him. I felt very positive about taking him, but I was shocked when I actually saw him. I was used to looking at chubby little black babies with black curls and velvety brown skin. Aaron was thin and pale.

Ethnic differences aside, he was the palest, sickliest looking baby I had ever seen. Apparently the hospital he had come from felt the same way, because they had sent a nurse with the social worker.

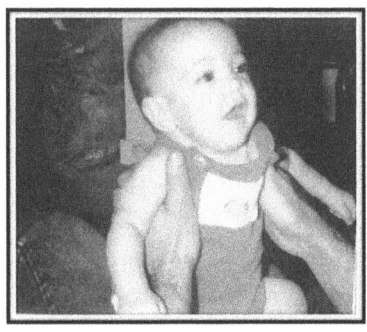

| Aaron talking to daddy.

Well, I thought, I have been brought babies with a police escort. I'm not intimidated.

Lying in the bassinet, he reminded me of a forlorn little mouse, and he was crying—a lot. Not to worry, it was physically impossible to outcry Micah, so I was still in control. I was sure I could handle this baby. Then the nurse announced that of course he would have to be suctioned with a suction machine like the one the nurse in the hospital demonstrated on the baby with the tracheostomy. Remembering the effect the suction machine in the hospital had on both the baby and me, I sat down. When the suction machine was actually produced, I had an anxiety attack. I felt nauseated, my face got cold and I began to perspire. I thought I was going to faint. My ears rang so loudly, I couldn't hear what the people around me were saying. I thought, "I can't do this! I really can't do this! This baby is too sick for me to take care of." I couldn't think of anything but getting away from that baby. I wanted to go home. I didn't care what they did with him, as long as they didn't make me take him with me. The nurse appeared to be demonstrating how to choke the baby to death by shoving the suction tube down his throat. As she was doing this she said something about the surgical gloves she was wearing, but I couldn't hear her because of the ringing in my ears. Too sick to talk, I got swept out the door with Aaron in my arms, while Hamp followed with the dreaded suction machine.

We always took a sick baby straight to the pediatrician's office so he could see him before he was in a crisis, so we drove straight to Bob Thompson's office. On the way I kept telling myself two things over and over: first, don't throw up! second, I could call as soon as I got home and tell Catholic Charities I couldn't keep him. By this time Hamp had noticed how pale and quiet I was and said, "What's wrong, Sweet?" When I told him how I felt, he was shocked. "This isn't like you. I think you are being attacked by Satan," he said. The instant he spoke the words, I knew he was right. My anxiety was out of proportion to the situation. I began to pray, and reaffirm my determination to take this baby.

By pure willpower provided by the Lord, I got through the examination with a new doctor. Bob was not there that day. I couldn't hear most of what he said because of the ringing in my ears, but my only concern by this time was to get home with the baby so I could lie down. When we left the doctor's office I told Hamp it didn't matter if I threw up all night and couldn't hear for a week, I was keeping this baby. By the time we got home I felt fine. As with baby David, when I realized I was being attacked by the enemy all power over me was gone. "Resist the Devil and he will flee from you," (James 4:7). I was shocked by the terror I felt that night, and for several months I had no idea why Satan was so overt in his attack over this particular child. The suctioning I was so afraid of was much easier with a child who only had mucus in his throat instead of a tracheostomy. In fact, it turned out Aaron *never* needed to be suctioned. I did it for several days, never getting anything up and finally just stopped it altogether. He never needed the thing that had frightened me so.

> *JOURNAL: My sin nature is like a skin I keep trying to get out of. Dare I hope if I stay "In the Light" long enough, it will just burn and peel off?*

The next day, Hampy and I took Aaron to the cystic fibrosis specialist. She examined him and expressed concern over his obvious frailty and also over his trachea. X-rays showed it to be almost closed by scar tissue from previous intubations. He made a noise when he breathed much like Micah, but not as bad.

"If he gets an upper respiratory infection, it could kill him," she said. "His trachea is barely open enough for him to survive now. If it swells at all, he will die."

She considered admitting him to the hospital, but knowing the awful affect being back in the hospital had had on Nathan, I begged her to let me take him home. I promised to call every four to six hours and tell her how he was. If he got worse I promised to bring him straight to the hospital. We spent a watchful two days as Aaron seemed to wilt like a little flower. He lay listlessly in his bed or in my arms, scarcely bothering to eat. He didn't get any worse, though, and after two days he began to perk up. In another day or so he began to show interest in the things around him and even smiled a little when the children played with him. Like most of the babies, he had only been reacting to the stress of new surroundings and was not actually sick.

The doctor had put him on enzymes to digest his food, medications to aid his breathing, and three different vitamin preparations to be sure he got the vitamins he needed to stay healthy. Like Micah, he frequently had thrush in his mouth but Aaron's was caused by the strong antibiotics he took to ward off the lung infections he was so prone to.

I had expected stays in the hospital for Aaron when he first came to us because I knew he would be susceptible to lung infections, but we were able to avoid any hospitalizations, at no small expense to my nerves. One Saturday a few weeks after he came to us, Aaron's nose was running and he was coughing, so Hamp and I met the doctor at the hospital. She heard enough congestion in his chest to want to put him into the hospital and give him antibiotic injections every six hours. Seeing the dismay on my face at the thought of leaving him at the hospital, she said, "Unless, of course, you want to learn to give the injections at home."

"Me?" I said. "Shots? Oh no, I don't want to stick this baby with a needle!"

"Then I have no choice but to admit him. He has to have the antibiotics," she said.

We waited for two apprehension-filled hours before a nurse had time to show me how to prepare and inject Aaron's medicine into his leg. I discovered giving shots was very time consuming. It took about three minutes to prepare an injection, but it took much longer to steel myself to actually stick the needle into the baby.

That night when it was time to give Aaron his shot, I felt like a surgeon about to attempt his first operation. I practiced repeatedly on an orange, observing to myself that oranges don't cry. We chased the children from the room so I wouldn't have to perform before an audience. With Hamp holding Aaron's leg tightly, I took a deep breath, pulled up the flesh and jabbed his leg dart like with the needle. It bounced back, breaking the skin just enough to bleed and hurt. Aaron started crying.

"I can't do this!" I said. "Why did I think I could do this!" Hamp tried to reassure me and then suggested we pray before we tried again.

"How did I even try to do this without praying?" I said. I couldn't believe I had been so wrapped up in my efforts to do it right, I forgot to ask the One who actually knew exactly how to do it.

After we prayed, Hamp said, "Let me see that needle, Sweet." I handed it to him. He was a tool and die maker after all, accustomed to making things perfect to $1/1000^{th}$ of an inch. "Look, see the end of the needle? It's slanted, with a sharp point at one end where the opening for the medicine is. You have to turn this side of the needle to the skin. Hold it like this." He showed me, turning it around.

"If I don't get it right this time," I said to Aaron, taking the syringe from Hamp, "you are going to the hospital." This time the needle went right in, I injected the antibiotics, and Aaron hardly whimpered.

"I wonder what would have happened if we had prayed before we started," Hamp said in an exaggerated musing tone, when it was all over.

"You could have suggested it sooner," I snapped. "You knew I was scared to death." Aaron's legs were like pincushions sometimes, but every time he seemed to be getting a cold, the doctor had me inject him with antibiotics, and he was never admitted to the hospital.

> *JOURNAL: Lord, I am ashamed to tell You I have no pleasure in Aaron. I am grateful to be entrusted with him, but the glow is gone. I don't have the feeling of challenge and accomplishment I have always felt with a baby. Does this mean the ministry to the babies is only now becoming a pure service to the Lord? John McArthur says when he first went to pastor Grace Church he thought it was like a honeymoon; it was fun and challenging. Then it got to be work, a job. Now he knows it's a warfare, a fight he must enter into daily. Is this what is happening with the babies? Do humans want to serve You as long as it feels good, is fun and gets strokes from other people? Then when our flesh is tired of it, do we want to put it down and run after something new that feels spiritual like our old ministry used to?*

> *JOURNAL: I think the thorns of self are being uprooted in the ministry to the babies. The pleasure of doing it is gone. I pray it may be replaced with a holy joy from the Lord. "Oh, send out Thy light and Thy truth, let them lead me, let them bring me to Thy holy hill and to Thy dwelling place. Then I will go to the altar of God, to God, my*

exceeding joy; and upon the lyre I will praise Thee, Oh, God, my God." (Psalm 43:3-4).

> JOURNAL: I got tense and upset with Aaron when he woke up just as I was going to bed. After about thirty minutes of speaking what I wanted to feel to the Lord, as I rocked him, I felt a gentle release of the anger and I was content to do whatever Aaron needed. He went to sleep immediately afterward. So very often, when I agree with what the Lord wants of me, even though I don't want to, He doesn't make me actually do it.

> JOURNAL: The works of my flesh are like unproductive labor pains; they exhaust me and bring forth no life.

When we had had Aaron about six weeks, the doctor commented to me there was a laser surgery which could be used to remove scars and she wanted to ask some of her colleagues what they thought about using it on Aaron's trachea.

A FEW DAYS LATER, I SAW SOME FRIENDS FROM OUR CHURCH AT THE mall. When they asked how Aaron was doing, I heard myself say calmly I wasn't worried about him because I felt God was going to heal him. I couldn't believe I said it. It had come unbidden out of my mouth. The surprise on their faces almost matched my own. I felt more affirmative about God healing Aaron than otherwise, but I was still shocked such a definite pronouncement had come out of my mouth. I had never been a "name it and claim it" person. I knew there was much more to being healed by a supernatural touch from the Lord, than just trying to believe it would happen. I had prayed my heart out for Micah to be healed and he had died. I did not feel good about having spoken so definitely to these people.

They had not walked with the Lord as long as I, and I was afraid they might be hurt by my pronouncement if Aaron wasn't healed.

On our next visit to the doctor, she related she had discussed Aaron's case with the other doctors, but they had all felt his trachea was too small to risk the laser. "It could cause swelling, and that could kill him," she said. "It's just too dangerous to try." I had no feeling about the news one way or the other, because I knew the Lord was not hindered by technology. If God wanted this baby healed, all He had to do was touch him. I had forgotten all about the laser God had shown me the past December.

SEVERAL NIGHTS LATER I WAS BRUSHING MY HAIR BEFORE GOING TO bed, when the Lord broke into my thoughts. "It doesn't matter the doctors can't use their laser on Aaron. Remember I showed you I have a laser and I am going to use it." I had not thought of the laser and the crystal since we had gotten Aaron. I stopped brushing and sat staring at the mirror. Had the Lord really shown me the crystal and the laser because He was going to heal a baby unborn at the time? Would He tell me before hand? It was too much for me, but the words were so clear, and so shocking I recorded them in my prayer journal. Even though I still couldn't believe the Lord would take the trouble to show me this, my heart seemed to accept it quite easily. I found I couldn't stop telling people the Lord was going to heal Aaron. I told everyone at church to pray for him if they wanted to be blessed, because God was going to heal him. I felt uncomfortable feeling so positive about it, but I couldn't stop myself from telling everyone Aaron was going to be healed.

On July 19, Aaron had a late morning appointment with the cystic fibrosis doctor he saw every two weeks, due to his compromised trachea. I took him out for an early morning stroll while it was still relatively cool. He loved riding in the stroller, but we had to walk while it was cool because children with cystic fibrosis sweat heavily and lose too much salt if they become overheated.

It was a beautiful morning and I had taken my Walkman to listen to a teaching tape. This really spoke to me afterward about the sovereignty of God. I was not praying when the miracle happened; I was not even thinking about Aaron. I had nothing to do with it at all. I walked along looking at the pavement in front of us, listening to the tape. Once when I glanced up to watch for cars, what I saw stopped me in my tracks. "In the spirit" as clearly as I had seen the crystal eight months before, I saw Aaron lying on his back and the same laser-looking light coming down to his throat. This time there was no crystal, only God's healing light and the child. I stood looking at this incredible sight, afraid to move or look away, for fear I would somehow upset what was happening. Finally, I had to look at Aaron to see if he felt anything. He was lying quietly looking up at the trees, seemingly unaware of anything unusual. When I looked up again, the vision was gone.

For some reason I felt responsible to do something to insure the reality of what I had seen, so I prayed. I prayed without stopping all the way home. As I bathed and dressed to go to the hospital for Aaron's appointment, I prayed. I only stopped praying long enough to write down exactly what I had seen, before I could forget or confuse it in my mind. As I dried my hair, I reminded the Lord that Aaron was an innocent baby and it was not his fault he had cystic fibrosis and a scarred trachea. Actually I was babbling, afraid if I stopped praying and started thinking and analyzing, I would talk myself out of what I had seen.

Then the Lord spoke again. He quoted His Word in John 9:2-3. "Who sinned, this child or his parents that he should be born blind? It was neither...but that the works of God might be displayed in him." He substituted the word child for man, but the rest of the scripture was quoted exactly, and I knew the Lord had intended to heal Aaron for His glory before he was ever born, and nothing I did was going to change His plans for him.

At the hospital, the doctor asked if I thought Aaron's noisy breathing sounded any better. "I'm not worried about it," I said. "I think God is going to heal him." I had never made a statement like this to a doctor before, but today I just blurted out the truth and didn't care if she thought I was a religious fanatic. I knew what I had seen. There was no doubt in my mind I had witnessed the beginning of a miraculous healing.

She of course nodded slightly and said, "Ummm."

She sent us for our usual X-ray of his trachea, then we returned to the examining room. Normally she followed us quickly, read the X-ray and came right back. But this time she was gone such a long time, I decided she had been called away on an emergency. When she finally returned, I pounced on her. "How did his trachea look?"

"Better." she said quietly.

I knew it! I was ecstatic. The Lord had indeed begun Aaron's healing. I assumed the healing had only begun and would take place over a period of time, so I never would have asked for an illustration, but the doctor went on.

"This is how his trachea looked before," she said, taking a pencil and drawing two parallel lines on the examining table paper. "They were so close they almost touched. This is how they look now." She drew two more lines about a quarter inch apart.

I was shocked. "My goodness," I said. "How much more until they are normal?"

"That's about it." she said. "They are normal."

She told me she had been gone so long because Aaron's trachea had looked so different today. She had gotten a radiologist to view all of his previous X rays with her. All she could say was it had been nearly shut before, and now it was normal.

I suppose I was acceptably coherent for the remainder of the visit, but once I was alone with Aaron in the car, I started to laugh and cry at the same time. I laughed at the wonderful power of God, and how simple it is for Him to heal. I also rejoiced over God's willingness to cause the doctor to draw me a picture so I would understand his trachea had been completely healed, rather than just begun as I had assumed. I also cried because I realized how easy it was for Him to heal, and I knew He could have healed Micah and Nathan just as easily and He had chosen not to.

The Lord spoke one more thing to me that day about Aaron's healing. He said, "If you don't bear witness of this before men, don't look to see it again."

I promised him I would indeed tell people what He had done. When I arrived home I rushed through the back door screaming to the children, "Guess whose trachea is healed!" Then I called Hamp, Daddy and the church. It was the most exciting news I had ever had to tell. I shared it before the church that Wednesday night and reminded them I had told them about the laser eight months before. The entire church was blessed to hear the wonderful, merciful miracle, and the news of Aaron's healing has been told and retold to hundreds of people.

The stridor Aaron breathed with didn't stop when his trachea was miraculously opened. For reasons known only to Him, the Lord only healed the thing which was an immediate threat to his life. Aaron still breathed with a raspy noise and he still had cystic fibrosis. A couple of months later we determined his noisy breathing was caused by his trachea collapsing on itself a little each time he breathed. He eventually outgrew this as the doctors said he would.

The most dramatic evidence of Aaron's healing was his growth. He went from 0-3-month-size clothes to 9-12- month-size clothes in six weeks. His previous growth chart had shown a fairly straight line that rose ever so slightly over the weeks. After July 19, the line on the graph went almost straight up. Aaron became a downright handful on the increased oxygen. He learned to zoom around the house in his walker and played non-stop for hours without tiring.

Before his healing he couldn't play for an hour without needing a nap. Our sickly little boy was gone.

As soon as Aaron mastered the walker, he set his sight on Beth. He spent the last four months he was with us on a quest for her tail. It was a very tempting tail, with long pretty black and white fringe that swished the air like a fan. No red-blooded little boy could have resisted trying to grab a handful of it, but Beth kept a careful eye on Aaron when he was on wheels, and usually managed to avoid him. The only time she couldn't protect herself was while she ate. When she was hungry, Beth would ease quietly to her bowl, trying not to attract Aaron's attention, wolf down some food, then look back to see if he was coming.

John telling Aaron to wait his turn for the comics in the newspaper

If he was already closing in, she would shift her tail-end away from him, get another bite and look back to check his position again. Sometimes when she tired of eating this way, she would come and bark at me until I came to the kitchen and put my foot on the walker to immobilize Aaron so she could eat in peace. While I held him prisoner in his walker, Aaron would stand shouting at Beth, both hands reaching for her tail, even though she was three feet away. Fortunately for Beth, he never got more than a quick brush of her tail through his fingers.

> JOURNAL: Christ did not sweat blood in the desert when He was tempted at the beginning of His ministry. He did in the garden just before the crucifixion because the attack was so much stronger, the battle so much harder. The closer He got to the ultimate obedience, the worse the attack of Satan. I know this is true for us as well. The more we die to ourselves, the more Satan has to fear from us, hence the more viciously he attacks. This requires our staying as close to Jesus as we possibly can. Satan is not playing with us.

> JOURNAL: August, 1985. Lord, I desire not to be like a dumb animal, who is led without comprehension to the place of work by his master and then led step by step through the work his master desires to accomplish, never understanding his part in the work or even the purpose of the work.

I prayed this prayer one morning. And after spending some time thinking and praying about exactly what my place in the work of the kingdom of God was, I went on to my Bible reading, hoping the Lord might reveal the answer through His word. My Bible happened to fall open to Ezra 8, not a place I read often. Because I had not read Ezra in a long time, I read through the account of Ezra looking for Levites among the exiles who were finally being allowed to leave Babylon and go home to Jerusalem. He knew God's law allowed no one but Levites to touch the articles of worship which had been given as gifts from the Babylonians and the original articles of worship looted from the temple when Nebuchadnezzar's men had destroyed it. Artaxerxes, The king had returned those things for them to take back to Jerusalem for the new temple they would build. The scripture describes Levites being found and the articles of gold and silver being given to them to carry. When their journey was over, the Levites handed over their precious burdens to the officials of the temple in Jerusalem. I saw nothing there which applied to me, so after reading other scriptures for a while, I opened my prayer journal to read over some of my previous notes and prayers. Immediately I saw a quote from Ezra 8 in my notes. This seemed odd, so I read the chapter closely again. The only thing outstanding to me was that Ezra called for Levites to carry God's precious articles of worship, i.e. the things which belonged specifically to God. I was mildly interested that this passage had come to my attention twice in one prayer time, but I really saw nothing there for me. I did not see it was the answer to my prayer for understanding my place in God's work.

> JOURNAL: *I had to speak at a public hearing about federal funds for foster children. I had been at the hospital with Aaron for several hours for a check- up. I was tired and my neck hurt terribly. Aaron cried continuously as Hamp walked him back and forth in the back of the auditorium. I tried to tune him out as I spoke to about fifty state allocators of federal money. I wanted to tell them how much foster children needed the things the federal money buys. I took pictures of Caleb, Matthew, Micah and Nathan so they could look at the faces of the children we were talking about. This money was very important to foster children in Mississippi. Kathy Sones told me afterwards that she was amazed by how calm I seemed and how well I made my points, knowing my inexperience with public speaking at that time. I realized in spite of my not having time to pray right before I spoke, or even think about asking the Lord to anoint me to speak for the*

> *children, He had overridden my tired flesh and made me walk by the power of His Spirit. I thought of Lazarus (John 11:44). The power of Christ was so strong it literally picked Lazarus up and propelled him out of the cave, still wrapped in grave clothes. How wonderful to know He will do the same for us. If my flesh isn't "grave clothes" I don't know what is. It hinders me, trips me up, weighs me down and in every way impedes my following my Lord as I want to. Praise God, I don't even have to be able to walk on my own. He will "propel me" by His Spirit where He wants me to go. He is so sufficient. He is literally everything we need.*

In the months following his healing, Aaron became a vital part of the family. He enjoyed everyone and everyone enjoyed him. The teenagers from our church played with him when they came to see our children, and argued over who would get to carry him around at church. Aaron did all the fun things our last few babies had been incapable of doing. He played and squealed and laughed. He loved to be tickled and to splash in the bathtub. He particularly adored Stacey, and they were especially close. Everyone was always ready to stop what they were doing and take Aaron for a bathtub romp because he loved it so.

Whoever bathed him always got almost as wet as he did. There are pictures of Aaron on Stacey's bed playing with her stuffed animals, pictures of Aaron asleep in a pile of toys, and pictures of him sitting in the high chair making faces. At Christmas there are pictures of him helping everyone open gifts, and rolling in the wrapping paper under the tree. It seemed the increased oxygen had caused his little personality to bloom, and he threw himself into life with total abandon.

Aaron fit into our family so beautifully that people began to comment it would be really hard for us when he left. I don't know what they thought it was like when all the others left! Friends and strangers alike said he looked like our own child and we should

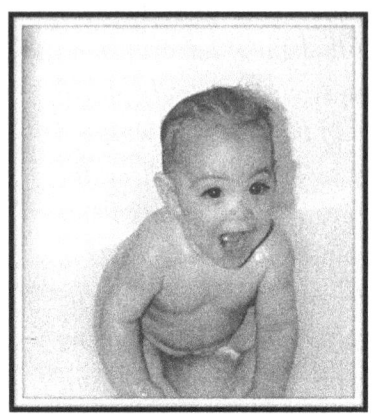

Aaron caught in the tub with no water flying.

adopt him. The children all thought it was a wonderful idea and begged to keep him. I asked Hamp what he thought, dreading myself, the thought of giving this precious little boy to strangers.

"No," he said.

"We are not called to adopt." Even though he loved Aaron as much as the rest of us, he was immovable on the subject. He was just positive we were not called to adopt. I wasn't convinced—I didn't want to be.

> JOURNAL: I am not giving Daddy enough attention. He comes and goes with just a greeting for days at a time. Lord, remind me to hug him and touch him. It seems as if no one touches him anymore.

> JOURNAL: Lord, I have fasted and prayed and had the elders anoint me with oil, but the pain in my neck and shoulders seems worse than ever. Please heal me so I can serve you better.

A couple of months after Aaron was healed, I was still praying to understand all that had happened in his healing and the significance of the crystal. As I prayed, it occurred to me that while I had been calling the beam of light I had seen a laser, I really had no idea what a laser was. I looked it up in the encyclopedia and was amazed to find my vision described scientifically.

It said a laser is concentrated light energy traveling in coherency. It is made by shining light into one end of a perfect crystal, usually a ruby. The beams of light bounce rapidly off of the smooth, flawless interior walls of the crystal, until they are tightly bound together. The hot, powerful beam which comes out of the opposing end of the crystal is called a laser. If there are flaws of any kind in the crystal, they will diffuse the light and it will not become a laser. A flawed crystal can only reflect light which feels warm and looks bright but has no power!

The Lord seemed to be showing me we are like a crystal which deflects the light of Christ with our flaws, sin. Jesus could heal because He was flawless, without sin. His life was perfect and His faith was complete. But in John 14:12, Jesus said, "...he who believes in me, the works that I do, he shall do also; and greater works than these shall he do, because I go to the Father." Doesn't this mean the incoherent glow that comes from us is really supposed to be a powerful light of laser intensity? This must be why the Lord kept telling me, "Whatever is not of faith is sin." (Romans 14:23). The sin that flaws our crystal is a lack of faith.

I think it is hard for us to have faith because of our awareness of our own sin. The Jews refused to go into the promised land because they were afraid. They knew how disobedient they had been all along the way and they knew in their hearts they didn't deserve for God to give them victory over the inhabitants of the land. I think this awareness of our sin makes it very hard for us to believe God will work miracles for us. We know we don't deserve it. But this is truly the essence of the wonderful gospel of Jesus Christ!

Ephesians 2:8-9 says, "For it is by grace you are saved, through faith, and that not of yourselves, it is a gift of God, not by works, lest any man should boast." By His grace, God gives us faith with which to believe Him, and Romans 4:4-5 says, "Now to the one who *works*, his wage is not reckoned as a favor, but as what is due. But to the one who does not work, but *believes* in Him who justifies the ungodly, his faith is reckoned as righteousness." And Jesus Himself said, "This is the work of God: that you believe in Him whom He has sent." (John 6:29). So believing the Father through

Christ has to be the only way we can ever have the power of God in our life. If Jesus said, "Greater things than I do shall you do," it must be possible. Surely even when we feel virtuous and deserving of God's power in our life, we are scarcely better in God's eyes than the worst sinner on earth. What we think makes us acceptable to God means almost nothing, compared to the huge mass of sin still in us we don't even recognize yet.

One morning in early October I was praying about the babies. It was becoming harder and harder to manage my family and the babies, especially now that the glow of ministry was gone. Our children were teenagers now and all the tension and concern adolescents cause in a family were being activated. My concerns for them alone needed an hour of prayer a day. Daddy was living with us and having problems with his eyes and his lungs which I had to help him deal with. And now with the constant pain in my neck and shoulders that had developed when we had Micah and grown slowly worse, the ministry to the babies seemed very heavy.

As I leafed through my prayer journal, I came to an entry made in August, which began with my asking the Lord to tell me what my work in His kingdom was. On the same page, under my prayer were my notes on Ezra 8, which described the Levites being summoned to carry the gold and silver vessels back to Jerusalem that had been stolen from the temple and taken to Babylon. This time I saw clearly what the Lord was saying. The babies were the Lord's treasure, like the golden vessels which belonged to God's temple. My service to God was to carry His treasure. I knew the Kohathite branch of the Levites carried the vessels used in the tabernacle, the forerunner of the temple, when they were in the wilderness, and that the articles were covered because no one but the sons of Aaron could look at them and not die. The Kohathite's job was to carry the burden assigned to him. The articles were wrapped carefully so he had no direct contact with the holy articles (Numbers 4:15 & 20).

Now I saw clearly that I was like a priest entrusted with God's treasure. I was called to carry it for Him until He asked for it, as the priests were to carry the gold and silver implements of worship. I smiled to myself as I noted gold is *very heavy*. One doesn't realize how heavy, until he has carried it for a long time and dealt with the reality of the weight. Mile after mile, day after day, they carried God's gold along with their own belongings, shifting it from arm to arm and onto their shoulder, trying to relieve their aching muscles. The gold was heavy, but they were privileged to be the ones to carry it and so are we privileged to carry His babies for Him.

Happy as I was to understand my service to God through His babies, it was like a delayed answer to a prayer, which wasn't as important now as it had been two months earlier. I didn't know God was building an explicit answer to a desperate prayer I would not even pray for two more months.

In a few weeks, Aaron's picture was in the newspaper saying he was available for adoption. I was still not sure we had to give him up. None of us wanted to even think about his leaving. Of course we always felt this way, so it wasn't significant that I almost cried just thinking about it. The newspaper article brought an immediate response from a family in a community very close to us. The couple was older than I had expected and they had teenage children. It was a different kind of family from those we usually placed with, and at first I made mountains out of every molehill of difference. But the Department of Human Services felt they would be a good family for Aaron, and were ready to begin working toward placement immediately.

In late November the day came for Aaron's social worker, Verna Gallagher, to knock on my door to make arrangements for his adoption. I cried and sniffled through the meeting, and when Verna left, I paced back and forth through the house crying. "I have to hear from You!" I told the Lord. "If I can't keep this baby, You have to tell me loudly enough for me to hear. I can't bear the thought of giving him up if I don't have to. Lord, please, speak to me." I cried and walked up and down for about thirty minutes, then I lay down on the couch to try to compose myself before the children came home from school. I didn't want them to see how upset I was over losing Aaron. I had just closed my eyes when the Lord spoke. I reached for my pen and a piece of paper. He said, "How much do you love My babies? How much do you love Me? Do you not know there is much to be done that can only be done by those who are willing to be hurt and to bleed?" Jesus was a man of sorrow, acquainted with grief (Isaiah 53:3). "How committed are you to giving babies a chance to live and love and grow? Are you willing to pour yourself out for them?"

The Lord has brought this one sentence back to my mind many times since then and it has always pointed me in the right direction. Though frightening, it is comforting to me because it tells me the Lord has come again to direct my faltering steps to do his will. Exodus 32:25-28 came to my mind. It says after Aaron made the golden calf and Moses returned from the mountain of God, there were several divisions of people. Those who had run to hide in their tents from shame for what they had done, those who were still drinking and reveling and partying, and those standing still, outside with the revelers, but listening to Moses and waiting to see what he would say. Then Moses addressed the people and said, "Everyone who is on the Lord's side come and stand by me," and all the Levites came. He told them, "Thus says the Lord, the God of Israel. Every man of you put his sword upon his thigh and go back and forth from gate to gate in the camp and kill every man his brother, every man his friend and every man his neighbor," referring to the ones ignoring Moses and continuing to engage in pagan revelry.

Only by being willing to kill even their own brothers and friends if it was God's will, could they be truly fit to serve and please God. Could I "kill" my love for Aaron and give him to the Lord? Was I willing to put an end to my love and desire for him, to let him be "dead" to me as my son?

As I thought about the Levites being called to sacrifice so much to obey the Lord, I thought of Ezra 8:15-34 again, and I immediately saw what the Lord had started showing me in August. I remembered Ezra had to find priests to carry the treasure from Babylon back to Jerusalem. It was not permitted for anyone to touch God's holy vessels except Levites. They carried it for the duration of the journey and turned it over when it was asked for in Jerusalem. If one of them had put a golden utensil under his robe and kept it for himself, it would have been unthinkable! Yet this was what I was thinking of doing. Aaron was God's treasure, and it could never be God's will for me to keep him for myself in light of all He had shown me concerning my service to Him. That is why the angel said, "This is pure gold to you," speaking of my service to God with Micah. I am like a Kohathite, called to carry the babies, which are worth more than gold to Him. I am to bear the burden of their needs, to be responsible for them and to count them precious vessels of the Lord's.

Now that I understood who I was, and what Aaron was, I knew my job of carrying him was over. I had been asked for him and it was time to hand my little treasure over to the Lord; to let Him place him where He wanted him. Aaron belonged to the dear couple who were preparing a place for him in their family, not to us...not to me.

In place of the terrible anxiety I had felt, now peace flowed in. I knew no matter how hard it was in the days to come, it was the Lord's will for Aaron to leave us and He would give us grace for it. I am still amazed by the mercy and compassion of the Lord to show me in His word a picture of my service to Him. He broke it down and explained it to me in the only way I ever could have been absolutely sure I was right to give Aaron up.

The weeks before Aaron left were hard for all of us. It is

easier to adjust to something that has happened, than to something that will happen. Knowing we soon would no longer be doing the things we enjoyed so much with him was heart rending. He was twelve months old and an active, precious little boy. He walked before he left us, something no foster baby had ever done. For the first time I had physical symptoms of the stress I was under. It was a hard time to get through, but knowing we were doing what the Lord wanted made it possible. "I can do all things through Christ who strengthens me," (Philippians 4:13).

If we never experience the Lord's will through obedient pain, I don't believe we will ever come to the place of being able to serve Him without being controlled by the needs of the flesh. As I was entrusted with Micah, and learned to carry him for Jesus, and to bear the pain of all that was required for him, I learned how faithful the Lord is to meet us where we are. When I could go no further with Micah, He sent an angel to tell me I was in His will and no matter how awful the situation was at the time, He was right there with me in it. Knowing that, gave me the strength to trust the Holy Spirit in me to keep me going.

IF I HAD ENTERTAINED ANY DOUBTS, AARON'S RECEPTION OF HIS NEW family would have banished them all. The Lord gave them such favor with Aaron he loved them from the moment he met them. After a look of mild concern, the first time they left our house with him, he always left for visits at their house with a big smile and a happy wave goodbye. Even their dog loved him. The family lived close enough for Aaron to be able to go back and forth between us for several weeks before his final placement. When the day came in January for him to leave us for good he was almost as comfortable in their home as ours. Watching his new parents leave with him was painful and except for Hamp, we all cried, especially the girls and I, but it was no worse than Caleb, Matthew or Micah, because we knew it was God's plan for Aaron and for us.

Having a former baby live just a few minutes away was a unique experience for us. Laura and her boyfriend, Pat, took him to the zoo and to see Santa at Christmas time, and I have seen him several times. His parents brought him for a visit when he was two, and when he has been very sick, his mother has called and asked us to pray for him. His cystic fibrosis is still a major concern and he wears glasses now, but Aaron has a loving, supportive family to get him through the rough places.

I can't help thinking of him when I hear the argument that children with birth defects should be aborted. Aaron has a genetic disease which can kill him, but I think of all the pleasure he brought our family and all the joy Ruby and Ray Gibson and their family have received from him, and wonder how many precious children have been denied the opportunity to live and bring love and joy to a family because of what might or might not lay ahead for them and their family.

> *JOURNAL: Isaiah 28:16 and I Peter 2:6 say Jesus is a tried stone, a precious cornerstone. The tried stone, or cornerstone had no faults or cleavages, like the vision of the crystal.*

> *JOURNAL: The underlying illustration of the laser is that our sin of faithlessness prevents our seeing healings and miracles. It is literally true whatever is not of faith is sin, and that diffuses the power He promised in the Bible. Faith is more than Hebrews 11:1. It is the total confidence that God is in control, and as we obey Him, He will reveal Himself in our life. And what more does a believer really want than that?*

7
JOHN MARK

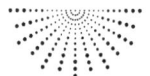

Six days later Catholic Charities called about John Mark. The baby in need of a home this time was in a different situation from anything we had dealt with before. He was a premature little black boy who had been given a tracheostomy to save his life soon after birth. He was eight months old and had been in the hospital most of his life.

> *JOURNAL: June, 1986. Last week at church prayer group I had to bite my tongue to keep from asking for prayer for our next baby. I had a strong sense that he was almost ready for us and in need of much prayer. But I was afraid to say it for fear I was wrong.*

Because of the trach, he was unable to vocalize. The only sound he could make was the sound of air blowing through the little plastic tube inserted into his trachea to hold it open. The trach itself required special care, not to mention the three machines necessary to keep him both alive and healthy. I had never cared for a child with a tracheostomy, and it was intimidating. But the thing which put me off the most about this baby was that his parents wanted him. He was to return to them as soon as he was strong enough.

The baby's parents were not married, but wanted their baby and had moved in together to take care of him. They had discovered his care was more than they were prepared to handle. He had been returned to the hospital twice in the emergency helicopter, and the fright of those experiences had forced them to agree to foster care for him until he was able to survive in their rural home without machines.

I had always said I would never take a child who would be returned to birth parents. I thought children who were returned to their parents were neglected before and after their foster placement. That made their time in foster homes a short experience in a secure, loving home, before they were returned to their deprived and unhappy childhood. I didn't think I could handle that. However, I couldn't escape the fact that this baby was in need of a loving home while he was getting well. I knew the hospital could never meet his emotional needs, and there were few foster parents in our area who were willing to take a child with such complex medical problems. My experiences with other babies and my knowledge that if we took him the Lord would be with us gave me the courage to step out in faith and begin a relationship with the baby.

ON MY FIRST VISIT TO THE HOSPITAL, JOHN MARK, THE BIBLICAL name we had chosen for him, only glanced at me once. He seemed much like Matthew, totally tuned out. On the next few visits he looked at me fleetingly, but mostly he just lay on his back with his head back and chin up, as if trying to make room for the cuff of the mist tube attached to his throat. His lack of interest in his surroundings made me feel certain he had brain damage. His head was flat on the sides, typical of premature babies, but he had pretty brown eyes and long curly eyelashes. As I leaned over the side of his crib to stroke and talk to him, I felt neither attracted nor repelled by him. I thought it would help if I felt one way or the other. Then I realized I had never felt any strong emotion on first beholding my "new baby," except Aaron, and he had terrified me.

The nurses showed me how to suction his trach and I found that being forced to face the suction with Aaron, had taken away my fear of harming the baby with it. It still wasn't easy to put it into his throat and suck out the air as well as the mucus, but it only took a few seconds and if he turned a little blue, they showed me how to give him a quick burst of air with a hand-held air bag. Learning how to replace the strings which held the little plastic appliance in his trachea was much harder. The strings had to be cut and looped and knotted a certain way, and the baby kept still enough so the appliance didn't come out while there were no strings around his neck to hold it in. I thought this was the hardest part of caring for him, but there was no danger of its being left undone. Trach strings on a baby develop a terrible odor if not replaced every day or two, so I was highly motivated to learn to do it efficiently. Because there was such a complex system of machinery needed to care for John Mark, it took several weeks for me to learn how to use all the machines and make the arrangements to bring him home. I also had to meet with his birth mother and make arrangements for her and his father to visit their baby in our home, which was much harder for me than learning to handle the medical equipment.

When we had been visiting for about a week, John Mark began looking at us and even turning his head so he could see us. Also the nurses, knowing now that he was going home to an active family, started working on helping him learn to sit up. Given the opportunity, he quickly learned to sit in a walker for short periods and the possibility of being mobile fascinated him. For weeks we kept a steady procession of people going to the hospital to see John Mark and play with him. By the time he came home, the whole family and half of the church youth group had fallen in love with him. The nurses also experimented with taking the mist cuff off of his trach to see if he would build up thick mucus and choke without it. He could go for an hour and a half when he came home from the hospital.

One afternoon right before we brought him home, a social worker brought John Mark's mother to our house to meet me and see where her little boy would be living. She was a quiet girl in her late teens, and she was very sad her baby was coming home to me and not her. She thanked me for taking care of him, but her eyes filled with tears when she saw the reality of a crib and toys for him. I thought how painful it must be to see another mother making preparations for taking care of your baby, especially one who could give him more than you could.

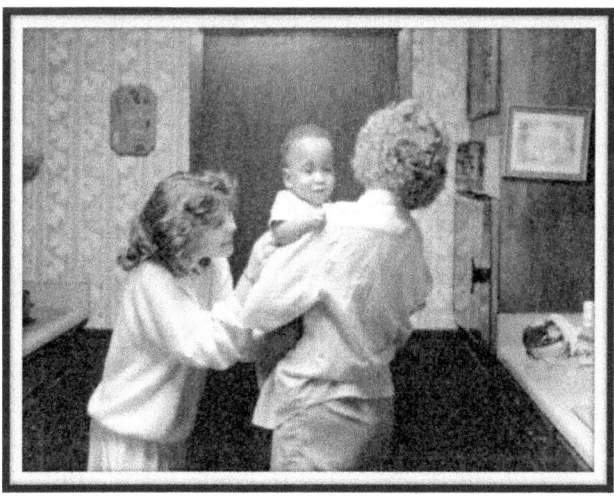

Laura stopping by for a tickle to John Mark on her way through the kitchen.

The dynamics between the baby's mother and me was another

reason I had always said I would never take a baby who would go back home. I tried not to worry about what would happen to our relationship as the baby grew and it became apparent he looked on me as his mother. I dreaded not only her anger and resentment, but my frustration and anxiety if it became plain to me she was not going to be able to give him what I thought he needed. I knew there was nothing I could do to prepare for it or avoid it, so I gave my concerns to Jesus and tried to concentrate on John Mark's needs.

TWENTY MINUTES AFTER I ARRIVED HOME FROM THE HOSPITAL WITH John Mark, the home health van drove into the driveway. I had been shown how to use the machines which kept John Mark alive and healthy in the hospital, but now I would be left alone at home with him. His life could depend on my ability to use them. I watched the technician bring in the three machines, cases of sterile water, distilled water, cases of tubing and catheters, trach kits and sterile gloves. My confident words to a friend recently, "I don't think I will ever be afraid of another baby," mocked me. With the baby alcove and part of our bedroom filled with machines, wires, tubes, boxes, and flashing lights, I was afraid, again.

When Hampy came home, his eyes widened in disbelief. "Good grief, Sweet. Do you really know what to do with all this stuff?" he said, standing in the midst of all the machines and boxes.

"I think so...I pray so," I said, trying to sound more confident than I felt.

The mist which kept John Mark's secretions fluid so his trachea didn't become clogged with mucus, came from a big machine in our bedroom and made swooshing sounds as it took oxygen from the air. The air was forced through a tube attached to a bottle of sterile water. From there the cool mist was pushed down a big blue plastic tube with a cuff on the end, which was attached under John

Mark's chin and held in place over the trach opening with elastic bands.

The suction machine was just like the one I had been given with Aaron, but suctioning a trachea was different from a throat because at that time doctors considered the trachea sterile. If I introduced any bacteria into John Mark's trachea, it was thought he could develop a deadly infection. Every suction had to be done with a sterile surgical glove on the hand holding the catheter, and then it had to be irrigated with sterile water. I could use one catheter for four hours, but then I had to throw it away and open a new one. Medical home health care has shown the trachea is not a sterile environment, as thought at the time, but that didn't help me then.

The third machine was an apnea monitor to track his heart rate and breathing. It was set to alarm if his heart rate or breathing changed drastically, as it would if his trach tube became plugged with mucus. If his heart rate or breathing changed that much, the machine would emit a horrible, high-pitched whistle. It was very efficient. Every time it went off, everyone in the house covered his ears and rushed to John Mark's bedside to turn it off. Fortunately, we discovered after just a few days that this child's breathing and heart rate both slowed so much when he was deeply asleep he made the machine alarm continually, not allowing him or us to sleep. At the time he wasn't having any problems, so the doctors and we agreed to leave it off for a while. It was a relief not to have to deal with the wires, lights and whistles of at least one machine.

I took copious notes on the use of all the machines and was delighted to learn the home health technician, Art Landry, lived only minutes away. His daughter and Laura were friends and went to school together. He promised to come day or night if I needed him, and he did.

It took me a day or two to relax with all the intimidating equipment, but John Mark was so stimulated by his new surroundings and the children playing with him, he didn't seem to suffer any stress at all from the drastic change in his life.

It was amazing how quickly we all adjusted to hearing the air passing through John Mark's tiny trach tube that signified crying. To our ears he was crying like any other baby and only strangers noticed there was no real vocal sound coming from him.

 JOURNAL: Lord, thank You for the ministry of Open Doors with Brother Andrew. Not just for their ministry to Christians in countries closed to the gospel, but also for their ministry to me. Without their teaching me what Your children suffer in other countries just for naming the name of Jesus, I would never have known what a child I am. I would have been tempted to think I was especially obedient and that sitting up at night rocking someone else's child was an enormous sacrifice. But I know there are Christian brothers and sisters all over the world, who have lost everything dear to them. Many are totally cut off from human comfort, and must depend totally on You. Thank You for their witness that wherever our obedience takes us, You are there.

Within a week of his arrival home, John Mark was pulling the mist cuff from his throat, taking the tubing apart and throwing it out of the crib. Sometimes he saved one piece to chew on, but the rest had to go. For a while I waited until he was sleep, and then stealthily slipped the cuff over his trach, but that didn't work long and we had no choice but to leave the mist off completely. This bothered me because I knew without the moisture from the mist machine, the mucus in his trachea would be thicker. One little plug of mucus in the tiny opening he breathed through could kill him in minutes. I knew if that happened, we could walk into the room and find him dead. There would be no warning. If the tube was blocked with mucus, he wouldn't even be able to make his quiet little crying sound to alert us that something was wrong.

The seriousness of his compromised airway notwithstanding, the stimulation of being in a family made John Mark so interested in the activity around him, he began to assimilate and apply knowledge with amazing speed. I saw again the truth I had learned with other sick babies. The more normal the baby's life, the more normal the baby. He went from an eight month old who lay on his back all day, never turning over, never watching what went on around him, to a little boy who was constantly moving and was interested in everything. I knew if I could expose him to the outside world, his development would blossom even more, but I was hindered by his need for the suction machine. I couldn't take him anywhere without it and the machine was both cumbersome and electric.

Finally, after weeks of inquiries, someone told me about DeLea catheters. They worked like a siphon. I put one tube in his trach, and I sucked the other. My suction pulled the secretions up his tube and into a little bottle in the middle. They were expensive and disposable, but they opened the door to the world for John Mark. With them I could take him literally anywhere and he could have all the experiences of a normal baby. Babies with trachs no longer have the opportunity of using DeLea catheters because of the fear of AIDS by medical workers. DeLeas were easy to use and Laura and I quickly got used to them, but no one else in the family would touch one. They and the rest of the civilized world thought the whole idea of suctioning was incredibly gross. When we were in public, I covered everything with a cloth diaper, and people around us never knew what I was doing. Once a friend from church was visiting me at home and we were deep in conversation. Without realizing she had never seen me suction John Mark, I picked him up and suctioned him with a DeLea as we talked. The color left her face and she put her head down on the table. I thought she was going to faint. It was a lesson I didn't forget.

JOURNAL: (Matthew 16:16-17) Peter's confession of Jesus as the Christ. Jesus said, "Flesh and blood did not reveal this to you, but My Father who is in heaven." The presence of Jesus in flesh and blood did not reveal the reality of who He was to Peter. That was done by the Father. Jesus said, "No man can come to me except the Father draws him," (John 6:44). If being with Jesus in the flesh couldn't save Peter, how can I bear the burden of being such a good example to my children that they desire to walk closely with Jesus? The Father and the Holy Spirit will have to reveal the power and reality of Jesus to them. I can't do it. What a relief not to have the whole responsibility resting on me.

 JOURNAL: The Lord had me put my church bulletin at II Kings 18, Sunday, so my Bible would open to it today. As I started to pray for the children, I was discouraged and depressed. I opened my Bible and read how the agent of the King of Assyria, Israel's enemy, stood outside the walls of Jerusalem and shouted what he had done to other cities. He said, "Do you really think because you trust in your god you will be different? They had gods and they didn't deliver them! Don't think your god can save you from me!" The people were sitting on the city wall hearing every dire prediction of what would happen if they trusted in Yahweh. Hezekiah, king of Judah, took the propaganda to God in prayer. The story ends with no attack on Jerusalem, God striking 185,000 Assyrian soldiers dead, and King Sennacherib assassinated while worshipping his idol god.

I take every word of this for my family. Hampy and I will trust in our God, and even though the enemy threatens us and courts our children with all of the allurements of the world, we will have faith in their commitments as little children to keep them in God's hand. We believe they will serve the Lord according to His determination when they are grown.

Because his trach made him so vulnerable, I got approval from Human Services to pay for nurses when I had to be away from him. There were about six nurses who came and went during his stay with us, one of whom prayed with me to receive the Lord. There were two who stayed with him the most, Joyce Butler and Jean Ferguson. They became like members of the family. They bought him clothes and toys and were more like his aunts than paid nurses.

> *JOURNAL: Lord, I have tried several medications, and all the doctors' suggestions for relieving my pain, but it grows steadily worse. When John Mark wakes me in the night, I often never get back to sleep because my neck hurts so. Lord, surely I could serve you better if I could sleep. Please show me what to do.*

In the fall when the weather changed, John Mark developed some congestion in his lungs, which was not unusual in our humid climate. It was inconvenient because it created more mucus in his trachea. There were days it seemed all I did was suction him, but I was not worried about it. He was fragile because of his compromised airway, but basically he was a healthy child.

While all the children did everything for John Mark, Laura was especially adept with suctioning. Stacey and John would do it with the suction machine, but being older, they were more often away at school or work. Since the suctioning didn't bother Laura, when I had to leave the house for a few minutes and didn't have a nurse, I made sure she was there.

JOHN MARK'S PARENTS BEGAN VISITING HIM SOON AFTER HE CAME TO us. They came weekly at first, but quickly tapered off to once every month or so. They were congenial and polite, but I had the feeling they really didn't understand his needs. They didn't seem to grasp the reasons behind the procedures necessary for his care, which caused them to be less diligent about them than I would have liked. His father was a particularly likeable and outgoing young man, and John Mark loved for him to come and play with him. Being a mother didn't seem to come so easily to his mom, and I had to show her how to stimulate and play with him. Her apparent lack of enthusiasm for her son weighed on my heart. I was dismayed to find she was soon pregnant again, and she often fell asleep while she was responsible for John Mark. I never left her alone with him. I left them alone in the house with him when they came together, so they could experience full responsibility for their baby without prompting from me.

When they asked to take him home for the day on his birthday so his extended family could see him, we agreed. We thought he was stable enough, and they understood sufficiently about his care that one day couldn't hurt him.

> *JOURNAL: John Mark is going home for his birthday. Aaron's mother called yesterday and wanted to bring Aaron to see us that day. Thank you, Lord, for Your perfect timing. It will be a blessing to see Aaron and his adoptive family at a time when I am trying not to worry about John Mark's future. I will not allow Satan to rob me of my joy.*

Wanting to be a blessing, I did everything I could think of to ensure success for John Mark's first trip back home. I packed bags of clothes, medicine, suction tubes, and baby food. I tried to send everything he could possibly need. Of course, I also wrote out when to give him his medicine and how much baby food he usually ate.

When his parents brought him back that night, they were three hours late and John Mark was exhausted, dirty and sick from eating foods he had never had before.

> *JOURNAL: Such confusion about John Mark. I sometimes feel we never should have taken him. Lord, you called me to John Mark for a purpose, please fulfill it. Deuteronomy 1:31-32 says, "Even though He carried you in His arms like a son and brought you this far; still you don't trust Him. Even though He goes before you to seek out a place for you to camp, you still don't trust Him." I think too often we give up half-way to where God is taking us, and begin to look to our own understanding for security.*

John Mark stood in his baby bed and leaned around the corner to look at me in the mornings. He beamed happily and bounced in his crib when I looked up and saw him. I couldn't keep the tears from my eyes; he thought he was my little boy. He only knew Hamp and me as Daddy and Mother, Stacey, John and Laura as sisters and brother. Our house was his home. His life was with us as far as he knew. How could it be possible he did not really belong to us? Over and over I told myself God had put John Mark into the family He wanted him in. I would have put Jesus into a comfortable affluent family in Rome, to make it easy for Him to influence the world. I would have ruined everything the Father had planned, because I could only see the small picture. The Father knew everything Jesus was called to do. He had important reasons for the family and location He had chosen for His Son. I knew that about Jesus and I had to believe the same thing for John Mark.

> *JOURNAL: Lord, I want to have a circumcised heart (Romans 2:28-9). I want my heart so unfleshly it shows on my body, on my face, in my eyes. "Let them who fear Thee see me and be glad!" (Psalm 119:24)*

I knew my feelings could cause real trouble in our relationship with his parents if we did not walk in strict obedience to the Lord. I tried hard to acknowledge and encourage his parents. When he was sick, I always called and gave them a report and asked them to pray for him.

> JOURNAL: *I am jealous of other women's relations with Jesus, my Redeemer-Husband. Lord, please show me scripture about sharing You with other women. I feel resentful when other women make me feel they know You in ways I don't, or have favor with You I don't have. Women are so emotional in our love for You, we give Satan a powerful weapon against us in this respect. It is all right for someone to teach scripture, but I don't want to hear about Your speaking to someone else's heart, or making Your presence felt with them as You do to me. I felt impressed that Jesus's answer to this problem was in I Corinthians chapter twelve, which describes the body of Christ. We can't function effectively in a body with other people unless we can put aside our selfishness and be willing for them to have as deep and intimate a relationship with Jesus as we have. I have lost all of this resentment now, as my willingness has grown to allow Jesus to work His will in whatever manner He desires.*

One Sunday afternoon in the fall, Hamp and I left John Mark with the girls to go to a run. Hamp would run, I would walk and sit. The weather was nice and John Mark was doing fine. We would only be gone a couple of hours. When we came home, we were shocked by what had happened in so short a time.

Laura had put John Mark in his bed for a nap, and then sat down on the other side of the alcove wall from him to talk to her boyfriend on the phone. As they talked, she became aware of a soft, high-pitched whistle.

"Richard, hush, shhhhh," she said. "Wait a minute." She dropped the phone and looked around the corner at John Mark. He was unconscious, his lips were blue and he was barely breathing. The mucus plug she knew had to be in his trach tube was allowing just enough air through to make the soft whistle. Forgetting the phone, she screamed for Stacey, who was at the other end of the house. She flipped on the suction machine and began to suction John Mark. Unable to move the plug, she dropped the catheter, ran to the door of our room and screamed as loudly as she could again. Then she ran back and continued suctioning, but without success. Richard, who was at our house a lot, knew something was wrong with the baby and quickly hung up. When Stacey got to our room, Laura said, "Call the rescue unit. I can't get his trach cleared!" Stacey ran to the kitchen phone where there was a sticker with the rescue unit's phone number and tried to call. "There's something wrong with the phone!" she screamed back to Laura. Still suctioning, Laura leaned back and looked around to the chair she had been sitting in. The phone was still off the hook. I had alerted the fire department before I brought Nathan and every baby after him home from the hospital. They had posted our address on their bulletin board for everyone to be sure they knew where we lived.

Within minutes the paramedics rushed in, oxygen in hand, only to find John Mark standing in his crib, holding on to Laura. The catheter with the mucus plug lay on the table by his bed. The paramedics turned immediately to Stacey, who at seventeen, was three years older and much taller than Laura, and began congratulating her for saving the baby's life. They were surprised when Stacey identified herself as the person who had called them, and her very small fourteen year old sister as the real heroine.

NOT LONG AFTER THIS, I DECIDED TO TRY TO FIND A SPEECH therapist to teach John Mark sign language. He obviously wanted to communicate with us and I thought he was smart enough to pick up some basic sign language, even if he was only twelve months old. There was no guarantee he would ever be able to have his trachea repaired and speak like a normal person, and I knew it would be devastating to him if he was unable to communicate or play with other children. Several weeks of perseverance found a speech therapist willing to work with such a young child. Sherry began coming twice a week to our house to work with him. Her ability to teach and his ability to learn were both incredible.

She began by showing John Mark toys and showing him the sign for them. He quickly picked up what she meant and learned to give her the toy she signed for. I was fascinated by his ability, and would watch from the kitchen so I wouldn't distract him. Sometimes he got bored with the game and refused to cooperate, or he would pick up the wrong thing, with a grin on his face, clearly indicating he knew that was not what she wanted. When this happened and he was unwilling to stop playing and get back to work, Sherry would put him in the corner, and hold him facing the wall.

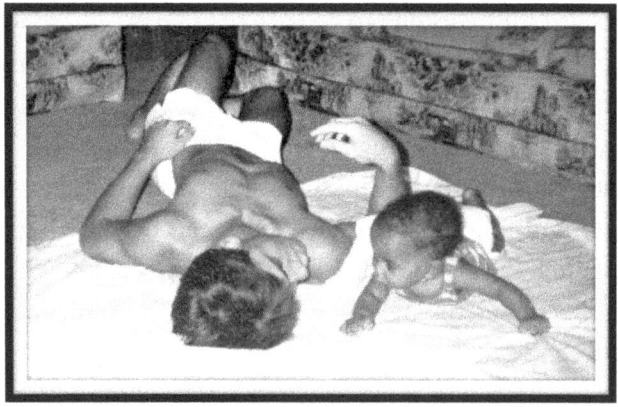

John Mark just able to push up. John is showing him how to stick out his tongue. It's therapy for the babies who can't vocalize.

The first time she did this I had to stop watching. He looked so tiny and miserable being forced to sit in the corner crying. I was sure he couldn't understand such discipline at his age. After several minutes, she had me suction him, brought him back to the toys, and asked him sweetly to give her the item again. Tears still on his cheeks, John Mark solemnly handed her the toy she asked for. I was impressed. I would not have believed it if I hadn't seen it myself. Thereafter, she rarely had to put him in the corner. All she had to do was mention it and he would get right to work. Sometimes of course, he was tired or didn't feel well, and those times Sherry would just stop. I learned all the signs he did, and a few more, so I could help teach him too. He learned fast and I knew he would be able to communicate at an early age if he had to keep the trach for a long time, or even the rest of his life.

One day, Sherry suggested we try to show John Mark he could talk. We could cover his trach with our finger and get him to cry, laugh, or cough. This would force air over his vocal chords and make a sound. If he knew he could make sounds, he could learn to cover the opening himself when he wanted to speak. His reaction was something I never expected from such a lively little boy. Instead of crying with anger or fear, or even trying to move our hand so he could breathe, John Mark did absolutely nothing. He just looked up at us with a look of abject sadness. He would sit there, unable to breathe, and look at us with an expression that said, "I can't believe you would do this to me, but if this is what you want to do, I won't fight you." He refused to push our hand away or even cry. I kept trying it for a while, but he always responded the same, and I finally gave up. I was accomplishing nothing, and I couldn't stand to see that expression on his face.

JOURNAL: Lord, make Your bride, the church, alert and expectant, looking for her husband every moment. Let us not be as one who has given up hope of His ever coming,

who lies on her bed trying to sleep and forget a groom was ever supposed to come for her.

As the fall weather grew colder, John Mark's lungs grew worse. The doctor gave him all the usual medications for chronic lung problems and he probably would have been all right, if he had not had the tracheostomy. While a normal child had his whole throat to cough up mucus, John Mark had only the tiny opening in the bottom of his trach tube. The presence of so much mucus in his airways was a constant danger.

One day I had to make a quick trip to the mall for something and left John Mark playing with Laura. I had listened to his lungs with the stethoscope and they sounded as good as they ever did. He wasn't sick and there had not been even a hint of a mucus plug.

When I came home an hour later, no one was there. On the kitchen counter was a note from Laura. "Mother, I have gone to the Baptist Hospital in the ambulance with John Mark. Granddaddy is with us, love, Laura."

Poor Laura, I thought. Not Again! And now Daddy has had to get involved. I should never have left her alone with him. I phoned Hamp to meet me at the hospital.

When we rushed into the emergency room, we found Laura sitting on the examining table holding John Mark. He was playing with her necklace, and had a big smile on his face. Granddaddy was relaxing in a chair. "Daddy, I am so sorry you had to do this," I said, angry with myself for causing everyone so much trouble.

"Well, they wouldn't bring him without an adult," he said, with a wave of his hand.

Laura said the situation had developed much as the one before, only this time it seemed to clear by itself just before the paramedics arrived. While they were writing out their report, the trach got plugged again and they brought him to the hospital when they couldn't clear it. Laura took a DeLea catheter in the ambulance and continued to work on him on the way to the hospital. Just before they got to the hospital, she got the plug out. Thank goodness for Laura's tenacious spirit. Twice she had kept working and enabled John Mark to breathe again.

Bob Thompson arrived and ordered an X-ray to check for pneumonia, but it was clear. "I think he has pockets in his bronchial tubes that are holding mucus," he said. "It's called bronchopulmonary dysplasia. It wouldn't be so bad if he didn't have a trach, but that little hole he has to breathe through makes any mucus build-up really dangerous." He increased the aerosol mist treatments I had been giving him for months and added a medication to it. He also changed one of his oral medications.

"You see if I turn my back on you again," I told John Mark as we left the hospital. From then on I didn't leave him at all without a nurse there. Laura had come through twice, but I wasn't going to put that responsibility on her again.

A FEW WEEKS LATER LAURA'S LOVE FOR JOHN MARK MADE FOR AN amusing encounter with a teenage boy who made the mistake of questioning John Mark's ethnic background. One afternoon several of John's friends came by to pick him up, and one of the boys noticed John Mark playing on the floor in the den. He walked around the couch for a better look, then squinting suspiciously at him he asked, "What color is that baby?" in a tone that implied there was no use trying to fool him, that baby was black.

"Oh, I'd say he's a rich chocolate brown," I said, smiling. I understood his amazement at finding a black child in our home, and was willing to meet him where he was. But not Laura.

She strode up to the boy, who was easily twice her size, and looked up at him with her eyes blazing fire. "He is black, he is my little brother, and if you don't like it, get out of my house!" she said.

The boy backed away, putting up his hands in defense, "I didn't say I didn't like it!" he said, and retreated to a chair on the other side of the room where he waited silently for John.

One afternoon in early December, I came home from working at Hamp's tool and die shop to find Joyce listening to John Mark with the stethoscope while he napped.

"He has been really congested since early this afternoon," she said. "It's almost time for a mist treatment. If he doesn't clear up after that, you probably should call the doctor."

As soon as she left, I gave him the breathing treatment, holding the mist in front of his face as he slept. He started coughing almost immediately as the mist broke up the congestion in his lungs. He coughed violently, bringing mucus up into the little tube in his trachea. Quickly I suctioned him, but the mucus kept coming up. He had plugged the trach and his lips had turned blue three or four times before I got Bob on the phone. Holding John Mark in one hand and the phone in the other, I told him I was bringing him in. In retrospect I should have called an ambulance, but I didn't realize how bad it was.

Laura came in and volunteered to come with me. "Good, you can lean over the back seat and give him air if he needs it," I said, handing the air bag.

It was getting dark and I wished fervently for Hamp to drive us as he always did when I had to rush to the hospital at night. Not having to drive let me to give my full attention to the baby. He was still at the shop though, and John Mark couldn't wait for him to get home.

We bundled John Mark into the car and headed for the doctor's office about twenty minutes away. We had gone no more than a block when I had to pull over and suction him. I turned on the interior lights to see if he was turning blue around his mouth. I couldn't be sure in the artificial light, but I thought he was. We drove on, only to have to stop again and repeat the suctioning. This time he looked limp, and I couldn't get anything up from his trachea. We drove on. Another block meant another stop to suction. I couldn't get anything up and he was definitely listless. The congestion rattled ominously in his chest and throat. I decided to try to just drive and let Laura give him little bursts of air with the air bag to be sure he was getting oxygen. We would never get to the doctor if we kept stopping every few hundred yards to suction. In a couple of minutes, I realized John Mark was not going to make it to the pediatrician's office. I swerved and headed for our family doctor's office which was only a block away.

Snatching him out of the car without even looking at him, I ran into the waiting room. "We need oxygen! Quick!" I shouted at the startled receptionist, "Quick!"

People started running. In seconds we were in an examining room with the doctor peering anxiously at John Mark.

"He sounds bad," he agreed, as he listened to his chest. "You were wise not to try to make it to the pediatrician." He ordered a shot of epinephrine and in a few minutes the baby was breathing easier. "If you leave right now, you will probably be all right until you can get to Bob's office," he said.

Greatly relieved and confident things were under control, we headed toward town again, but in less than five minutes John Mark was wheezing as badly as before. I couldn't believe it. Once more Laura leaned over the back of the seat blowing air into his trachea to give him the oxygen he so desperately needed. I prayed under my breath the Lord would keep him alive until I could get help for him. Laura gave John Mark puffs of air about every five seconds, until after what seemed an eternity, we finally reached Bob's office.

They were closed now, but both doctors who were still there looked at him. That he needed to be in a hospital was obvious, but we were all concerned with getting him there. More medication was administered and given time to take effect. John Mark's breathing greatly improved, but I hadn't recovered from his unexpected relapse after the first shot. I kept thinking about his parents and how they would feel if I let him die. Knowing there were parents waiting to get him back, increased the pressure when I was trying to make decisions. If I made a bad decision about an orphaned baby, I would feel heartbroken and guilty, but I knew the Lord would know I had done my best. Parents would not be so quick to forgive.

The hospital was only ten minutes away now, so I gathered up my courage and set out for the hospital. Compared with the ride to the doctor's office, the trip was uneventful. He was breathing much better, at least temporarily. He was put right into intensive care and a plastic tent was placed around his crib with a mist machine attached. This provided a cool, moist environment to keep his secretions liquid. The usual I.V.s were started, and he was given medication for his lungs, but to add insult to John Mark's injury, I could only see him every four hours. At least this was the same hospital Nathan had been born in, and I was consoled the same intensive care staff who had taken such good care of Nathan was now caring for John Mark.

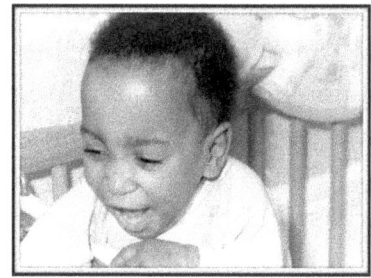

| Beautiful Baby!

The worst part of ICU for John Mark was being isolated in the cool, damp tent. He couldn't hear anyone talking because the noise of the mist machine sounded like a huge plane about to take off from his crib. No one could hear him crying for the same reason. When I went in to see him, he would press his face against the plastic and wail miserably, his little face telling me what his vocal chords could not, "Why do you keep leaving me here? Mama, take me home!" He was miserable and lonely, but the mist could save his life. I could unzip the tent and put my arms around him and kiss him, but my time was up all too soon, and I would have to leave him alone in his little tent. He would stay there nearly a week. Then he was moved out onto the floor.

After talking it over with the doctors and nurses, I decided not to take John Mark home without a mist tent like the one he had in the hospital. He seemed to need the mist too much and I didn't want a repeat of the trip to the doctor's office Laura and I had experienced. It was right before Christmas, and we couldn't get people to move quickly to get a mist tent delivered hurriedly. It would be two weeks after Christmas before we were able to bring him home with the tent. I hated for him to spend Christmas in the hospital, especially now that he wasn't any sicker than usual, but I wasn't willing to risk his life over it.

Because I couldn't stay with him all the time, the nurses put his bed in an observation room across from the nurses' station where they could watch him. This put him in view of people any time he wanted to look out, and he much preferred it to being in a room all by himself.

His parents said they wanted to come see him Christmas Day in the hospital. Hamp, the children and I decided they should have Christmas alone with him, and we didn't go to see him until that night. I waited anxiously for our time to go, but when we arrived at the hospital, we discovered they had never come! John Mark had spent Christmas Day all by himself. I was glad he was so young he didn't know the difference. Of course the nurses and hospital staff were wonderful at Christmas. The children who had to be in the hospital had all the treats and toys they felt well enough to enjoy. Churches and civic groups brought so many toys to the children, John Mark had more stuffed animals and toys piled in his bed than he could play with.

ONE MORNING ABOUT A WEEK LATER, I ARRIVED TO FIND JOHN Mark's bed empty. I started to look for a nurse to ask where he was, when he sped past the door in a little yellow walker. I stepped out of the room to see him go zooming down the hall, his tiny hospital gown with teddy bears on it flying in the wind.

"Where is John Mark?" One nurse asked when she saw me.

"There he goes!" said another, who had spotted him halfway down the hall.

"Boy, are we glad to see you," one of them said, laughing as John Mark was brought back, pushed from behind by the orderly who had intercepted him.

The nurses appreciated their respite from trying to keep him happy and contained, while I was there to bathe and play with him.

The next day when I arrived, I noticed every drawer and cabinet door at the nurses' station was secured with rubber bands to keep John Mark from opening them.

"He discovered the drawers and doors last night," a nurse told me with a sigh. Just then we heard a loud bang from down the hall. Following the noise, I discovered him in an empty room, pulling out a metal drawer for patient's clothes. He was slamming it as hard as he could. Since he couldn't make noise with his vocal chords, the loud metallic bang of the drawer seemed particularly satisfying to him and noise rang through the corridors several times before I could get to him.

"Don't you know there are sick people here?" I asked him as I spun his walker around with my foot and gave him a push toward the door. John Mark just grinned up at me. His forays in the walker, the hospital puppet, Bernard, and the play room probably made the hospital seem like a nice place to live, but I was anxious to get him home and our life back to normal.

FINALLY, HIS MIST TENT CAME AND WAS INSTALLED OVER HIS BED AT home. It was an undertaking to run and to keep clean, but we felt he would be safer sleeping in it. He was still in danger from mucus plugs, but they would have much less opportunity to form now that he spent ten to twelve hours in the tent while he slept.

A good while later, one morning before the children left for school, I heard the telltale sounds of a plug. I had been hearing a sound I didn't like off and on for a couple of days. I had suctioned and irrigated with saline, and even used the air bag, but I still couldn't get it cleared. Then just before the children left for school, the plug moved and John Mark began to turn blue. Fortunately, I was standing right by his bed.

While I suctioned, I screamed for someone to come and help me.

"Hold him while I get the trach scissors!" I said, shoving him into John's arms as soon as he came in. By this time, John Mark was unconscious. I cut the strings holding the little appliance in the hole in his throat and pulled it out. I had watched doctors take it out and had even done it once myself, but only to learn how. I had never done it under pressure. I had been told if I couldn't get the trach cleared, I could always take the plastic tube out and clean it. He was supposed to be able to breathe for a short time without the appliance, but when I pulled it out, the hole in his throat appeared to collapse on itself. It seemed to need the plastic tube to hold it open. There was nothing to do but clean the tube and put it back as fast as I could. I was committed now, and he couldn't breathe through the tube while it was plugged anyway.

John was holding the baby at arms' length, like he was afraid he would break. "Mother...Mother..." he said over and over, fear rising in his voice.

"He is supposed to be able to breathe like this!" I said, running to wash the tube. My hands were shaking as I ran hot water through the little plastic tube. "This water isn't sterile!" I said, suddenly realizing I might be contaminating his trachea. Nobody ever told me what to do after I took the tube out! They obviously thought I knew, but I didn't. I had no choice now but to rinse the tube in hot water and put it back into his trachea. He was barely breathing without it.

When I finally got it back in and he could breathe well again, John Mark came to life and started fighting. He wanted us to hold and comfort him, but that had to wait until I could secure the appliance with new strings around his neck. Eventually everything was in its proper place and I was able to pick him up and comfort him. This unnerving incident taught me to carry instructions to their ultimate conclusions in my mind. I should have asked exactly what to do after I took the appliance out. Fortunately, the hot water was all right and John Mark was none the worse. I could hardly say the same for John and me. I knew for a fact John was wide awake for his first class that day.

> JOURNAL: Lord, what shall I say to You about John Mark? I don't know what to pray for him. I feel that maybe You want me to fast for him. Maybe prayer and fasting are the only things that will change things for his future.

In the spring, John Mark's asthma improved dramatically and it was time for him to go home. He only needed the suction now and was doing well without the mist tent.

I had spoken to the doctors about having his tracheostomy closed so he could talk and a surgical procedure was done to see if the opening could be closed, but there was too much damage. A specialist I had consulted because of his lung problems contacted a doctor in another state who had developed a new procedure for reconstructing damaged tracheas and he was willing to see John Mark for an evaluation. It was arranged that his parents would take him to see this specialist as soon as he went back to them.

I was concerned about John Mark's going home to a doctor who didn't know him and it was too far for his parents to bring him to Bob Thompson. I asked our nurse, Joyce to see if Les Jones, the pediatrician she and Jane had gone to work for, would consider taking him as a patient. He and his partner were Christians, and their office was much closer to the small town where John Mark's parents lived. Private pediatricians didn't usually take Medicaid, but he and his partner agreed to help. I began taking him to them so they could get to know him before he got sick. They knew his background and the nurses had known him for months, and better still, he knew them.

The day came for John Mark's parents to take him home for good. We walked out to the car with them and as his mother sat him beside her on the seat (car seats for babies were not required then,) John Mark leaned over to grin at me and wave good-bye. He thought he was only going for a visit. He had no idea he was leaving me forever, and the pain of knowing he would feel abandoned when he realized he was not coming back was sharper than I had ever felt before.

All the other babies' placements had held the promise of happiness and a better life than they would have had if we had not intervened. Before, I had known the baby would feel betrayed because he could not understand why I had given him up, but this time I felt I actually had betrayed him. For the first time I was sending a baby into an environment in which I was convinced he would not be as happy as he had been with us. For John Mark, my consolation had to be that he possibly would not have survived his first winter if not for us. I told myself again God had given John Mark to his parents and not to us because that was what He wanted for him. I also comforted myself with the knowledge they did love him and want him.

My feeling of regret over John Mark never really left, but the following Christmas his parents brought him to see us and I was happy to see he had grown into a sturdy little boy. He pointed to a bottle of Coke on the counter and when I gave him some, he surprised me by whispering, "Thank you," without covering his trach opening.

About six months later, after much prayer and phone calls back and forth, his mother called to say he had gone back to the specialist for another reconstructive surgery and finally had the trach closed. At last John Mark could talk like a normal child. Only the scar on his throat bore testimony of his silent first three years of life.

Up to this point, John Mark was the only child I had regrets about. The sadness I felt the day he left us, came back whenever I thought of him. I pray the Lord will make him a great blessing. I also pray that someday I can tell him I loved him and would have kept him if I could.

8
BEN

*L*ate one afternoon in February, 1987, Daddy came downstairs complaining of a sore throat. He was susceptible to respiratory infections, so when there had been no improvement several days later, I convinced him to go to the doctor.

"Strep!" Daddy growled when he came back, prescriptions in hand.

"Well, at least strep is easy to treat, you should feel better soon," I said. But a week later his throat was no better and the doctor referred him to a throat specialist.

By the middle of March, we knew Daddy had cancer of the larynx. He had stopped smoking two years before, but he had smoked heavily since his early teens. His emphysema and enlarged heart made surgery contraindicated, so the only treatment recommended was radiation.

Daddy took his illness stoically, feeling he had only himself to blame, and when he started the treatments he accepted them gracefully, chatting with other patients and nurses as if he had come to visit, rather than be treated for cancer. I had not realized what a consistently cheerful person Daddy was until he became so seriously ill. He worked every day and went twice a day for treatments until he became so weak and sick I had to drive him. It was a tribute to God's perfect timing we had no baby. Daddy worked full time until the middle of the summer, then a few hours every morning, until he finally just didn't have the strength to get to the office.

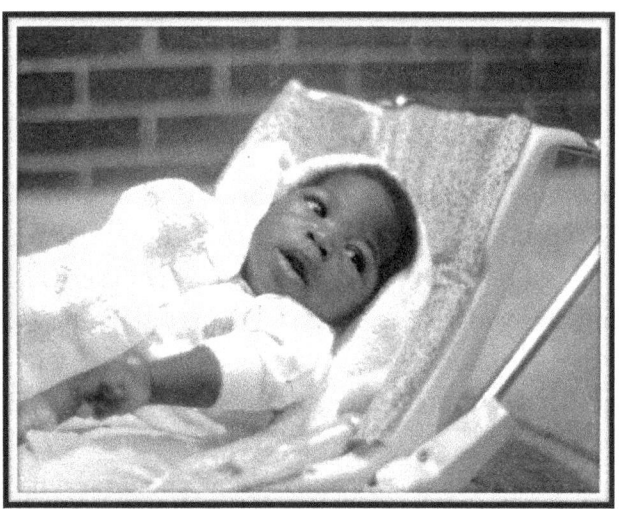

| Ben having a slight seizure, wide awake.

As the radiation took its toll, he lost the ability to taste properly. No matter what he tried, his reaction was the same. A look of intense disgust, spitting into a napkin and a shake of his head. "It tastes like hell." His throat became too sore to swallow and in June he had to have a tube put into his side for me to inject Ensure. His weight went down and down. His hair lost the last of its color and became iridescent white. He seemed to age twenty years in three months.

I prayed for the grace to be the daughter Daddy needed. I wanted to be supportive but not controlling. I knew he would do what I wanted, just to avoid being a problem, but I didn't want to rob him of his autonomy. I stayed out of his decisions until he asked for my opinion. He usually did.

BY THE END OF THE SUMMER, THE WORST WAS OVER. DADDY BEGAN to regain his strength, and best of all, his sense of taste. The doctor had told us he felt he could cure Daddy with radiation, and by the end of the treatments, there was no sign of the lesion. The doctor pronounced Daddy cured, but said the cancer could come back. If it did, it would probably do so within eight months. We all gave a sigh of relief and thanked God for bringing Daddy through such a horrible ordeal.

> JOURNAL: Lord, your Word says in Psalm 125:2 that you surround Your people as the mountains surround Jerusalem. Please surround and defend my family from Satan for the sake of Your Son, Jesus, and for the sake of Your name. I especially pray for Your protection for John while he is so far away. Let him feel Your presence with him, Lord. Help him find Your will for his life.

In May, soon after Daddy's treatments began, John graduated from high school. One week later he left for basic training in the Air National Guard. He was only seventeen. I knew he was strong and capable for his age, but it was so hard to put my son on a plane and send him to experience the same thing Hamp had. He had gone to Air Force basic right after we married, for the Air National Guard. I knew what awaited John. Basic training turned out to be a great experience for him, and he saw God's provision for him again and again. He wrote and called home often, and also wrote and called his grandfather. John was very worried about Daddy and anxious to get back to him. His letters to him spoke of things they would do together when he came home in October.

JULY, 1987: DOLLY HAMBRICK CALLED ABOUT A LITTLE BLACK BOY today. He weighs twelve pounds and is nine months old. He is spastic, quadriplegic, and has minimal brain function. I felt reluctance in my flesh as she described him, but when I thought and prayed, I felt the anointing rising in spite of myself. Lord, I want Your will for my family and me. If this is our baby, please bring him and prepare a place for him in our hearts. If not Your perfect will, please stop it on the other end.

> *JOURNAL: We have decided to name the baby Benaiah, after one of David's mighty men. It means God will strengthen. Benaiah was one of David's mighty men, a powerful soldier, strong and courageous. It is a hopeful name for a little boy who is nine months and can neither sit up nor roll over. Lord, please honor the name we give this baby and strengthen him for Your glory. There is a human spirit in Ben's suffering little body. Please keep that before me. Ben is to me as I am to You. Please send Angels to Ben to calm him, and tell him You are coming to help him. Tell him You will take him to people who will love and care for him.*

I had the elders pray for my neck again Sunday. It seems impossible I could care for a baby with no improvement in the pain. I don't know how I will handle it with another baby, but I know You will give me the grace if for some reason You still aren't ready to heal it.

> *JOURNAL: Last night at Bible study I taught on sacrifice.*

Solomon offered sacrifices at the dedication of the temple and God filled it with His shekinah glory (I Chronicles 7:1-2). In Leviticus 9:24, Moses's offering was accepted by fire from God. David's sacrifice on Ornan's threshing floor (I Chronicles 21:26) was accepted by God. When He is pleased with a sacrifice, God accepts it, so we mustn't offer something we don't really want to give. When Ornan offered to give him the oxen to sacrifice, David said, "I won't offer that which costs me nothing." David paid for the oxen, because he wouldn't offer a sacrifice which wasn't really a sacrifice for him, and we shouldn't either. Malachi 1:7-14 speaks of blemished offerings being sacrificed to the Lord, as if they were "good enough" for God. The people even began to complain about having to offer sacrifices, and said, "My, how tiresome it is." We shouldn't offer less than our best to God. We offer rushed time, half-hearted praise, uninterested Bible study, and we even begin to say, "My, how tiresome it is," about the ministry He allows us to perform. It is a privilege to offer sacrifices to God and have Him accept them. It is a privilege to serve the living God. If we take this baby, it will be a privilege to carry him for the Lord, not something we do because we are good, or capable, or doing God a favor.

> *JOURNAL: There has been so much tension in the family lately, I fear having a new baby here at such a time; but the babies are what have taught us so much about Jesus. If we don't take this baby, what blessings and lessons will we not receive? Lord, please especially bless us all with this baby.*

I spoke with social workers several times before Ben came to us, and learned he had been left on his father's carport after an argument between his unmarried parents over who was going to take care of him that night. A neighbor, hearing his crying, called police, who took Ben to a shelter. His parents' lack of commitment to him prompted the court to put him in foster care. I discovered his mother had reportedly used alcohol and taken drugs during her pregnancy, and when she was ready to deliver, suffered a premature rupture of the placenta which deprived the baby of oxygen. He was actually stillborn and had to be resuscitated. Some or all of these circumstances combined to cause irreparable damage to his brain.

> *JOURNAL: Walking and praying the day before Ben came, I thought of the Jews in Egypt staying under the blood of the lamb during the Passover. If they had run out of the house, the blood over the door posts would have done no good, because they would have removed themselves from it. The Angel of Death didn't look into the houses to see who was there, he only looked at the blood, and whatever firstborn was under that blood was passed over. I had never thought of their temptation just to run, to try to get away from the death. The fear, not only of the first born, but of their families, must have been terrible. They were surely afraid for the firstborn in the house, and also for themselves. What if you could catch it? What if Moses had misunderstood God about what He wanted done? Moses's record of speaking for God had not impressed the Jews very much up to this point. How terrifying to stand and wait for death to come to you and deliberately pass over you without killing you, especially when your guilty heart tells you that you don't deserve special protection. It is hard to stand trusting Jesus, only Jesus and nothing else. I feel rather like that taking this baby at this time in our family's life. In the natural it doesn't seem to be the thing to do, but Hampy and I have peace about it.*

JOURNAL: The day Ben came. Lord help me put the needs of my family first and also to be able to continue preparing Bible study lessons as I care for this new baby. I stand on the conviction this baby will not got to a nursing home. I pray by the power of God, he will become a baby that people of God's choosing will not be afraid to adopt. Please, Lord, no nursing home.

Ben had been in a shelter for at least a week before they brought him to us. It was not for babies, and they didn't know what to do for a baby in his condition. It was a blessing we got him out when we did. His needs were so unusual he would have died there. When Hamp and I met the social worker at Catholic Charities to pick him up, we were amazed by how much he resembled Micah. They could have been twins. Like Micah, Ben looked like a chubby baby doll. His body was well proportioned and seemed perfect. It was hard to believe anyone so healthy looking and cute could be so badly damaged. He appeared to be sleeping deeply and felt icy cold to my touch. The social workers had driven for several hours in the summer heat with the air conditioning off and the windows down trying to warm him up, but it had not helped. I immediately looked through his diaper bag and put layers of the warmest clothes on him. They reported he had not eaten all day and repeatedly ignored the bottle they had brought. I knew he couldn't generate any heat without food, so I poured out half of the thick, creamy formula and replaced it with warm water from the restroom sink. Then I got some sugar packets from the coffee machine in the hall, poured in a couple and shook it all up. Taking Ben on my lap, I squeezed enough sweetened formula into his mouth for him to taste the sugar. His eyes opened and he began to suck. "I never met anyone under thirty inches tall who didn't love sugar." I told the surprised social worker.

I had made an appointment with Les to see Ben as soon as I got him, so we went immediately to his office. While I explained what

I knew of his background and diagnosis, Les took his temperature and checked him over. His temperature was 93 degrees! Ben had not responded to anything after he drank the bottle; he wouldn't even open his eyes again. His breathing was so slow and shallow it was hard to detect without a stethoscope. There was obviously something terribly wrong with this baby.

Les told me to take Ben to the hospital and go straight up to the pediatric floor while Hamp checked him in downstairs. He said he would follow us as quickly as possible. As I walked down the hospital corridor so familiar to John Mark and me, the nursing supervisor recognized me and came to meet me. I looked down into Ben's still face and felt his icy cheek with my hand. "I don't know if he's breathing," I said. She snatched him from my arms and ran to a treatment room with several nurses behind her. They brought warmed blankets and a heat lamp, but several hours of warming only elevated his temperature a few tenths of a degree. In the meantime, Les came and did a spinal tap and took blood, which showed nothing, but everyone agreed a child who seemed comatose and had a body temperature of 93 degrees belonged in intensive care, so I never got home with Ben that day. It felt strange to pick up a baby, take him straight to the hospital and go home empty handed. In about a week they felt sure his symptoms were caused by severe damage to his brainstem and not some type of infection and let me take him home.

For the first few weeks, we spent much of our time trying to keep Ben warm. I dressed him in winter clothes and hats, even though it was the middle of summer. I kept him wrapped in blankets, but it didn't help. With the use of a heating pad, we finally warmed him to 97 degrees, but were surprised when he began screaming and having seizures. We discovered not only was he perfectly happy at 93 degrees, he actually couldn't tolerate normal body temperature. A temperature of 96 or above would send him into a crisis of seizures and crying. After trying different things, the heating pad became my most constant resource in the battle with Ben's temperature, even though we learned early not to let him get too near normal. Whenever his temperature dipped below 93, I usually put him on the heating pad for a few hours, but he had to be watched closely and his temperature taken every hour, because once he began to warm up, his temperature continued to go up even after he was taken off of the pad.

| John and Ben in their favorite nap place together.

While he always felt cold to the touch, we never actually found out how cold Ben could get, because thermometers only went to 90 degrees. One day I took his temperature with a new digital thermometer and the read-out screen was blank. I tried it again, but still it didn't respond. "I can't believe this thing is broken. I've only had it a few months," I said in disgust, and went to the drugstore for a new one. I put it under his arm and waited expectantly. The screen remained blank. It finally hit me that Ben's temperature must be below 90 degrees! I wrapped him in blankets and put him on the heating pad. In a few hours he began to warm up. I have no idea how cold the child was that day, but I realized then he could slow down, and cool down enough to make his heart just stop one day if I didn't watch him closely. For the rest of his life, Ben's temperature would be a major concern in keeping him alive.

The other immediately observable effect of Ben's brainstem damage was his chronic sleep state. When he first came home, Ben slept most of the time, but would wake sometimes and be mildly responsive, even smiling and cooing, but by summer's end, waking usually triggered seizure activity. His arms would pull up, his back arch and his eyes would roll up and to the side and jump as long as he was awake.

> *JOURNAL: There is a "place of faith" and it is in the presence of God. Nowhere out of His presence will I find real faith. That is, total trust I am moment by moment in His hand. When I am in His presence through prayer, there is no doubt, no fear, only the comfort of His reality.*

In the middle of August, Hamp and the girls and I drove to Illinois to see John. We left Ben in the care of some of the nurses who had helped us before, who knew Daddy well enough to keep an eye on his health too. Daddy had planned to go with us, but we decided he was not stable enough to go so far away from home and his doctors.

We picked John up at his base and drove on to Chicago for the weekend. When we picked John up at the airbase, he came out with his gym bag in one hand and a model airplane in the other. He had made his grandfather a perfect model of the plane he had flown in WWII. It rode all the way back to Mississippi on a pillow to insure its safe delivery to Granddaddy.

> *JOURNAL: "And they who worship Him must worship in spirit and in truth" (John 4:24). How glibly the words roll off our tongues. Worship Him in Spirit and truth. What does that mean? Lord, show me what it means to worship You in spirit and in truth.*

Ben seemed to live on death's doorstep. His heart could barely be heard with a stethoscope, so I got a prescription for a heart monitor. I had one for John Mark at first and was sure I remembered how to use it. When the technician from the home health service brought it to me, I assured him I already knew how to use one and as soon as he was gone, I put it on Ben. It immediately alarmed. The girls rushed in holding their ears. "Mother, turn it off! What are you doing?" I kept trying the leads in different positions, but it would not stop alarming. Severely frustrated with myself, I called Art Landry, the technician who lived nearby. He came over on his way home from work that night and patiently showed me everything I already knew-again. I was sure he had done nothing different, and when he turned it on, the monitor alarmed immediately. "The unit must be the problem," he said, going to his van for another.

"I'm glad it's the monitor," I told Hamp. "I was feeling really stupid." Art tried a second monitor on Ben, but when it alarmed immediately too. I said, "I know what's wrong. The monitor can't hear his heart either!"

ART CHECKED EVERYTHING AGAIN AND AGAIN. FINALLY, WE ALL HAD to agree the problem was not with the monitor, but with Ben's little heart. Right then it was too faint and slow for a monitor used to detecting normal babies' heartbeats. Ben's little brain caused such abnormal conditions in his body, the usual treatments and safeguards available to babies and their parents were not applicable to him. We knew unless the Lord healed him, Ben would remain alive as long as the Lord wanted him to, and then he would go home. There was nothing man could do for this baby.

Because Ben ate baby food well and drank from a bottle when he was hungry, I did not anticipate trouble with his eating. He never spit up, and didn't drool as many brain damaged children do. In fact, we never had a drooler. But by late fall his appetite was waning and he gradually ate less and less. I did everything I knew to find something he really enjoyed to encourage him to eat. Ben just wasn't interested.

> JOURNAL: Hampy's birthday. God bless this wonderful man and make me worthy of his love. I praise You for the godly man You have made of him. He calls me his little pile of rubies (Proverb 31). I feel sometimes more like a bag of rocks around his neck, but he chooses to think of me as worth more than rubies.

At the end of October, John came home. Daddy was almost back to normal and I was glad John had not had to witness the effects of radiation at their worst. John enjoyed his Granddaddy's wonderful cooking again after a summer of military food, and they spent hours together rehashing Daddy's old Air Force stories. Because basic training had caused John to miss the beginning of the fall semester of college, he worked at a part-time job and had plenty of time to spend with his grandfather before leaving for college in January.

John also used this time to forge an amazing relationship with Ben. He had the responsibilities of a grown man now, working and preparing for college. He was often out with friends and dating. I had wondered if he would have time for a baby who slept all the time and could do nothing to attract his attention. But I underestimated John's love for babies. He was drawn to Ben like a magnet, and even more surprising, Ben responded with equal force. Every night after work, John came to our room to see Ben and kiss him goodnight, sometimes taking the sleeping baby to spend the night in his bed. On one such occasion, we discovered John had a strong physical effect on Ben. He came home one afternoon when Ben was crying and seizing, and not responding to anything I tried. He was agitated and tense. His breathing and heart rate were erratic and rapid, for him. Babies all tend to respond to the rhythms of another person's body, and often I could hold Ben close and rock him and calm him down, but there were other times it took valium, or John, to relax him. That afternoon John said, "Let me take him, Mother." He went to the couch and lay down with Ben in his arms. Ben squirmed until he had his nose almost touching John's. Then he lay motionless, as if he was listening to and feeling John breathe. No matter how agitated Ben had been, within forty-five minutes his heart rate and breathing had slowed to match John's. John enjoyed sleeping with Ben too, and often I would find the two of them asleep nose to nose on the couch. I have lots of pictures of the children asleep with babies in their arms, but Ben's response to John was amazing.

> *JOURNAL: I want to keep my focus "heavenly", to see things in eternal terms. How would Jesus respond to my children and my husband? He would take pains with the family's meals, He would be encouraging to Laura and supportive of Stacey and John and it would all be motivated by love, not duty. The Bible seldom speaks of duty, but repeatedly speaks of being motivated by love. Lord, motivate me by love! Help me unclutter my mind and concentrate on loving. I want to be single minded like Daniel the prophet. He set his heart to reject the things of Babylon and never wavered from that course.*

One afternoon in mid-November, Daddy came downstairs with his hand on his neck. "Baby, feel this lump," he said, leaning down.

"I don't know what this could be, Daddy," I said as I ran my fingers over the large lump on the side of his neck. "I think you had better check with the doctor." I could not let myself know it was a recurrence of the cancer.

The day of Daddy's appointment with the doctor, I went to

work at the shop, telling Daddy to call me with the doctor's diagnosis. I had often scoffed at people for refusing to see what was obvious to everyone else, but I discovered that I too was capable of totally blocking from my mind what I did not want to face. I had known immediately on some level of my mind the lump had to be cancer, but I couldn't allow the knowledge into my consciousness. As the time for the appointment drew nearer, I became incredibly anxious. I couldn't focus on what I was doing. Suddenly my concern for Daddy overcame my denial and I ran out to my car and raced to the doctor's office to be with him. Daddy was sitting in the waiting room looking as calm as could be and he grinned when he saw me as if he had no idea why I had rushed over. Now I think he knew exactly what was going on.

The examination was short. Putting his hand on the lump, the doctor closed his eyes for a second, then said, "Mr. Murray, I'm sorry, your cancer is back." I looked out the window, gritting my teeth to keep from crying. There was a dreary little tree standing all alone in the late afternoon shadows of the courtyard. I can see it now as clearly as I did that day years ago. I knew in that instant I was losing my daddy. I told myself that was ridiculous, there was no way I could be sure of that. Still, I knew neither the doctors nor the Lord were going to keep Daddy with me. I had an overwhelming conviction that he was going to die very soon.

I was glad we had gone to the doctor's office in separate cars so I could cry my heart out on the way home without Daddy seeing me. When I got home I went automatically to Ben's crib to check on him. Ruth Enlow, one of Ben's sitters provided by Human Services was with him. She was a lovely Christian grandmother and had become like a member of the family. When she asked what the doctor had said, I dissolved into tears again. I was absolutely sure my father would be dead within three months.

When Daddy got home, he went upstairs for a little while. When he came down, he was very calm and acted as if nothing unusual had happened, so I chatted with him about the arrangements for the needle biopsy the doctor wanted to be sure of his diagnosis. No one mentioned cancer. After supper, Daddy went upstairs. I was used to being completely open with Daddy about what was on my mind. I wanted more than anything to talk to him about it. But I knew I couldn't bring myself to say what I was thinking. After a verbal altercation with one of the children, which made me feel even worse, I picked up Ben, who felt colder than usual and wrapped us both in an afghan and sat down to rock him and try to warm him up. His chubby little body nestled against me was amazingly comforting. The more I rocked with his little face against my neck, the calmer and more peaceful I felt. The calming effect was so strong I told Hamp about it.

> JOURNAL: Daddy had a bone scan this morning and I woke up with, "Have this mind in you which was also in Christ Jesus..." (Philippians 2:5) repeating in my mind. I don't understand, Lord, show me what You want me to see.

Later, I saw the answer was to give up my instinctive desire to be my own God. Philippians 2:5-8 says Jesus did not think equality with God a thing to be grasped, and laid it aside. So when He came to earth, He had already conquered the greatest desire of man's fallen nature. He had already rejected equality with God. He was willing to be perfect man. I knew God was showing me how to function in the midst of watching my precious father die, caring for baby Ben, and trying to be a good mother to my teenage children. He was showing me I must be an obedient servant, and resist the temptation to try to deal with my problems in my own strength and my own intellect. He knew His plans for all of us and I did not. There had to be reasons for all of the hard things in my life at that time and only He understood them and could bring good from them.

> JOURNAL: I see that many things experienced with God

> must be personally experienced. They are felt, rather than understood. It is in no way essential or even possible to understand all that we feel with God. When younger believers say to us, "Tell me what He is like? How did this or that experience feel?" Often we can only say, "Take His hand. He must show you. Words are not adequate to tell."

Daddy's humor was macabre as he joked to his friends he was "on his way out." He replied to the doctor's admonition to call if he felt worse with, "If I get any worse you can come to my funeral!" I knew Daddy always made jokes about things that made him uncomfortable, but it bothered me to hear him joking about his impending death. I wanted to shake him and scream, "You are dying! How can you joke about it? My heart is breaking." The seriousness of his illness still had not been acknowledged between us, and even though I knew there were things we needed to say, I could not make myself bring up the possibility of death with Daddy. At last, a week after we had seen the doctor, Daddy broached the subject himself.

He put his arms around me and said, "Baby, I'm not afraid to die; I know where I'm going. I just hate to see you crying and unhappy. I know you don't think it's funny, but I have to joke about it. It's the only way I can deal with it. Please don't cry."

"I can't help crying, Daddy," I said, choking up. "I love you and I don't want you to leave me." We finally agreed that I would allow him to make awful jokes about his death, and he would allow me to cry whenever I wanted. It was the last agreement we ever made.

> JOURNAL: Lord, thank You for the amazing comfort of Ben. Every time I hold him I feel better. He seems to radiate peace. I don't understand it, but he has the same effect on everyone. Every time I let someone hold him, I almost have to fight them to get him back. Everyone loves to just sit and hold him. Now that it is cold, Hampy and I

put him between us in bed to keep him warm at night, and we fight over who gets to sleep holding him like children fighting over a teddy bear. If one of us wakes in the night and we don't have Ben in our arms, we try to inch him over next to us without waking the other.

> JOURNAL: November 1987- Thank you, Lord, for: Daddy being saved, medicine to relieve his pain and his being here with us.

> JOURNAL: December 1, 1987- Lord, please cause us all to grow through Daddy's illness. Use this awful thing to teach us more about You and what we are supposed to be becoming. It is so easy to forget why I am here. I am here to bless, to love, to pray, to tell other people about You and to be conformed to the image of Christ.

> JOURNAL: It was not the power of the Lord to do miracles that saved people, but His power of self- sacrifice to die on the cross. Only our ability to sacrifice our self has the real power to witness. This is why Micah was such a blessing to people. The Holy Spirit gave us such an anointing of self-sacrifice that people could see the power of God.

While I knew Ben needed to be moved and turned often to prevent his developing pneumonia, my concern for Daddy and dealing with trials that come with any family, distracted me. One afternoon a routine check of his lungs with the stethoscope revealed a crackling noise I had not heard before. A trip to Les and an X-ray confirmed pneumonia. Daddy was to check into the hospital on December 5 for his first chemotherapy treatment to slow the cancer and prevent pain, not to cure. Because Ben had an infection, we decided he should be admitted to the same hospital so I could be with them both. It was easier for me and safer for

Ben to have him in the hospital on the floor above Daddy, and it saved me much driving back and forth from home.

For the first couple of days, the chemotherapy didn't bother Daddy, but the third day he started vomiting and nothing they did stopped it. I stayed with him most of the days and both nights while he was so sick, with Hamp and the children relieving me long enough to go home to shower and change clothes.

One time during the entire miserable treatment he snapped at me, and only as I retreated from his sharp words, did I realize they were the first I had heard from him in years. I had not appreciated Daddy's gentle, patient spirit until it left for a moment. Never again did a harsh word come out of my father's mouth, and as I watched him struggle with the pain and the nausea, I thought, not only did he teach me about life, now he is teaching me how to die.

On the fifth day, the doctor and I decided the chemotherapy was making him too sick to continue and it was decided that as soon as he recovered a little strength from all of the vomiting, I could take him home.

Upstairs, Ben had taken a turn for the worse and been moved into intensive care the day after Daddy was admitted. By the morning of Daddy's fifth day in the hospital, I was afraid we might actually lose Ben. I was especially distraught over him because I felt the need of his special comforting presence now more than ever. I had come to think of him as an angel sent from God to minister to me during Daddy's sickness and the struggles of motherhood in my own family.

> *JOURNAL: Do children hang back from commitment to You because they know the price of discipleship may be high, as it has been with Hampy and me? I think many Christians' children in America only know Christianity on a superficial level that costs them nothing.*

Because Daddy was so weak, there was no discussion of

going home yet, so late in the morning I told him I wanted to go home and change clothes and eat. I would be back in a couple of hours.

Daddy said "Go ahead," then opened his eyes. "Will you wait until I am asleep before you leave?" he asked.

"Of course I will," I said. I knew he had to know, as I did, the next weeks and/or months were going to be hard. After the extreme sickness he had just endured, I shouldn't have been caught off guard that my Daddy didn't want to be alone in a hospital room at 63, facing death, but I was. I have wished a thousand times I had not left him, and after all these years, I still cry almost every time I think about it. I wish so much I had been older than 42 when this happened to him. I would have had much more maturity and understanding of his feelings simply as a human being if I had been older. But I still only saw my daddy, the man who could withstand anything and couldn't possibly really be afraid. So after about five minutes I told myself he was asleep and without waiting to be sure, I quietly left.

I was gone longer than I had meant to be and was hurrying down the hospital corridor when I saw Chuck Frost, the pastor of the church we had been attending for several weeks, coming toward me. We had left our church of fourteen years in July and had been looking for the new church home we knew the Lord had for us. I stopped him, explained who I was, and asked for prayer for Daddy and Ben. He took Daddy's room number and promised to visit the next day and to pray for them both in the meantime. When I got upstairs, Daddy was asleep, so I went up to check on Ben. He was not doing well at all, and I leaned against the wall of the empty elevator with tears streaming down my face and begged God not take them both from me. Daddy was still sleeping, so I quietly sat down and started reading. When several minutes had passed, I glanced at him. He didn't seem to be breathing. I got up and put my hand on his chest; he was warm but totally still. I felt as if I were dreaming.

"He has to be breathing," I said out loud. "There is no reason for him not to be."

I walked quickly down the hall to get his nurse. I couldn't bring myself to call the nurses' station and say he wasn't breathing. The nurse raced to Daddy's room and one look told her what I could not accept. Daddy was not breathing.

I was led into the hall as nurses ran into his room. His doctor had just arrived when the call went out for the STAT team. As she came down the hall, she looked as surprised as I.

"You and your dad and I are supposed to have discussed what you both wanted done when this happened," she said after she had looked at Daddy. "You are going to have to tell me what you want me to do."

Daddy's sudden death was so unexpected by everyone, I had neither been prepared by the doctor, nor prepared myself for this kind of decision. I didn't want to make it alone, but I had to, quickly. I said, "Give him a chance to come back, but don't work on him for forty-five minutes trying to force him to live."

Other nurses took me to the nurse's station and sat with me. They were very compassionate and supportive, but my mind kept going back to what I had told the doctor. I realized the Lord had given me what to say. If I had said, "Don't help him, let him go," later I am sure I would have felt I had killed my father. If I had said, "Bring him back no matter what you have to do," and he had died a slow painful death, which was expected, I would have felt responsible for denying him a quick and peaceful death. Of course, theologically I knew those weren't really my decisions, but the heart can feel guilt, even when the mind knows it is innocent.

The doctor returned shortly to say they had done several things to revive him and he just did not want to come back. My daddy was gone. His nurse went back into the room with me and actually wept with me as I told her how precious he had been to me. I was amazed by the staff's ability to care so intensely for each patient day after day. They were truly wonderful. This was at Mississippi Baptist Medical Center.

I wanted to call Hampy because I needed him, but I dreaded telling the children their granddaddy was gone. Hampy said he would pick up Stacey at the drugstore where she worked after school. I called Laura's boyfriend, Pat, and asked him to get Laura and bring her to the hospital, but I sat for several minutes before I could bring myself to call John. Of all the people who loved Daddy, John's pain at losing him would be the closest to mine. Finally, I picked up the phone, held it for couple of minutes, and then called him at work.

"No, no, NO!!" I heard him slam his fist down on something. John had lost as much as I had.

"John, promise me you won't leave there until you can calm down. If you have a wreck on the way to the hospital I don't think I can take it." He promised me he would calm down before he drove.

IN LESS THAN AN HOUR THE FAMILY HAD GATHERED IN DADDY'S hospital room. We all wanted to say goodbye to him there, where we had last seen him alive. We all were crying. Even Hampy choked up, and as I looked around at the tear-streaked faces, I wondered if my children and grandchildren would weep so for me when I died. I wondered just how much sense of real loss they would have when I ceased to be among them.

Sometimes tears are shed when someone dies just because death is such a shock, but the tears my family were crying were from a deep sense of loss. We had lost Daddy's cheerful voice, his smiling face, his beautiful photographs, his wonderful cooking, his total support of everything we undertook .... We had lost so much. Not only had I lost my best friend, who supported me even when I was wrong, I had lost my only complete connection to my past.

There was now no one with whom I shared history. My childhood and youth with my parents existed now only in my memory. It was a strange and lonely feeling. At home that night, I was unable to focus on anything, and I thanked the Lord Ben was not depending on my care that night.

> JOURNAL: *Lord, call me out of the grave, though I be wrapped and muffled with grave clothes so I cannot even call to Thee. Thou knowest the grave wherein I am hidden and none but Thee can call my deadness to life again.*

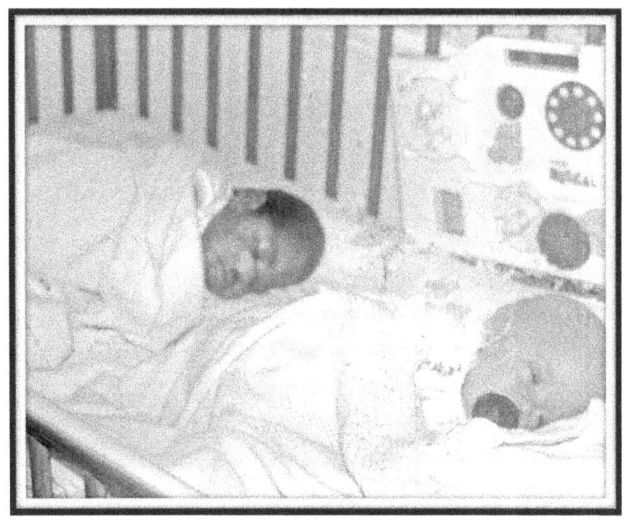

Ben sharing his bed with the new guy.

The next morning, I was anxious to get to Ben at the hospital. He had been moved out of ICU to a room and Ruth was sitting with him. His I.V. had come out and the nurses were starting the ordeal of looking for another tiny fragile vein. It was so painful it always woke him, which brought seizures and crying.

"Have you tried to feed him?" I asked, "Are you sure he can't eat enough by himself?" I didn't know if I could stand to see any more suffering just then.

"He won't suck on the bottle at all," one of the nurses said, handing me a bottle with full strength formula and a Nuk nipple.

"He doesn't like Nuk nipples," I said, looking around for one I had brought from home. I found it behind some things on the table, poured out a little formula and replaced it with water, added some sugar and put on the nipple he was used to. I got him to drink just enough of the thin sweet formula to avoid a new I.V. Ben was so different from normal babies with his inability to keep warm, unwillingness to eat, his seizures and chronic sleep. Good nurses kept treating him like a baby whose body functioned normally, but normal child-care could kill Ben. He stayed in the hospital nearly a week until the pneumonia no longer showed on X-ray, and then I got to take him home. I spent hours rocking, wrapped in a blanket with him, soaking in his peace.

> *JOURNAL: How much healing would we see if the whole body of Christ gathered around the sick and handicapped, loving them, carrying them, praising God with them and for them when they can't. We are all looking the wrong way. We pursue money, advantage and security, when the real power of God would come if we would but live quietly and love and nurture the good and godly things in life.*

> *JOURNAL: Daddy went home December 8, 1987. He died in his sleep. I can hardly believe he did not have to suffer through weeks or months of pain, slowly dying. How unfathomable are Your mercies, Lord! How I praise You. You spared Daddy and me. You kept me at the hospital when I was tempted twice to go home to sleep, thinking I needed my rest to be able to care for him when he came home. I would feel terrible now if You had not made me stay there. I don't understand why You showed us such mercy, but I bless You for it, Lord. You did beyond what I could ask or think (Ephesians 3:20).*

I never asked the Lord to spare Daddy unless there was more He wanted him to do on Earth. I could see no reason why we should be spared the suffering so many other believers have had to go through. People usually suffer when they are dying, it is part of our humanity, Christian or not. My prayer was that we should all profit from the experience as much as possible. It never occurred to me the Lord would just take Daddy home with no warning. I felt for a time as if I had been blindsided by the mercy of God. I knew it was a mercy, but it was a shock to lose him so suddenly.

For several weeks I would not allow myself to grieve. It seemed ungrateful somehow after the Lord had spared Daddy so much suffering. One day a friend called me and picked up on my dilemma. "Carlene, everybody grieves when their daddy dies! God doesn't expect you not to suffer!" she said. I realized she was right, of course and I admitted to myself and the Lord how lonely I was for my daddy. It was strange that one of the best lessons the Lord ever taught me, I didn't apply to my most intense loss. I knew better than to run from pain, but I did when I thought I had no right to feel it.

> JOURNAL: Lord, I have been thinking about an older Vietnamese child again. Are you really bringing this to my mind? How on earth could we take an older child into our family? I am tempted to reject the very thought, except that it is so strong, and I have felt it on several occasions over a span of three or four years when I have been praying.

> JOURNAL: Lord, I went with You so willingly, thinking You were going to make me into a great warrior for God. But I have "become" nothing but wholly dependent on You. You made me back into a child, who can only run to you and ask You to come and do battle for me. We are all children, holding our Father's hand.

> *JOURNAL: As God is eternally present, so my relationship with Him is also in the eternal present. There is no middle, no end, no change, even though my body ages and dies. My relationship with Him will remain constant. I will never know another moment without Him.*

9
DANIEL

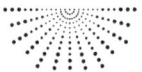

I was sitting on the floor trying to coax Ben to eat when Laura handed me the phone. It was late January; almost two months had passed since Daddy's death. I took a break from spooning food into Ben's mouth and catching it as it ran out, and leaned against the couch to ease the pain in my neck. The call was from a hospital social worker who was looking for a foster home for a newborn white boy who had anencephaly. Anencephaly means the baby has no brain. Usually there is no covering of what brain tissue may have developed, and the baby dies very quickly. This baby had a well-functioning brain stem at the very top of the spine where it joins the brain. This area controls breathing, heartbeat and other life functions. The babies who actually survive, have enough of a cranium to protect the brain stem and hold spinal fluid. As I listened to the sad story of this baby, a small voice somewhere in my mind was saying, "Name him Daniel; his name is Daniel."

"I would be happy to take him," I told her, ignoring the voice, "but I already have a baby who takes all my effort just to keep alive.

I couldn't possibly handle two babies, much less two who are so damaged."

A week later I received a call from someone else about the same baby, and as I explained my situation again, I heard, "Name him Daniel; name him Daniel." It was annoying to keep hearing a name for a child I had no intention of taking, especially Daniel. I knew a mean little boy named Danny when I was a child and I had disliked the name since. If I were going to take the baby, the last name I would give him would be Daniel.

In three weeks I received five calls about the same baby, and each time my mind told me to name him Daniel. It had become irritating.

| Someone just washed her hair, but look at that little face!

It seemed no other foster parents would take the baby because doctors expected him to live only a few months. No one wanted a baby who would die in their home. Nathan had died in my arms, so I was not afraid of his dying. I refused because my hands were full with Ben. It was utterly impossible.

Then a social worker from Catholic Charities called again. "Carlene," she said, "I know I am asking a lot, but this baby's mother is going to keep him and lose her chance to go to college if we can't find someone to take him. Isn't there any way you could take him? It probably wouldn't be for long. His life expectancy is only a couple of months."

Trapped, I told her I would pray about it, something I had carefully avoided doing before. I had not even wanted to discuss the possibility with the Lord that He might be calling me to take this baby.

When I asked Hamp what he thought, he wanted to take the baby, but since I would be the principal caregiver he deferred to me.

Eventually, I called Kathy Sones to ask her to agree with me in prayer about the situation. She stunned me by saying, "I think God has been preparing me to help you mother this baby. I have been receiving a baby in my spirit for several weeks. I can't believe you called about this."

"Tell me you are not serious! I can't handle two babies no matter how much help you give me," I said.

"Well, let's ask Larry," she said. "If God puts it in his heart to allow another child in our home now, we can feel certain it is the Lord's will."

Great idea, I thought! Kathy and Larry already had six children, and I was sure he would never agree to a newborn with no brain coming into their home. Relieved, I hung up the phone confident Larry would say, "No."

Fifteen minutes later Kathy called to report Larry said it was fine with him. I couldn't believe my ears. What was the Lord doing to me!

"I am going to have to hear directly from the Lord about this," I told her. "I don't want another baby, and I don't see how I can possibly take care of two of them." But when I squeezed open a tiny portion of my mind, I was amazed to feel the gentle drawing I had felt so often before when I was afraid to take a baby. Automatically I started praying and realized the Lord wanted good for all of us and He would provide whatever I needed to care for two babies if that was His will.

THE NEXT MORNING, I PRAYED ABOUT THIS CHILD AGAIN, ASKING THE Lord to be very clear. Even if I accepted the continued phone calls, and Kathy's willingness to help with him as indicators of God's will, there was still the name. "Lord, You know I don't like the name Daniel," I said, "It is not a name I would ever choose for a baby. Is that why You gave it to me? So I would know it was You speaking to me? If that is the case, may I accept the name as confirmation of Your will, but name him something else? I waited, silent before the Lord for a long time. Then, the word, "Justice," filled my mind. Justice? You want me to name the baby Justice? This is not the Lord, I said out loud. I'm not getting anywhere. I decided to stop praying for a while and try again later. After I put my Bible and prayer journal away, I went to the bookcase to look up the meaning of Daniel. It had finally dawned on me maybe God had a specific reason for naming the baby Daniel. Incredibly, I found that Daniel meant "justice" or "God is my judge" or "Judge of God." It was the crowning and unmistakable confirmation I needed. I knew no matter how impossible the task appeared to me, for some reason the Lord wanted the little white boy with no brain in our family and He wanted him named Daniel.

 JOURNAL: Lord, Daniel has not come into the world for no reason. He is not just an accident. He was made in Your image. You knew him before he was in his mother's

womb. You know his spirit, and why he is here. Please cover him as he does what You have sent him to do and allow Satan no opening to him. Make me sensitive to Your desire for him, and Lord, please, if he is going to die, don't let it be at Kathy's house in front of her little children.

I knew it would be less traumatic for my children, who were older and had already experienced a baby's death.

> JOURNAL: Night before last, I couldn't hear Ben's heartbeat with the stethoscope. I asked the elders to pray for him. The presence of the Holy Spirit was strong as those dear men laid their hands on Ben and entreated the Lord's mercy for him.

> JOURNAL: (February 8, 1988) Lord, teach me how to worship You in spirit and in truth (John 4:24). Teach me to obey, not out of duty, but out of love. Duty is spoken of three times in the Old Testament and twice in the New. There are pages and pages of references for love.

Because Laura and Stacey were sick with strep and mononucleosis respectively, Kathy and I decided she would get Daniel from the hospital and take him to her house at first. Then we would move him by stages to our house as I learned to manage both babies.

Not having had a baby in their house for a while, Kathy's family was excited over the prospect of Daniel coming to stay and I was glad. Every baby deserves to be the center of attention in a family who fight to hold him and think he is the most beautiful baby in the world.

The day Daniel came home to Kathy's, the difference between my feelings for him and Kathy's was obvious from the moment she held him up for me to see. Kathy looked delighted as she sat him up to give me a better view. "Look at him! Isn't he gorgeous?"

"Yeah," I said, slouching into a chair not even asking to hold him. "I didn't know his head would be so big."

She cradled his head protectively and said, "It's not so big; I hardly noticed it at all."

Kathy loved everything about Daniel and everything about him irritated me. To her he was a precious little boy made in the image of God; to me he was a noisy little white boy with an inconveniently large head. I knew my feelings were ungodly, selfish and not at all what the Lord wanted from me, but I couldn't help it.

> JOURNAL: I had the elders pray for Daniel. They prayed the Lord would be glorified in his life.

The day after Kathy brought Daniel home, I took him for Les to see him before he got sick. I commented that except for his unusually large head, Daniel looked and acted like a normal newborn. Les switched off the light and held a flashlight to his head to see if we might see any dark areas of functioning brain tissue. The light went right through his head. There was nothing in there but clear spinal fluid and some pieces of cartilage. "Do you mind if I call the nurses?" he asked gently. "I would like for them to see this; it is the most dramatic case of hydranencephaly I have ever seen."

Les explained that Daniel seemed so normal because he apparently had a well-functioning brain stem, which controls the basic life systems. He said as Daniel grew older, if he grew older, his behavior would remain that of a newborn in spite of his age. On the way home, I looked over at Daniel in his car seat. He looked like any other baby except for his large head. Daniel is whole, I told myself. He just lives in an imperfect body. I knew that was true, because Micah had had virtually no functioning brain either. I also knew the fact that he had no brain was not what was making it hard for me to bond with him. It was my love for Ben and my contentment in mothering him. I was happy with Ben. I didn't want to be burdened with another baby.

I decided to give Daniel a bath before taking him back to Kathy for the night. Laura and Pat came in from school just as I was putting him into the baby tub. They both thought he was wonderful. They exclaimed over how tiny he was and what a beautiful little face he had.

"Mama, he acts just like a normal baby when you give them a bath," Laura said. "I thought he wouldn't know or care what you did to him, but he is scared of the water just like every other baby."

I was surprised too. I had not expected him to react to anything like a normal child, but Daniel immediately let us know when he was hungry or had a tummy ache and he remained terrified of baths until he was over a year old. I thought he would never overcome his fear, because he had no brain to remember from one bath to the next, but after about a year and a half, he lost his fear of the water and seemed to enjoy his baths.

Daniel was a fussy baby from the start and Kathy's co-mothering was invaluable, especially overnight. Together we fought colic and changed formula and bought toys that made soothing sounds, all trying to get him to sleep at night. Kathy discovered although there was no evidence of brain tissue to allow Daniel to hear, he reacted noticeably to the tapes of praise music and scriptures she played beside his crib. Sometimes he quieted immediately when he heard the tapes and lay perfectly still, as if he was listening with his whole being. This worked consistently at Kathy's house but seldom at mine.

While we were dealing with Daniel's sleep problems and learning how to care for him, Ben's deteriorating brain function was becoming a major concern. He had been eating less and less for several months, and by the end of January he had essentially stopped eating. Les Jones and I had discussed feeding him with a naso-gastric tube, but we were reluctant to do anything so drastic. I tried every trick I knew to entice Ben to eat, but with no success. I didn't want to keep him alive if it was time for him to go home, but I didn't want to make my own decision to let him die either. Hamp, our pastor and I prayed specifically for guidance from the Lord for two weeks. None of us received any indication one way or the other from any source God might see fit to use. So, hoping the increased nourishment would stimulate his appetite, I asked Les to put in an "NG" tube. I knew Ben would pull the tube out if he could, and I would have to learn how to put it back. It was frightening to think of putting a tube into a baby's nose, down his throat and into his stomach, while missing his lungs, but it turned out to be easier than learning to give Aaron injections. The tiny tube slid easily into his stomach if it was properly lubricated and Ben's chronic sleep state proved a blessing to both of us when it was time to put a tube back in. He usually stirred and sometimes fought me, but it was still easy compared to putting in a tube on a healthy, active baby. The outside end of the tube was taped to Ben's face to keep it out of his way, and like Nathan, he hated the tape. When he was awake he often worked until he got the tape off and the tube out. Then he waved it triumphantly in the air. Some thought it was the spasticity, but spasticity drew his arms up with his fists down when he was awake. But he never waved his arm unless he had an NG tube in his hand, and his hand was not turned down either.

The machine controlling the liquid nourishment dripping into Ben's stomach was far more troublesome than the NG tube. It worked like an I.V. machine at the hospital; and once I mastered threading the line, like a sewing machine, it was easy. Tube feeding showed us just how much Ben's digestive system had deteriorated. The body normally pushes food from the stomach into the small intestine, etc. through the gut, but Ben's system had slowed so, the food seemed to seep into the proper place, if it got there at all. If feedings were given faster than one drop every five seconds, the food would come out his nose. The lack of digestive action meant it took almost all day to get one bag of liquid nourishment into him. The machine had to run all day for Ben to get enough. Unfortunately, the sitting service did not authorize the sitters to handle medical equipment. Human Services paid for sitters now instead of nurses, because of the expense and because, really, skilled nursing care would do neither Ben nor Daniel any good. This meant when I had to be away from home for hours at a time, I fed Ben until I left. Then I turned off the machine and left a big note on the kitchen counter saying FEED BEN. Whichever of the children got home from school first, turned the machine back on. The whole family had to work our schedules around feeding Ben because it took all day every day. I could have fed him at night and maybe gotten more food into him, but I was afraid something might go wrong while I slept and choke him.

    I had already almost done that with my eyes wide open once. I forgot to pinch the clip on the tube shut when I attached the bag of Pediasure to the machine. All the food ran straight down the line and into his stomach. I was looking at the machine and the bag, not Ben. I came back a few minutes later to find Ben's eyes wide open and his arms waving frantically. This was the only conceivable good thing about his food being absorbed so slowly. The whole day's feeding was all over him. I couldn't believe I hadn't killed him. My hands shook so I could hardly hold him while I called Les's office to tell them what I had done. He could have aspirated some of the liquid into his lungs, which would surely have caused pneumonia. But he suffered no ill effect beyond being shocked into wakefulness.

While we were learning how to handle Ben's tube feedings, Daniel made his transfer from Kathy's house to ours. Even though he still slept at Kathy's several nights a week and visited her some during the day, the stress and weariness of grieving for Daddy and trying to deal with my children, plus the two babies, finally boiled over. One day I blew up at Kathy on the phone. I told her our arrangement was not working. I just could not handle Daniel, as I had tried to tell her—and God—from the beginning, but no one would listen to me. When she asked if I would help her if she took Daniel and became his legal foster mother, I said, "No. If I could handle more than Ben I could keep things the way they are." I wanted my life with just Ben back.

When Hamp came home I confronted him with my feelings, wanting him to agree that I should send Daniel away. "I have no anointing for this child!" I told him.

"The Bible doesn't say take the homeless poor into your house if you feel anointed for it," he said, calmly putting his wallet and keys on his dresser, with his back to me.

"I don't love him!" I said angrily. "You should see how Kathy loves him!"

"You know even adoptive families don't always feel love for the new child right away; that doesn't mean anything," he said, finally turning slowly to look at me. His calm was infuriating.

"I already had Ben and I loved him. I didn't want another baby then and I don't want another baby now!" I was almost screaming.

"Well, I don't think that matters, Sweet. God made it very clear He was calling you to be Daniel's mother, not Kathy."

I sat on the bed, my head in my hands. I knew it was true. For some reason the Lord had called me to mother Daniel, not Kathy. I wanted to love him or at least to be able to act like I did, but all I felt was resentment and frustration.

> *JOURNAL: Lord, I prayed before Daniel came that You would motivate me by love. I see now unless I am motivated by Your love I will fail You with this baby. I don't love him. You must love him through me. I almost feel I have a human baby and an angel baby. Ben is so sweet and lovable. Comfort radiates from him.*
>
> *Daniel is so human. He screams and waves his arms when he is not satisfied. He wakes me at night with his crying, his screams saying, "Do something for me! I can't tell you what! You figure it out!" He seems to personify humans in their natural state: demanding, impatient, loud, selfish, and unreasonable. Ben is just the opposite: sweet, docile, cuddly, and undemanding.*

> *JOURNAL: My heart and my spirit run to You, Lord, but they are forced to drag my mind and soul behind them as dead weight. They pull back and faint and can only be brought by being pulled bodily along.*

As I continued to pray for grace and strength and love for Daniel, things slowly got better. Kathy and I realized God had to have plans for Daniel we could not see yet. We both knew Kathy had the expertise to mother Daniel by herself, and she had the mother love for him I did not. I knew that feeling—I had it for Ben. But try as I might I could not find it in my heart for Daniel. It was obvious to both of us God seemed to have given the baby to the wrong mother. I am sure she asked the Lord more than once why He had given her so much love for Daniel when I was the one He had made responsible for him. We both had known how hard mothering Daniel would be for me because I already had Ben, but neither of us had expected the experience to be so painful for Kathy. While Kathy learned more about serving the Lord in frustration and sorrow, I learned an extremely unpleasant lesson about myself. I was ashamed to find I could be so cold and unloving to a little child. With the stress of caring for two fragile babies and my own family and the resentment I felt for having to do it all, I discovered a dark spot in my heart I had never suspected. I was unbelievably selfish and a completely unworthy servant when I didn't want the job. Ben was precious to me and I loved him. My flesh was comfortable with my ministry to him. My flesh had never wanted Daniel and I resented his crying, his keeping me up at night, and many of the normal things he did made me angry.

> JOURNAL: I drew an analogy between Ben and Daniel being an angel and a human. Am I rejecting the human baby because humans aren't nearly as easy to love as angels? Maybe the Lord is showing me the meaning of unconditional love. Ben draws my love almost supernaturally. There is no effort for me to love him, but Daniel is demanding and not satisfied by most of what I do for him. II Corinthians 7:1 says, "Therefore, having these promises, beloved, let us cleanse ourselves from all defilement of flesh and spirit, perfecting holiness in the fear of the Lord." I know my feelings for Daniel are not holy. They are as dark and ugly as fleshliness can be, and my spirit seems to be sitting somewhere inside me with its arms crossed in rebellion like a five-year-old.
>
> Paul said in II Corinthians 7:2, "Make room for us in your hearts, we wronged no one, we corrupted no one, we took advantage of no one..." When I read these words I feel so guilty. Daniel has never hurt me or done anything to me that I should lack love for him. Lord, make room for Daniel in my heart.

One morning in early spring, I gathered up papers I had no time to read and headed for the trash. As I threw them in, the headline on *The National Right to Life Newsletter* caught my eye. The story told of anencephalic babies being killed and their organs "harvested" for other children whose birth defects did not involve their brains. It said there were bills being proposed in seven state legislatures to allow two doctors to agree that a living child was dead, because he had no functioning upper brain. Once the two signed a death certificate, the doctors could cut the baby open (without anesthesia, because they didn't think newborns felt pain yet), remove what they wanted and throw the baby into the incinerator. I could not believe what I was reading. They were talking about Daniel. I called Kathy to come over and read it. Neither of us could believe people could be so blind to a child's worth as a human being. "If they decide a person has a right to live depending on what he can comprehend on a given day, I'm in trouble too," I told Kathy.

"This is incredible," she said.

That afternoon I gave Daniel a bath. As he squirmed and made faces, whimpering in protest as I washed his face, I thought, If only the legislators considering those bills could see Daniel. They would realize they are talking about killing little children. I knew I had to express my firsthand knowledge of anencephalic babies to someone who could do something. I got the phone number for Dr. James Wilke, head of the National Right to Life association, and called him

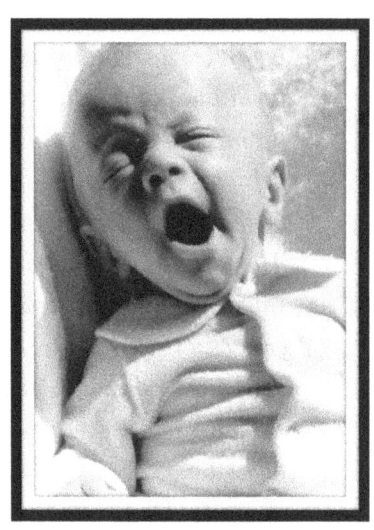

| That's a yawn, not a cry. :)

at home. I told him about Daniel's disliking baths, his crying for his bottle and calming when he was held and comforted. I told him how he liked the baby swing and enjoyed being rocked. In short, what a little person Daniel was, cognitive capacity notwithstanding.

"I want to do an article about Daniel in the *National Right to Life Newsletter* he said, "and send copies of it to all the legislators who are considering bills on infant organ harvesting. I want them to see this baby."

I called Catholic Charities and asked Father Elvin Sunds for permission to use pictures of the baby in the newsletter. I realized then why the Lord had given custody of Daniel to Catholic Charities instead of Human Services. Had he been in the custody of the state, they never would have given permission to use his picture in a "politically controversial" newsletter.

Late that night, Daniel woke me crying, and while I was changing his diaper a realization began to dawn on me. Exactly what did his name mean? I went through the dark silent house to the bookcase, flipped on the light and looked up the name again. Now I understood why his name had to be Daniel. How disgusted the Lord must get with me for being so slow on the uptake, I thought. This child had to be named Daniel because it means *"God is my judge."* No man has the right to judge Daniel unfit to live. God has given him his life and no man has the right to take it from him because he doesn't come up to that man's standard. Daniel's ability to understand has nothing to do with his right to live. He is a person made in the image of God, and God has a purpose for Daniel's life. The second interpretation of the name, "Judge of God" also spoke to me now. When doctors, legislators, legal experts, etc. who had seen Daniel's picture and read about him in the newsletter stood before God to be judged, would God hold up Daniel and say, "Do you remember this child? I sent him to Earth so those with eyes to see would see. If you refused to see the worth of this child of Mine, then you will be judged guilty by what you allowed to be done to My children who were like him." The name Daniel was packed with more meaning than any name I had ever given a baby. Then again, I didn't give him his name. The Lord did.

A reporter from the *National Right to Life Newsletter* interviewed me on the phone, and I sent her pictures of Daniel. Within two weeks Daniel's face graced the front page of the Newsletter. The article, titled, "When I look at Daniel..." beautifully portrayed Daniel's humanity, and pointed out he was made in the image of God, and was not a malformed mass of tissue to be used or destroyed as man pleased. In the month following, I received mail from all over the country. Most of the people said they were so blessed by Daniel's picture they had cut it out, and put it in a prominent place so they could see it often. Also, none of the states with bills pending to allow the killing of anencephalic babies for organ harvesting passed the legislation.

> JOURNAL: Lord, I see that You had all these things prepared for Daniel to be used for Your purposes. My inheritance from Daddy to pay for his needs and for sitters to help me since there was no financial help from the state. You provided Kathy to help mother him, and Les to treat him free until he was covered under Medicaid. You saw to it he was in the custody of a private, Christian organization which would give permission for him to be used in a pro-life publication. I also see Your perfect timing again. I see if Daddy had slowly died with cancer, he probably would have died in February or March and I would not have been able to mother Daniel.

> JOURNAL: I took Daniel in obedience to what little I saw You had prepared for him: Kathy, the name Daniel, etc. Having been obedient to what I knew, Your plan began to unfold in spite of my attitude. James 2:22 says, "You see that faith was working with his (Abraham's) works, and as a result of his works, faith was perfected." Praise You, Lord. I see I took Daniel strictly by faith, and the work of ministering to him in obedience to You, has caused my faith to grow as I have seen You use all of these things to complete Your purposes for Daniel for Your glory.

Daniel was healthy, and although he was still the size of a newborn, his growth was steady. Unfortunately, his head was growing faster than his body because of spinal fluid continuing to fill his head. By early summer his head, which he could not control, outweighed his body, making it very difficult to hold him. It was only a matter of time before the weight of his head caused someone to drop him. Even though the doctors felt the pressure of spinal fluid enlarging his head was not causing him pain, Kathy and I hoped they were wrong. We hoped a shunt to drain the fluid and relieve the pressure in his head would make Daniel more comfortable and less fussy. While most doctors thought a shunt was a waste of time for a baby like him, Les found a neurosurgeon willing to operate. But they would require someone to be with Daniel nearly all the time. That would be difficult for me because of Ben, but we felt we had no choice. Daniel's head seemed to get bigger every day.

In June, Daniel went into the hospital to have his shunt put in. He would have to be in the hospital for three days after surgery and Kathy and I, with the help of our families, were able to work out schedules to stay with him.

The surgery went well, and when I took my turn with him in the recovery room, the nurses were gathered around his bed, expressing surprise at his normal behavior. Daniel was fussing and whining like any baby who had just had surgery, and he was obviously as miserable as everyone else in the recovery room.

"I thought babies with no brain didn't feel pain," one nurse exclaimed.

"So did I," said another.

"He looks like he feels like everyone else in here," said another.

"Well, it's obvious having no brain doesn't keep him from feeling pain," I said. Then I told of incidents at home and the doctor's office showing us he did feel pain. They didn't argue. The evidence was lying in my arms whimpering.

Because my mother had become a semi-invalid in her late thirties, I had spent long hours staying with her in hospitals. This had given me an aversion to the confinement and boredom of sickroom sitting. I contemplated my turn to stay with Daniel his second night in the hospital with dread. Kathy of course had asked to stay the first night after surgery when he would feel the worst because she knew she was more attuned to his needs than I.

It was early summer, and already extremely hot. In spite of the air conditioning, Daniel's tiny room was hot and stuffy when I arrived to spend my night with him. "Wonderful," I grouched aloud. "Twelve hours in a steam bath." I complained to the nurses, who promised to have it checked in the hopefully not-too-distant future.

By eight p.m., I had shed my jeans and was standing by Daniel's bed barefoot wearing only my long shirt. I stepped in a pool of water on the floor at the end of the crib. The air conditioning had stopped up and was overflowing. A call finally went out for a repairman, who arrived at one a.m. with ladders and tools. At three a.m. I was holding a hose out the window to help him drain the water. By six a.m. the room was cool, and by seven a.m. Kathy was back. I couldn't say it had been boring.

The surgery left Daniel with a tiny tube just under the skin, running from a hole in his cranium to his abdomen. The excess spinal fluid drained into his abdomen where it was picked up and excreted in his urine. I marveled at the mechanical efficiency of it, but unfortunately it had no effect on Daniel's crying. In fact, he seemed more uncomfortable than ever.

> JOURNAL: *Looking back over my prayer journals, I was shocked and appalled by the distance I have fallen. It breaks my heart to see where I was before spiritually. There was a time when the physical presence of one baby, much less two, would be enough to keep me "up" in the Lord. Now nothing but a warm, loving exchange with Jesus*

> will keep me going. Amazing that with Ben and Daniel here, with all the activity I know is here for them, I am so dry and unaffected by it all. Lord, please change this.

Less than a month after Daniel's shunt surgery, Ben's digestive problems became acute. For days I had noticed his lungs sounding increasingly congested. I gave him his medicine and breathing treatments, but he continued to get worse. Finally, we put him in the hospital, but still couldn't find out what was wrong. Within a couple of days, his stomach grew extremely distended and he became uncomfortable enough to awaken him. Food came out his nose no matter how slowly the machine dripped it into his stomach. A battery of tests showed his digestive system had all but shut down. His intestines and stomach had swelled and were pushing up on his lungs. Ben lay in the observation room once occupied by John Mark. He was propped with pillows to make him as comfortable as possible with his bloated little tummy puffed out like a balloon. He was so miserable he awoke often and was always unhappy if I wasn't there. He couldn't reach for me or call for me, but he would cry and have seizures until I came or they gave him valium.

One afternoon I arrived to find Ben miserable and agitated. I was alarmed to see his hands and feet were swollen now, and the nurses reported he had been awake and crying for hours, in spite of a small dose of valium. I was angry they had not called me, but they took good care of my babies and I didn't say anything. I would have found a way to be there hours sooner. I quickly sat in the rocking chair by his bed, grabbed a pillow to put on my lap and asked the nurses to put him in my arms with all the tubes and monitors attached. Resting on the pillow, cradled in my arms, he went immediately to sleep. My neck hurt terribly, but Ben had always been there when I needed him. Now that he desperately needed my comfort, I couldn't risk waking him to shift my position. We sat for four hours without moving, while Ben drew peace and rest from me for a change.

Finally, with prayer, medication and enemas, we were able to relieve his bloating and reduce the pressure on his lungs. At last, Ben felt well enough to descend into his usual sleep state.

While he was there, many people had the opportunity to pass the observation room and see him. Any hour of the day or night I would arrive to find people watching him through the glass. They would tell me they had been in the intensive care waiting room or elsewhere, when they thought about Ben and came to check on him. Even people in elevators stopped me to ask if I was "Baby Ben's" mother. When I answered in the affirmative, total strangers, as often white as black said, "I don't know what it is, but I feel very drawn to him. There is something comforting about him. He seems so peaceful." People all over the hospital were talking about a little black boy who simply lay in a bed. He couldn't speak to them or even look at them, but he somehow touched their hearts with his helpless innocence.

THE LACK OF BRAIN IMPULSES AND POOR MUSCLE ACTION IN HIS GUT had finally caused Ben to stop having bowel movements, and for the remaining four or five months I had to give him enemas twice a week. This grossed out everyone in the house but Daniel, Ben and me, but it really wasn't bad if properly done. The secret was in being adequately prepared for the inevitable. After administering the disposable enema, I would put a disposable diaper on him, then a cloth diaper, then wrap him with a towel, diaper style.

Then I just checked every few minutes to see if it was time to change him yet. It was very efficient and once I became used to it, I didn't mind it at all. It was simply one of the strange routines that are commonplace in homes with handicapped children.

After Ben came home, life swept along for several weeks, a haze of tube feedings for Ben in the den, while Daniel fussed nearby in the swing. Stacey and friends from college were in and out. Laura and Pat going and coming and John breezing through long enough to play with Ben and ask Daniel what his problem was. Hampy held and rocked and comforted as much as he could, sometimes a child—sometimes me.

Daniel and Kathy Sones, the friend God blessed me with to get me through two babies at once. See the shunt behind his ear?

In July, Human Services was ready to feature Ben for adoption in the newspaper and on television. I felt sure no one would be found in Mississippi to adopt him. I had a sense that Ben would never leave me except to go Home to God, and I was glad. He seemed to be uniquely mine as no other foster baby had been. I truly believed he had come to bless me, rather than vice versa.

On the appointed day for the TV taping, the news crew from one of the local stations came to our house. The newscaster, Maggie Wade, admired Ben and talked to him and tried to coax his eyes open, but he ignored her. I tried to wake him by combing his hair, something that almost always got an indignant response, to no avail.

John had been in Atlanta for two weeks and arrived home just minutes after the news crew. As soon as he heard John's voice, Ben's eyes opened. As long as John held him, Ben smiled, eyes wide open, obviously delighted to see his big brother. But when John tried to hand him to Maggie, Ben's eyes slammed shut. It was frustrating because it was their policy never to show the foster family with the child. They needed to get Ben to look alert away from John. I left the room in the middle of the struggle and went to our bedroom to check on Daniel. When I returned to the den, the cameraman was closing up his equipment.

"Did you get anything?" I asked, surprised they were finished so quickly.

"Yes, I think it will be good," he said, heading for his van. Maggie and I walked outside, talking. I was about to ask how they had gotten Ben to stay alert without John holding him. We looked up to see Laura's best friend's car, blocking their van at the end of the driveway. It had quit just as she started to turn in. The cameraman volunteered to push the car until she got it started. He came back minutes later red faced and sweating profusely. In all the confusion I forgot to ask about the tape of Ben. We had no idea what we would see when Ben appeared on television the following Wednesday.

On the appointed evening, we gathered to watch Ben on the 6:00 news. John was at work and didn't even know Ben would be on TV that night. A close up of Ben's face showed him with his eyes open looking beautiful. Then John, who was not supposed to be in the picture, was holding Ben and talking to him, while Ben looked up at him attentively. I suppose Maggie decided it was important to show Ben recognized people, since everything else about him was so off-putting. But the love between a young white man and little black boy was so striking and so sweet, I couldn't have been happier they had shown it. Meanwhile, John was at work at the video store out front, while other boys were watching TV in the back room. "Hey, John! You're on TV," they called to him.

"What?" John said, going to the back room. There he was, on the news with little Ben, and his co-workers staring at him for an explanation. They had no idea John had a black little brother. It hadn't come up.

> JOURNAL: *Feeling great condemnation for not being able to get time or energy to pray, I read II Corinthians 2:14, "But thanks be to God, who always leads us in His triumph in Christ, and manifests through us the sweet aroma of the knowledge of Him in <u>every</u> place." How it comforted me to know I "smell like a Christian" because of His Spirit in me. Even when I am not walking in the power of His peace, I still manifest the knowledge of Him that is in me.*

A week later, the Lord used an infection in Daniel's shunt to give more people an opportunity to see a child most people would think was useless, a mistake, a freak of nature. It was the furthest thing from my mind, but the Lord was going to show Daniel's humanity to lots and lots of people.

DANIEL HAD BEEN CRYING STEADILY FOR ALMOST TWO DAYS, AND although he had no symptoms of illness, his fontanel seemed full, which I knew might mean the shunt was infected. I took him to Les, who also feared an infection in the shunt. There was no alternative but to take him to the neurosurgeon, as in straight to the hospital from the pediatrician. No time to stop for food, drink, or meds for either of us.

I expected a long painful afternoon as I sat holding a crying baby, and I prayed for grace to stand the pain in my neck and shoulders. It was a hundred times worse than I had thought. Daniel and I waited several hours before even seeing a doctor, and then waited alone in the exam room the rest of the afternoon and into the night for the tests to come back. Except for brief naps from exhaustion, Daniel cried the entire day. God bless the nurse who looked in and asked if she could get me a cold drink. It was all I had to eat all day. I had formula for Daniel, but he wouldn't eat. The day that began at ten a.m. in Les's office, finally ended at ten p.m. with Daniel's admission to the hospital for an infected shunt. I had known he would have to be hospitalized for the replacement surgery, but I almost cried when the doctor said he would have to be in the hospital for *five weeks* before it could be done. It would take that long a course of I.V. antibiotics to be sure the infection was completely gone before they could risk a new shunt.

Before Daniel was taken upstairs, the doctor asked an almost elderly nurse in the ER to start his I.V. Her fingers were stained with nicotine and she had a bad smoker's cough. I wondered why he didn't let a nurse upstairs try to get a needle into Daniel's tiny vein. Surely there is someone younger with better eyes and a steadier hand upstairs, I thought. I was angry he didn't care enough to think of Daniel's suffering to let someone so old stick him. I knew how painful it was for Daniel to have a nurse probe and poke in his arm with a needle only to have the vein burst and the process have to be repeated. His veins were so fragile no one ever was able to get a vein on the first stick.

As the nurse prepared her instruments of torture, I sank into a chair beside the table, trying to brace myself to hold and comfort Daniel through the coming ordeal. The nurse began by slapping Daniel's hand and wrist, then pinched and mashed his skin until I grew impatient to get it over with. "His veins are tiny and break easily," I said, letting her know I knew what to expect. "Everyone has to try multiple times before they find a vein that will hold."

"No, this little fellow feels bad enough, I am not going to stick him but once," she said, squeezing his arm and putting on a tourniquet. Then she heated a towel and wrapped it around his wrist. I had never seen anyone do most of this prior to sticking a tiny baby. After ten minutes of her careful preparation, we could see one little blue vein standing out in his wrist. The nurse took a needle and gently pierced the vein. We both held our breath as blood flowed up the tiny tube. The vein held. I watched her secure the I.V. as if she were handling nitroglycerin. So much for young eyes and steady hands, I thought as I thanked her. When I was leaving the hospital, I saw her outside smoking a cigarette to celebrate.

> JOURNAL: Father, I pray today and every day Daniel is in the hospital, You will anoint him with Your Spirit. Let everyone, believers, and non-believers alike see You in him. I agree with You that people will be convicted by him and have their minds set solidly against abortion and infanticide.

> JOURNAL: I sense as one area of my life is magnified before men to God's glory, my personal life will be as tormented by Satan as much as God will allow. There will be a price to pay to give this witness with Daniel. If I don't witness about the babies, my life will be quieter and more uneventful, but my family will be less zealous for the Lord. The price of serving and witnessing will ultimately make all of us stronger in the Lord.

Soon after Daniel was admitted to the hospital, I was talking with a visitor when I saw a nurse about to give him a dose of Phenobarbital four times his proper dose. He had been taking it at home to help him sleep, but she had enough to make him sleep for a week.

"Wait a minute!" I said, "What is that?" "It's his Phenobarb," she said.

"Look at the amount in the tube and look at the size of the baby," I said.

"It's an awful lot for a baby this little, isn't it?" she replied. "But that's what the computer said was prescribed." "Well, you need a new computer. I know Les never prescribed that," I told her. When she checked the computer, the nurse found a blotch on the printout that had caused her to misread the dose. I had to bite my tongue to keep from saying, "Any nurse with half a brain should have noticed the dose was enormous enough to have him put into ICU for being comatose. We would be here that many more days before they got back the blood work and saw he was overdosed." The near overdose underscored Daniel's need to have someone with him all the time, but Kathy and I knew we could not possibly do it alone for five weeks even with our families' help.

Kathy was younger than I and she was still in an overachiever mode, but the years between us, and my fibromyalgia had slowed me down considerably. I was still a bit of an overachiever but I was no longer compulsive about it. I knew when to admit I was in over my head, and forced myself to ask for help. I called my church, the Right to Life office, and several friends, asking them to please pass the word we needed people to stay with Daniel in the hospital.

The response was overwhelming. Several people took copies of the article on Daniel in *The National Right to Life Newsletter* and showed it to people at their churches. Some announced it at their prayer meetings, and others put it in their church bulletins.

Soon people from churches all over Jackson began calling to offer help. Several even offered to spend the night. Husbands and wives, widows, single men and women and even some teenagers volunteered to stay with Daniel. Hampy made a chart out of poster board and asked people to designate the times they could help. I could hardly believe so many people were arranging their lives to make time for little Daniel. Because no one had cared for him before except Kathy's family and mine, I made a two page care sheet and taped it at the end of his bed. It detailed how to obtain, mix and feed him his food, how to calm him, etc., and everyone did a wonderful job. It was a unique sensation to come into my foster child's hospital room and have to introduce myself to strangers who were acting as family for him. In all, twenty-nine people stayed with Daniel, not counting Singletons and Soneses. Seventeen of them were strangers to me. All were Christians, many were pro-life activists, who contrary to popular belief, care very much about children already born.

One volunteer family took up such a burden for Daniel they considered adopting him. They were Donnie and Kay Crawford, friends of ours from Right to Life. They felt a responsibility as pro-life activists to help care for him. They became my case in point.

"I have to admit I was apprehensive before I came," Donnie told me. "I wasn't sure I could handle a baby with no brain. It was a frightening idea. But when I looked at his little face, I realized he was a little boy, just like my own son. The fact that he had no brain didn't make him any less human." They felt exactly what I believed God wanted everyone who saw him to see. Donnie and Kay were at the hospital almost as much as I was. They came to check on Daniel at least once a day. Sometimes I would go to the hospital at ten or eleven at night to be sure he was all right and see which nurse he had. I stopped being surprised to find Kay and Donnie there with their children.

Hearing the comments from volunteers, nurses and doctors about what they saw in Daniel, made all the discomfort of mothering him worthwhile. They all learned things about anencephalic babies they had not known, and most of them applied their new knowledge to God and His will. Many changed their minds, or thought for the first time, about what handicapped children are and what they aren't, and most became firmer in their convictions against abortion, if that was possible. As Daniel's stay in the hospital unfolded, Kathy and I saw clearly the power of God being channeled through Daniel.

> *JOURNAL: I am seeing something I never saw before about the babies. The Lord brings children, little human beings to me to receive love. There is a string of little individuals in my mind, children I loved and was mother to. I had the most influential, most intimate relationship there is with them outside of marriage, but I never saw myself from their prospective. They are people—afraid, lonely, in pain, desperately needing a mother to love and protect them, and the Lord brings them to me. What an unbelievable privilege. What a totally unwarranted blessing. I remember my babyhood and my intense attachment to my mother. When I put myself in their place, I know surely I must protect this ministry and guard my actions to be sure I never jeopardize it in any way.*

When Daniel's infection did not respond to the antibiotics, they decided to take out the tube draining the fluid to see if the bacteria had colonized on it. I held him as the resident anesthetized the site and cut a tiny hole in his upper chest, to expose the tube and pull it out. The sharp instrument made a scratching sound as he carefully stroked it against Daniel's skin, to be sure he didn't cut too deeply. As soon as he pulled the tube out, Daniel calmed down. This reaffirmed my deduction the tube was touching something it shouldn't have been. From then on he seemed to feel much better, and came home a happier calmer baby. I don't know why the Lord allowed Daniel to suffer so. It seems God requires sacrifices from people sometimes we never would have expected. Or maybe it is part of a deep spiritual truth we are not capable of understanding on this earth.

> *JOURNAL: I fear being without Ben. He is surely an angel, and I don't want to be without his presence. How quickly we begin to worship angels, or anything symbolic of Christ! I suddenly realize feeling Ben is an angel has*

> become a snare for me. Thank you for showing me this, Lord. I know I don't have to have Ben or anything symbolic of Jesus. I have Jesus Himself.

As the summer drew to an end, Daniel continued to thrive. The second surgery had made him more comfortable and he was growing and eating well. All body systems seemed to be strong, healthy and as stable as a normal child. Ben on the other hand, was losing ground.

He had no concern about wet or dirty diapers, and certainly cared nothing for food. If I had stopped feeding him, he probably would not have noticed he was starving to death. He seldom woke unless John played vigorously with him. I knew Ben was dying. He had done what he had been sent here to do, and it was close to time for him to go back to the Lord. I was glad the Lord had shown me not to look to Ben for comfort, but to Christ Himself. It gave me the grace to loosen my emotional bond and to be willing to let the Lord accomplish His will for Ben.

In August, we learned a family in Pennsylvania wanted to adopt Daniel. They were a big, happy Catholic family with several birth children and several handicapped adopted children. The parents were Drew and Maureen Buccarro. Maureen and I spoke several times on the phone, and like Suzy Walker, she and I had much to share about the Lord. We could not have asked for a better family for Daniel. Even Kathy felt good about Daniel's placement with them.

When we made plans to fly Daniel to Pennsylvania, we decided to take Laura with us. Stacey and John were in college and it would be a fun trip for Laura. She had never flown before and like us, she had never seen Pennsylvania.

In early October, a reporter for *Mississippi Today*, a Catholic Newspaper, called and asked to do an article on the babies. The reporter came to the house a few days before our trip and took some pictures of Daniel and completed the interview with me. She planned to come back when we returned home from Pennsylvania and get some pictures of Ben.

Finding someone both capable and willing to care for Ben while we were gone was a problem, but the Lord provided the perfect person for that too. Isobelle Pointer, the wife of an old friend of the family, Malcolm Pointer, was a retired pediatric intensive care supervisor. She was eminently qualified to care for Ben, and she agreed to keep him at her house while we were gone. She visited Ben and we talked extensively about his needs, so they would feel comfortable together. She prayed for the Lord to help her take care of Ben, but I knew I could find no one to give him better, more loving care, than she.

Late in the afternoon, the day before we were to fly to Pennsylvania, I loaded the car with toys, clothes, food, medicine and Ben, and drove to Isobelle's house. When he was settled in and everyone felt comfortable, I kissed Ben and left. I still had a million things to do before our flight to Pennsylvania the next morning. As I backed out of lsobelle's driveway, I had an overwhelming desire to run back inside and kiss Ben one more time. How silly, I thought, I'll only be gone three days.

Daniel was very good on the trip and traveled surprisingly well. Laura turned out to be a faint-hearted flyer, asserting frantically just as the plane took off that she was sure people were not meant to fly and she didn't want to go. She relaxed once we were airborne and enjoyed flying when she had lost her opportunity to back out. She was also a big help with Daniel in what turned out to be an unbelievably long day.

We were delayed leaving Jackson and Atlanta, and arrived more than two hours late in Cincinnati, where of course we had missed our flight to Philadelphia. Drew and Maureen had been expecting us at two p.m. and had let their children stay home from school to greet their new brother. The little ones were ready for bed when we finally reached their house after 9:00 that night.

The Buccaros were a precious brother and sister in the Lord and they and their children were thrilled with Daniel. We spent two days with them, sharing fellowship in the Lord and showing them Daniel's routine and likes and dislikes. Then Hamp, Laura and I took a day trip around Lancaster County and returned for one more night. The next morning we left Daniel with his new family and drove to Philadelphia. I tried to feel sorrow at leaving a foster child with his new parents as I always had before, but I didn't. My heart was with my Ben at home. I would have been terribly upset if the family had been less than we had hoped for, but I was very happy for Daniel because I knew he would get the love he needed and deserved with the Buccaros.

Hampy, Laura and I drove to Philadelphia, and toured the Liberty Bell and Constitution Hall. We packed a lot into our time in Pennsylvania and really enjoyed each other. We checked into a hotel and wearily fell into bed. Our flight home was at 8:00 the next morning, which was a Sunday.

The next morning when the phone rang at 5:00, I assumed Hamp had asked for a wakeup call. I picked up the phone, but it was Les Jones, Ben's doctor. "Carlene," he said, "something terrible has happened." "What?" I asked, thinking Ben must have become ill. "Ben has died," he said. "Mrs. Pointer feels awful, but there was nothing she could do. He apparently had a massive seizure and just stopped breathing." He told me Ben had awakened Isobelle with a strange sound about 3:00 a.m. He was sleeping right beside her bed and she had picked him up, patted him and put him back down. As she sat on the side of the bed watching him, he stopped breathing. She immediately began CPR and told her husband to call an ambulance, but Ben was gone. Les met them at the hospital and assured them it was not their fault, but they were still distraught. I was sorry I had put them in a position for this to happen to them.

When Les called our home to learn how to reach us, he woke John, who was home alone. Les asked John if he wanted to see Ben's body and John said, "No." He told me years later he thought he would feel better just remembering Ben alive.

When Les told us he had talked to John, I knew we needed to call him. I was upset he was at the house by himself now. He had loved Ben as much as I did. I was weeping uncontrollably and went into the bathroom and sat on the floor to cry, so Hampy could talk to John. I could not believe my Ben had died and I wasn't there. I wanted desperately to see him alive just one more time, or at least hold him one more time. I got up and went to the phone where Hampy was talking to John. I took the phone and said, "John, please go to the hospital and hold Ben and kiss him goodbye for me. I want to so badly, and I can't. Please go and do it for me." John promised to do as I asked, and he called his girlfriend and took her with him. John never told me how wrenchingly painful it was for him to see Ben's lifeless little body until we were discussing it for the book. He said his legs nearly gave way when he saw his sweet little God-given brother's body. But he held him and kissed him and thanked him for his love, just as he had done with Nathan. I never would have asked John to go by himself and hold and kiss a dead baby he loved, had he not already experienced Nathan's death.

I felt awful, hearing how it had made him feel to see Ben's body. At the time I was so desperate to hold Ben just once more, I only remembered how well John had handled Nathan's death.

On the plane, I had to fight a frantic desire to turn back time and do things differently. If I had had any idea Ben would die while I was gone, I never would have left him. I couldn't believe I would never hold him or see him alive again.

The house was unbearably quiet and empty when we got home. Thursday we had two babies, but Sunday we had none. I was tempted to ask the Lord why Ben had to die during the three short days I had to be away from him. But Nathan's death had taught me to trust in His love for me, and the baby and my family, and I didn't question. I knew there was a very good reason. I just couldn't see it from where I was.

I kept myself busy the first few days planning Ben's funeral, which we did as if he were our own child. I made the arrangements at the funeral home that had held services for my parents, and asked our pastor to officiate. Catholic Charities asked Bishop Houck, Bishop of the Jackson Diocese, to represent them and word passed slowly that Baby Ben had died.

The day before the funeral, I was told both of Ben's parents and other members of his family would be coming for the service, which unnerved me completely. I felt much too upset to have to meet them under those conditions, but I had no choice. They were his birth family and they had a right to be there.

When we arrived for the funeral, we were surprised to find people we didn't know gathered around Ben's little coffin weeping. They were white, so we knew they weren't his birth family. We discovered they were people who had heard about Ben, us, or who had seen him once somewhere, but we didn't actually know. Many had seen the obituary in the newspaper. Of course there were also people from our church and our neighbors, anti-abortion people from Right to Life of Jackson, who we knew well, our friends and our children's friends and many of their parents.

The chapel was full, and many of us were moved to tears to see so many people who had taken time out of their busy schedules on a weekday afternoon to come and acknowledge the loss of a little person who had never turned over or spoken a word. He was important to them simply because God had made him.

Not only were there people, but there were flowers also, many from people we didn't know. Nathan's funeral had been quite small and simple with few people and no flowers, except the blanket of roses we supplied. Ben's funeral was nearly as large as if we had truly lost a family member.

The meeting with Ben's family was very uncomfortable for me.

I was so distraught over losing Ben that my grief was too strong to allow me to behave as empathetically as I would have liked. They were cordial and expressed appreciation for our love and care for their child. Ben's brother and sister were there, along with his grandmother and a few assorted aunts and uncles. Ben's birth family sat on the front row of one side of the chapel and we on the other. I suppose it looked strange to have the black immediate family on one side and the white immediate family on the other side, but that was the case.

In the service, Chuck spoke of the love of Christ, of compassion for the needs of the helpless and the beauty of the life of every child and Bishop Houck commented it blessed him to see that one little black child was so important to so many people. Ben's family appeared to be touched by the genuine love so many white people obviously had for their little boy.

I have no memory whatever of the hours, days or weeks following Ben's funeral. I believe I must have blocked them out of my mind, or God took them from me for my own good.

> *JOURNAL: Lord, there were probably lessons to learn from Daniel that I won't see for years. You packed so much spiritual activity and spiritual truth into that one little boy's life, I can't take it all in. I am especially impressed with Your choice and insistence on the name, Daniel. I am also impressed with the circumstances You provided to help me. Kathy, and all the other people who helped with Daniel, the way You caused him to be shown to so many people, and finally the wonderful, loving family You provided for him in Pennsylvania. Maureen has written to me about all the people there who have been dramatically affected by Daniel.*
>
> *Thank You for allowing me to have a part in Your plan for his little life. I repent with all my heart my unwillingness to serve You through him as You wanted me*

to. I pray the next time I am faced with obeying You in a situation I want nothing to do with, I will act more in accordance with Your will.

Aaron Daniel Buccarro (Daniel) died on January 15, 1990, one week before his second birthday. Like Ben, he died in his sleep.

10
DAI

*T*his chapter is not about a foster baby. As far as our hearts are concerned, it is not even about a foster child, because our Vietnamese son is more than a permanent foster son to us. Hamp and I call him our son and our children call him brother. In the heart of every family member, Dai is one of us.

It had been only two weeks since Ben's death, when a friend at church asked me to pray for a boy she was tutoring in English. His name was Dai Le, he was fifteen, Amerasian (a child with a Vietnamese mother and an American father) and had been in America for only eighteen months. He was living in a children's home, going to junior high school, and struggling to learn English, all while he tried to deal with his grief over leaving his mother, stepfather and siblings in Vietnam. His mother had sent Dai and his sister Kim to America because they were both Amerasian and they could come with virtually no red tape and obtain a good education and easier life. Once here, they also hoped to be able to apply for the rest of the family to come too. There were legal problems, though, which made their family's coming impossible. The two teens had no means to go back home, and they knew they could help their family more by sending money from America. Now Kim was away at college, and Dai found himself alone and living in a children's home. When Amy asked me to pray for him, I nodded and said, "Sure." When she mentioned him again the next week I realized I had only prayed once, so I wrote his name down to remind me to pray.

Several nights later as I was taking a bath, something was trying to break into my thoughts. I lifted my head, searching my mind for what my memory was trying to tell me. Then it came to me, the Vietnamese boy, Dai. The Lord had spoken to me several times about our fostering an older Vietnamese child. But this is a boy, I thought. I had always assumed if we took one in, it would be a girl. I wondered aloud to Hamp if the Lord could possibly want us to take a fifteen year old boy into our home.

| Dai shortly after coming to us.

"We would really have to be sure it was the Lord before we brought a teenage boy into our family with our two teenage daughters." He looked at me gravely over his glasses.

"I can't imagine bringing a boy that age into our home with the girls and the babies. It would just be too complicated," I said, shaking my head.

> *JOURNAL: October, 1988. Lord, have You caused my friend to speak to me about this Vietnamese boy? Is it Your will for us to take an older child—and a boy? There seem to be so many obstacles: the girls, the foster babies, our plans*

to sell our house and move. We don't even know where we will be living yet. I know You can work it all out if it is Your will, but please be very clear and specific about this. I would not want to put him through the stress of visits with us that didn't develop into a home for him.

After several days of thought and prayer, we decided I should call Catholic Charities to see if they could help me find out anything about Dai. They had a foster care program for Vietnamese children who had no families in America, and an old friend of ours was the director. When I called her, she told me she had met Dai's plane from Vietnam, and she had custody of him through the program.

She said Dai had been reared Catholic, not Buddhist. He was a quiet boy who never had given Catholic Charities any trouble. But his deep grief seemed to keep him from bonding with new people. It had been a factor in both of his prior foster placements being disrupted. After the second foster home had disrupted eight months before, Catholic Charities had placed Dai in a children's home until another family could be found for him.

"I would love for you and Hamp to have one of our children," she said. "I have thought about asking you to take one before, but I knew you were committed to the babies. I also knew how demanding they were. I didn't want to put pressure on you to take more than you could handle."

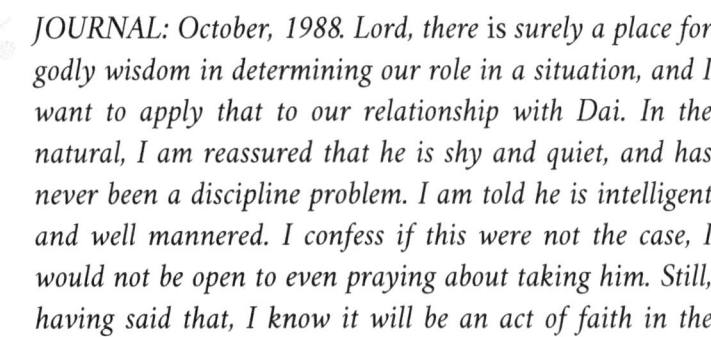

JOURNAL: October, 1988. Lord, there is surely a place for godly wisdom in determining our role in a situation, and I want to apply that to our relationship with Dai. In the natural, I am reassured that he is shy and quiet, and has never been a discipline problem. I am told he is intelligent and well mannered. I confess if this were not the case, I would not be open to even praying about taking him. Still, having said that, I know it will be an act of faith in the

end. We can look at his records and his behavior, but we can't see into the future and know how he will fit into our family. We can only do what we believe You are saying.

We asked each of our children separately what they thought of taking a fifteen-year-old Vietnamese boy into our family and to my surprise, they all thought it was a great idea. Laura especially was thrilled with the idea of having a little brother. It seemed there was nothing else to do but arrange for him to come for a visit and see what we all thought of one another.

When we made the arrangements for a weekend visit. Dai was told we were a "visiting family." That is a family to spend weekends and holidays with, to experience American life and get away from the home for a while. He had no idea we were thinking of inviting him to live with us. We didn't want him to feel more pressure than he already would, being in a strange home with people he didn't know and whose language he could barely understand.

WHEN HAMP AND I PICKED DAI UP FOR HIS FIRST VISIT, HE LOOKED nothing like I had expected. The housemother disappeared and came back with a small, dark haired boy, who looked South American to me. I would never have guessed he was Asian. He smiled and greeted us in formal English, which he spoke with a very heavy accent. I tried to talk to him in the van on the way home, but he spoke so softly and his accent was so strong, I could barely make out his answers to my questions.

At home I discovered how limited Dai's ability to communicate in English really was. His English vocabulary was small, but communication was made even harder by his insistence on looking at the floor when he spoke to me. His voice was so low, and his accent so strong, that with his head lowered, I could neither hear nor understand him. He told me months later, in

Vietnam it is rude for a young person to look an adult in the eye when speaking. Looking down was the respectful behavior that had been expected from him all his life. My requests for him to raise his head and look at me when we talked, didn't compute in his nervous confusion. We didn't understand each other well enough to be able to communicate about the communication problem. But the Holy Spirit dealt with it for us.

I soon just reached out and put my hand under Dai's chin and gently raised his head when he spoke to me. Then I smiled, to show him that I really did want him to look at me when we talked. At the same time, the Holy Spirit urged him to allow me to lift his head, and helped him believe I really wanted him to be rude and look at me when he talked to me. Repeatedly, the Lord gave Dai the grace to trust us, even when he didn't understand what we were saying, or why we wanted him to do something. He was so uncomfortable with us on his first visit, he would stand wherever I left him, rolling his shirt tail into a tight little roll until I told him to sit down.

His anxiety made me feel tense and anxious for him. When I tried to mentally put myself in his place, I realized not only were we strangers to him, but he didn't understand most of what we said. He also had no idea what we expected or wanted from him. I knew I could not have stood such a pressurized situation for an entire weekend as a grown woman, much less as a fifteen-year-old.

For his first visit I tried to think of something that would entertain someone who barely spoke English. I finally rented *Harry and the Hendersons*, thinking the action would not require understanding the dialogue. Dai watched it politely and understood enough to laugh quietly to himself a few times. It was a relief to see him forget where he was long enough to laugh at a movie. He was so nervous the entire first visit with us he couldn't eat enough to count as one full meal. I knew he had to be starving. By Sunday night I was anxious to get him back to the children's home so he could relax enough to eat.

A week later Dai came for Thanksgiving and over the long holiday he began to relax, at least with me. Because we had just sold our house, we knew we would have to move in January. I started the arduous process of packing over the Thanksgiving holiday.

One night, while packing books in the den, I found a *Good News for Modern Man* Bible. I asked Dai if he had a Bible. He said he did, but he didn't understand enough English to read it. Taking the little Bible, I sat down by him, and asked if he had ever prayed to have Jesus come into his heart. I knew he had been reared Catholic and had gone to church a lot, but I wasn't sure exactly how salvation would have been explained to him, especially since at that time South Vietnam was completely dominated by North Vietnam and Russia. I showed him several scriptures pertaining to salvation and explained them. He said he understood. Then I asked if he would like to pray with me to ask Jesus to come into his heart. When Dai said, "Yes," I offered to say the prayer for him, using words he understood, so he could repeat the words after me. I was amazed by the volume with which he repeated the prayer. I had not realized he had such a deep, beautiful voice. When we had finished praying, I said, "Dai, I am so happy that you have Jesus in your heart. Now you are my brother. We are in God's family together."

He said, "I'm happy, too," and from the look on his face, I had no doubt the Lord was in his heart.

Dai visited twice between Thanksgiving and Christmas, and his grief for his family and other broken foster placements notwithstanding, he was slowly settling into the family. The children all three loved him and even Beth quickly decided he belonged with us and paid no attention to him unless he was willing to play with her.

Although Hamp and I still talked as if it was not decided that Dai would come to live with us, my heart wanted Dai to be my son after the second visit.

Over the Christmas holiday, we involved him with shopping and decorating and making cookies. He felt guilty having fun and receiving gifts while his family was doing without so much in Vietnam. I kept reminding him he couldn't change things for the present, and his family would want him to be as happy as he could. I didn't know if he felt better, or smiled more to shut me up.

> JOURNAL: *The One who would be both mother and father to me came at Christmas, just as my earthly mother and father left me at Christmas. Lord, help me focus on that when I miss my mother and especially my father at Christmas time.*

One night during the holidays, I went up to Daddy's empty apartment, where I always went to pray now, and I prayed about Dai one more time.

"I want him so much, Lord. I feel as if he were mine already," I said, "but I don't want to do the wrong thing for him or for us. He has already lost two foster homes, and I want to be sure that doesn't happen to him again. Lord, please show me if we are supposed to take this child into our family." Tears ran down my face as I gathered my courage to say, "Lord, I give Dai back to You. I take my hands off of him. If You want him with us, please do something to let us know it is Your will."

I felt I had to receive Dai from Jesus, not just take him for myself because I could have him. That was the only way I could know we weren't acting in our flesh. There was no red tape, no process of approval to be gone through. We were already a Catholic Charities foster family. We had known the woman who had custodial authority over him for years, and she wanted us to have him. It would only require papers being signed, and Dai's things being moved to our house, for him to become ours. It could be so easy to make a mistake.

When I went back downstairs, I found Laura and Dai watching

Dai's senior picture.

TV in the den. As soon as I sat down with them, Dai initiated a conversation, which was very unusual for him. He talked about his unhappiness at the children's home. "Well, when they find you another foster family, you will have a family and new friends to be with," I said.

"They don't find other family for me," he said sadly. "I think sometime I run away, but I don't have money or anywhere to go."

The social workers at the children's home had asked us not to say anything to Dai about coming to live with us until we could talk to them after Christmas. But Dai knew we were a foster family already and we could have him as our foster child if we wanted him. I knew if I let this opening pass, he would feel certain we didn't want him and the door that had opened between us would begin to close. I also felt this was an answer to my prayer, because it was so uncharacteristic of Dai to begin a conversation about anything, especially his feelings. The only thing he had really tried to talk to me about up to this point was soccer, something I knew absolutely nothing about.

"Dai," I said, choosing my words carefully. "Daddy and I think Jesus wants you to come and live with us. Do you think you would like to do that?" Dai looked at the floor and nodded his head. "Are you sure?" I asked.

"Yes," he said softly.

"You will have to leave your school and your soccer team. They are too far from our house to go there," I said. "I find other school. I find other soccer team," he said, still looking at the floor. I breathed a sigh of relief. I hadn't been sure we were worth leaving a good soccer team.

That night before bed, I opened my Bible and started reading in Ephesians where I had stopped the night before. It was Ephesians 2:15-22 and it spoke strongly to me of Dai. It spoke of making two into one, establishing peace.

Dai had been divided his whole life, half Vietnamese and half American. It spoke of one new man. Then it spoke of peace preached to those far away and peace to those who were near. He had been taught about Christ in Vietnam and had heard the same good news here, both bringing the peace he needed so much. Finally, in verse nineteen it spoke of no longer being a stranger and alien, but a member of God's household. I felt this was a final confirmation that God had indeed brought Dai to us, and us to him.

WHEN IT WAS TIME TO TAKE HIM BACK TO THE CHILDREN'S HOME AT the end of Christmas vacation, I had to force myself to tell Dai it was time to go. Even though I knew he had to stay there for a couple of weeks while the papers were being drawn up, I felt he belonged with us already. I hated taking him back there. I missed him already. I cried when we got out of the car at the children's home, and when I looked at Dai, there were tears in his eyes too. "Don't cry," he said as he hugged me, "I come home soon."

> *JOURNAL: Lord, you are giving me a blessing with Dai I can hardly grasp. He is loving and intelligent and capable of having a deep reciprocal relationship with me that I will never have to lose. You are giving me a foster child I can keep. Even if he goes back to Vietnam when he grows up, or his family comes here, I will never have to lose my place in his heart. How can I thank You for so wonderful and unexpected a gift?*

The next time I saw him, I asked Dai if he felt it would bother him to call me "Mother," since he had a real mother in Vietnam. "It's impolite to call your mother by her first name," I told him. And since I will be a mother to you now, you will have to find some word for "mother" that you feel comfortable with." A few days later while we were shopping, he called to me from the dressing room. The name he had chosen for me was "Mom," a word he knew my own children didn't call me. The girls called me "Mama" and John called me "Mother." I knew Dai didn't feel he had the right to claim the privilege of using one of their names for me. He was very sensitive about how they felt about him. It would be two years before he addressed me as "Mother" for the first time.

Later that week, while he was still living at the children's home, Dai called and asked if I would take him to his soccer game at school. I had known he loved soccer, and was a good player, but watching him play that day, even I could see he was exceptionally good. When I commented on the way home about one particularly spectacular goal he had made with his back to the goal, kicking the ball over his own head to score, he looked at the floor and said softly with a smile, "Well, I'm show off for you." Every time I was with him, he did something to make me love and trust him a little more.

Although I had told Dai I loved him during Christmas, I had been cautioned by the social workers not to expect him to show any affection for us. Overt shows of affection were uncommon in Vietnam, even between parents and children. When he got out of the car that night, and leaned over and hugged me and told me he loved me, I knew the Holy Spirit was prompting both of us to do things to let the other know how we felt. Dai's place in the family would evolve slowly, but the Lord cemented his relationship with me before he ever moved in with us.

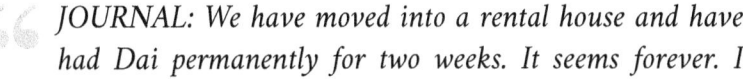
JOURNAL: We have moved into a rental house and have had Dai permanently for two weeks. It seems forever. I

> can't believe three months ago I didn't even know him. He is acting more and more like a kid at home, complaining about chores, resisting homework and even arguing with the girls. Lord, bind us together with Your love. Give him a genuine love for all of us and help us all to be patient with each other. Make me a good mother for all my children, Lord.

As soon as we settled into our rental house and established a family routine, conflicts between Dai and the girls began to escalate. John, our most easy going child was away at college and only came home on weekends. That left the girls at home all week with Dai.

Soon the three of them were arguing about everything. The girls argued with Dai about whether he had known Beth long enough to know what her whining meant. "I've known Beth all her life. That whine means she's hungry!" Laura would storm at Dai.

"She not hungry, I feed her already. She want to go out!" Dai would yell back. They fought constantly over the bathroom they had to share and the girls complained about the smell of oriental noodles cooking in the morning. Even worse were the television wars. Dai couldn't understand drama or comedy shows yet, so of course he wanted to watch sports, continuously. The more he voiced his opinions of the girls' viewing preferences, the more disenchanted they became with their new brother. I began to wonder if they would ever be able to form a positive relationship.

Fortunately, John, who only saw Dai on the weekends, was able to maintain a good relationship with his new brother. He took Dai to the school parking lot and taught him how to drive, and retrieved soccer balls for him behind the fence while Dai practiced shooting goals. It was good for Dai to have a brother who accepted him and agreed the girls could be real pains, even if he was only there on the weekends.

> JOURNAL: Dai has spells of being very withdrawn, almost angry. I felt the Lord said, "Allow him to hurt. He hurts and you have to accept it and allow it. Don't ask him what's wrong. It hurts in ways he knows no English for. Not only does he hurt because he is separated from his family, who love him, but he is also angry that he has to be an outsider in a family he doesn't belong in yet. He is odd man out, and he did nothing to deserve it." I know I can only be constant with my love and pray that Jesus' love will heal him and make us all a family.

> JOURNAL: Lord, the pain in my shoulders is spreading to the muscles in my arms. They ache as if I have the flu. The pain specialist wants to inject me all over my back and neck with something to kill the nerve endings and stop the pain. The shots are painful and expensive, but I can hardly function for the pain. It is such a drain on my energy. If You will allow this to work, I will praise You for it.

As the girl's disenchantment with Dai grew, they went through a stage of even resenting the time I spent teaching him English and helping him understand his school work. One night while I was helping Dai study for his final exams at school, the girls came into the room and began talking to me about nothing in particular. I chatted with them for a little while, then told them Dai and I needed to finish his studying. Their resentment of my sending them out so I could devote myself to Dai was obvious, and after they left, he turned to me and said, "They hate me; you know they do. They never going to want me here."

"They don't hate you," I said. "They resent my time with you. They probably wouldn't have even wanted to talk to me if I hadn't been in here with you studying. Besides, it takes time to become a part of a family, and it doesn't happen in a few weeks."

I drew on Kathy and Larry Sones's experiences with integrating their adopted children into their family with their birth children and said, "It takes experiences together; it takes all of us sharing things and helping each other, to make a new member a real part of a family. If you try to be a good brother to them, the time will come when they remember good things that happened and fun we all had in the family, you will be part of their memory. It's called shared history, and you don't have any with us yet, but you will, and it will make you part of our family. It will happen, I promise," I said. Dai didn't look convinced, but I could see he hoped I was right.

> JOURNAL: Funny, Lord, I thought when I was forty-four I would be older. Do I have time to grow up before I die?

After he had been with us for several months, I became dissatisfied with the fact that Dai never kissed me. I knew he had seen John kiss me when he came home from school, or when he left the house, and I wondered why Dai would hug me, but never gave me a kiss, which I often did to him. One night I just asked him for a kiss before he went to bed.

He surprised me by flushing deep red and pacing up and down in front of me, saying "Oh, no! Oh, no!"

I was mystified, so I just stood looking at him. "What's wrong?" I finally said.

"Oh, I never kiss anybody before!" he said.

"You never kissed anyone? Not even your mother?" I said in disbelief.

"Well, maybe my mother sometime," he said, "but never anybody else."

"Well," I said, "that's silly. I really want a kiss. It's no big deal."

Seeing he had no recourse, Dai took a noticeably deep breath and brushed his lips against my cheek as if it were white hot metal. He explained later that kissing was just not done in Vietnam, even between mother and child, unless the child was a baby. Of course, I knew that meant kissing must be kept to a minimum in front of his contemporaries, which is generally the rule with teenage boys anyway. Because of the kissing episode, I was touched by his lack of reserve a few weeks later when I took him to school. I was very upset over something that didn't concern Dai. I had sniffled all the way to school, with Dai watching me uneasily out of the corner of his eye. We pulled up at the curb in front of the school where several hundred students stood around casually scanning everyone as they arrived. He leaned over in full view of everyone, put his arms around me and kissed me on the cheek. "I love you," he said. "Will you be all right?" It was one of numerous instances that showed his capacity and willingness to love and extend himself in spite of all he had been through.

Because of the loss of his family in Vietnam, for the first year he was with us Dai watched over me like a mother hen. One night at the mall when Hamp and I decided to separate to look for what we needed, I asked Dai with whom he wanted to go. He thought a minute, then said, "Daddy can take care of himself," and fell in step with me.

"Wait a minute," I said, stopping suddenly. "Does this mean you love me and want to protect me, or you don't think I have enough sense to wander around the mall by myself?" I joked about it, but I knew his anxiety for me was rooted in the loss of his mother and family in Vietnam. Another day, after I had gone out to the mailbox and then upstairs to my bedroom, Dai came rushing up the stairs, anxiously calling me. When I answered and asked what was wrong, he said he had suddenly realized he had not seen me come in from the mailbox and was afraid something had happened to me. These were not isolated incidents. It was well over a year before he stopped having episodes of separation anxiety.

> JOURNAL: Lord, my children need to see Your power in me. They need to see Your love in my eyes, hear Your love in my words, and know that You will always be there for

them in me. Lord, I give you all the problems I see in every one of our lives. Please use Hampy and me to make the children feel loved and supported.

Although Dai was basically a normal boy, he had a keen sense of discernment that was very different from American boys. Asian people don't come right out with what they think as Americans do. In Vietnam even small children learn to read between the lines to understand what people mean and what they are really thinking. This had made Dai extremely wise about human nature, and I had noticed early in our relationship that he was usually very guarded about people's motives and intentions until he had been around them for a while. On the other hand, his lack of "education" by American television made him surprisingly innocent.

>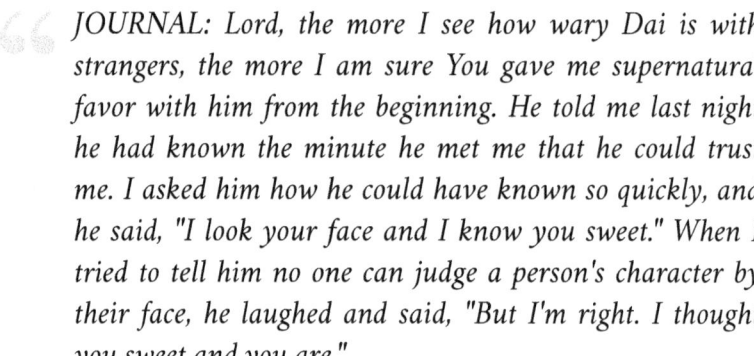
> JOURNAL: Lord, the more I see how wary Dai is with strangers, the more I am sure You gave me supernatural favor with him from the beginning. He told me last night he had known the minute he met me that he could trust me. I asked him how he could have known so quickly, and he said, "I look your face and I know you sweet." When I tried to tell him no one can judge a person's character by their face, he laughed and said, "But I'm right. I thought you sweet and you are."

Because his family thought he was coming to America soon, Dai stopped attending school in the third grade. His family lived in a village not far from Saigon, and even in Saigon for three years, trying to arrange to get the whole family out of Vietnam. The combination of poverty, bureaucracy, and a very different social structure from ours, allowed Dai to spend most of his childhood roaming his village, or Saigon, with other boys who didn't go to school. He worked to help his family build their new house out of wood and bamboo, and often spent all day looking for firewood for his mother. Sometimes he even loaded bananas to get money to help his family, but there was little work for grown men, much less for little boys. So he did what little boys the world over do best, he played.

He was very streetwise, as one would expect from a child accustomed to roaming free with other boys. But my expectations of having to teach him American middle class values were for naught. He surprised me constantly with his sense of honor and trustworthiness. Dai had been exposed to dishonesty, violence, and desperation that comes from extreme poverty and oppression from a Russian backed communist government. But his heart was tender toward the Lord and his fellow man. He stopped to help everyone he saw in need. He loved little children and was protective of women. He was uneducated, but he seemed to know the correct answer to every moral question. In the natural, this strength of character seemed to stem from three sources. The first was a devout Catholic mother who loved him, and a stepfather present in the home, who had given him the opportunity to learn love and a sense of responsibility. The other was the loving attention of an old Catholic priest, who had spent many hours with Dai instructing him in God's truths. "Even when I'm very small, I always want to be good," he commented to me one night.

It was a blessing to see traces of the innocence of childhood in Dai that all children share, and it was encouraging to see that honor and morality are the same in the hearts of all people. It was the difference between thinking and knowing. Dai's family spoke a different language and lived in a culture totally foreign to us, but I found that compassion, fairness and understanding of human feelings needed no common language in order to be shared. I once asked Dai if the love of Jesus coming from Christians felt the same in America as it had in Vietnam. He smiled and nodded. "Yes, it the very same."

Because he had a strong fear of forgetting things about home, for the first two years he was with us, Dai educated me about Vietnam. He seemed to be trying to hold on to his memories and at the same time explain to me what he had lost. He told me how babies in Vietnam loved to play outside in the dirt all day and how poor boys went to church wearing nothing but a pair of shorts, and neither God nor the priest minded a bit. He showed me how to make mangoes ripen by putting them in rice and told me how to tell when coffee beans were ripe. He showed me how to make a kite with bamboo, newspaper, and rice flour paste, and taught us to eat with chopsticks.

When he first came to live with us, I had hoped Dai would learn to feel at least a little American, because genetically he was. But his stories of Vietnam soon made me realize no matter how long a child lives, or where he goes, that place where he first felt love and security will always be home. He described games played with his friends, and beautiful fish they caught and put into old glass jars. He told of dangerous snakes he was too young to be afraid of. He laughed about eating until he was sick when giant mango trees were heavy with fruit, just waiting for little boys to eat until they couldn't eat any more. Equally happy childhood memories were of broken glass he cut his feet on, and rusty barbed wire. He looked for old shell casings from the war to sell for a few pennies, and swam in water so dirty that now he wouldn't touch it. He remembered sporadic electricity, no hot water, and soap that didn't seem to clean anything. He also remembered lice and poisonous spider bites so painful he couldn't sleep at night. Nevertheless, it all added up to the first place a child had known love. And I finally realized it didn't matter what else happened, or where he decided to live when he was grown. Dai was Vietnamese in his heart and he always would be.

The hardest thing for Dai and other Vietnamese refugee children to get used to in America was the "aloneness" in which we live. He had spent his early years surrounded by people: his seven brothers and sisters and mother and stepfather, his grandmother, and his neighbors, who considered everyone in their village as more-or-less family. Security to Dai was being with people all the time. He couldn't understand all the big empty houses mostly left vacant during the week, or that Americans stay inside their houses and hardly ever even sit outside and talk. Most of the children are in daycare now and aren't home to even play together after school. Security for a Vietnamese child was sleeping on a pallet with his brothers and sisters, and always being in earshot of other people talking. A nice room of his own with furniture just for him was very pleasant, and he expressed appreciation. But there was no comfort in it. He learned quickly the material wealth he had heard about in America was useless. It couldn't love you.

> JOURNAL: To be able to view my own culture through the eyes of a very intelligent, albeit ignorant teenager from a third-world country, is a tremendous blessing. Dai's insights cut right to the heart of the truth.

Before he even came to live with us, we had noticed that several times a day, a cloud would come over Dai and we knew he was thinking about his family. The pain on his face was terrible to see and I could only deal with it by looking away. Often we would miss him and find him asleep in his room and we soon realized this was the way he dealt with his pain and confusion. When it became unbearable, he went to sleep to block it out. The depth of Dai's profound feelings of loss became even more evident the first Easter he was with us, when he received a big packet of pictures and letters from his family. There was so much about his feelings and inability to express himself I still didn't understand, I misread him completely.

We had all looked at the pictures from his family and Dai had told us the news from Vietnam and I thought everything was fine. When he came and asked me to take him to the mall several hours later, I was ironing and said I was busy and it was too late to go to the mall. Again he urged me to please take him to the mall.

"I want to go the mall. I can't stand to stay here anymore. I am always unhappy here," he said miserably.

"What? You are always unhappy here?" I demanded, offended. We had done everything we could possibly do to make this boy happy, and now he was telling me he was always unhappy in our home. "Well, I guess we have really made a big mistake!" I stormed out the front door. I needed to walk off my anger before I talked to him anymore. I walked rapidly for a few minutes, then realized I should be praying instead of thinking. I had no idea what to do. Dai had said he was always unhappy with us. I assumed that meant he had tried hard to like living with us, but he just wasn't happy. I jumped to the conclusion that he had decided he didn't love us after all, and was so unhappy he wanted to leave.

"Lord, please let me understand what is happening. Let me see this from Dai's point of view." I prayed out loud. Immediately, the Lord reminded me of the pictures from his family. That was it. Dai had not known the right words to express what he was feeling. The pictures had made him long for his family and he wanted to go the mall and play video games to distract himself from his homesickness. He didn't mean he was always unhappy in our home; he meant he was so unhappy right then, that nothing he did at home made him feel better.

"I am so stupid," I said as I turned around and started back.

I went upstairs to Dai's room, but there was no light coming from under the door. He was lying in bed face down in the dark even though it was only 7:00 at night. I sat on the side of the bed.

"Dai, were you trying to tell me the pictures from home made you unhappy? Is that why you wanted to go the mall?"

"Yes," he said softly.

"Honey, is it like this? Did you think you could love me and have a home in America, and maybe things wouldn't be too bad; but then you saw your real mother and your family, and you knew you didn't really love me and you felt if you didn't have them, you didn't have anything?"

"No, I always love you," he said, his voice muffled by the pillow. "I don't know word to tell you anything, but I love you."

What terrible pain and frustration to have to deal with at fifteen, I thought. The only family he had ever known or wanted was on the other side of the world. The pictures had shown his parents and siblings getting older, changing, and so was he. Time was passing in Vietnam without him. How could he ever get back what he had lost? Where did my family and I fit into his life? How could he belong in our family, and if he did, where did that leave his love and commitment to his birth family? How could a person have two mothers—two families? As if his pain and confusion weren't enough to deal with, his English was not good enough for him to be sure he could say what he meant if he tried to share it with me. He had already made me angry by trying to tell me how he felt.

I had believed since I met Dai that he needed to cry for his family. He had told me he almost never cried, because his mother had told him not to cry when he was getting on the plane to leave. It seemed the only thing he could do to please her now, so he tried hard never to cry. I had attempted to coax him to cry several times before, when he talked about his family, but he always stopped himself before the tears came. This time I knew Dai had to cry. The intensity of his pain and confusion were too overwhelming to keep inside.

I began to talk about mothers and children, and how I thought I would feel in his place, and what would worry me, if my mother was far away. I felt cruel saying things I knew would focus him on his pain, but I was convinced he needed the relief that only tears could bring. Finally, he had all he could take. He began to sob. I lay down beside him and put my arms around him. I couldn't give him back his family, or take away his pain, but I was willing to be his mother for as long as he wanted, and I loved him dearly. I prayed that counted for something.

> *JOURNAL: Lord, I see what a tool of Satan worry is. When I see Dai downcast and worried about his family, I know he feels compelled to worry because it is all he can do for them. When I tell him his worry does no good and only makes him unhappy, he acknowledges that I am right, but emotionally he still feels driven to it. Jesus specifically said not to worry. In Matthew 6:27 He said we can't add an hour to the span of our life or a cubit to our height by worrying. He went on to say not to be anxious for tomorrow, and Paul said in Philippians 4:6 to "be anxious for nothing, but in everything with prayer and thanksgiving let your requests be made known to God." I know Satan wants us to worry because it is sin and because it is harmful to us. Worry keeps us from bearing fruit for You, it robs us of our joy and can ultimately damage our spiritual and physical health.*
>
> *Lord, please give Dai the grace not to worry about his family, but to pray for them when he is tempted to worry. Help us to find ways we can be of tangible help to his family.*

> *JOURNAL: The girls are angry that You, let me suffer pain for caring for Your babies. Doctors have found that being deprived of deep sleep is a major element in fibromyalgia and everyone thinks You should heal me since I probably wouldn't have the pain if I had not lost so much sleep for so many years. They don't understand the principle of suffering. As Peter and John felt in Acts 5:41, I count it a privilege to suffer if it is what You ordain. It is better to suffer for serving You than to suffer for seeking my own pleasure. Twelve years later, I know that I inherited a gene that was just waiting to give me fibromyalgia. My mother and her mother both had it. The doctors just didn't know what was wrong with them. The*

pain I suffer now, is much worse, but I believe if I had not taken the babies, I would have felt such frustration and stress by feeling useless to the Lord, I still would be as sick as I am now. I feel more than ever that the scripture above holds true for me and for anyone else who finds their body damaged from serving the Lord. I haven't been stoned or whipped or beaten or imprisoned, and I know that many others suffer everyday much more than I, because they belong to Jesus.

Because Laura had had bouts with strep infections for years, four months after Dai came to live with us, we decided she needed her tonsils removed.

Laura and I got up very early that morning to go to the hospital, and went through all of the paper and blood work preliminary to surgery. I knew something bad was wrong when after the lab tests had been done, the doctor called me out the nurses' station. It's her heart or she's pregnant, I kept thinking as I walked toward him.

"I can't operate on your daughter today. Her blood work shows that she is pregnant," he said bluntly. I sank into a nearby chair to keep from falling. I asked him to call my friend, Beverly McMillan, who was an ob-gyn, and arrange for her to see Laura as soon as possible.

Hamp and Stacey joined us at the hospital and together we went straight to Beverly's office. On the way I thought about the conversations I had had with Laura and Pat about God's good plans for their lives and how his rules about our conduct support that plan. I shook my head as I remembered the concern Hamp and I had felt about this happening, despite Laura and Pat's assurances they weren't doing anything.

Dai's graduation. (L to R: Hamp, Dai, Dai's sister, Kim, & me (Carlene))

By the time we arrived at Bev's office I was shaking uncontrollably and was relieved to see my dear friend, Pat Beasley, Beverly's nurse, beckoning from a private entrance to the office, so I wouldn't have to sit with people staring at me, knowing from Laura's and my eyes red and swollen from crying, that she was pregnant and unmarried. Pat had been a close friend since her days as a social worker at Catholic Charities.

I tried to talk to Pat, but I could only cry. She wrapped me in a blanket and put me in a quiet room in a recliner, promising to come back as soon as she took Laura for a sonogram to confirm or deny her pregnancy. It was only a formality. I knew the blood test wasn't wrong.

Because Beverly and her associates were all Christians, there were framed scriptures on almost every wall, but my eyes were too blurred by tears to read them. I couldn't seem to stop crying and gather my thoughts to consider what this meant for Laura's future, what affect it would have on our family, or what people would think of us. Our whole family had been active in the pro-life movement in Jackson, and we were well-known in the Christian community. What on earth would people think about our not being able to keep our own child from getting pregnant before she was married.

When I leaned back to try to relax my neck, I looked up and saw there was one scripture close enough for me to read. It said, "Fear only the Lord, and serve Him in truth with all your heart; for consider what wonderful things He has done for you." (I Samuel 12:24). After I had read it through twice, a peace settled over me. I knew the Lord had put it there for me. I was not to fear what people would think about our witness for the Lord. I was to be truthful about what had happened. The Lord had done wonderful things for us, and I knew He had known this was coming, and He could handle it.

> *JOURNAL: I have lost Ben, I have a teenager whose language I can't speak, we have moved to a rental house, I have no foster baby, which has often been a comfort to me spiritually, and my seventeen- year-old daughter is pregnant. I feel totally empty. I feel cut off from the One who kept me through whatever came. The constant pain in my neck even prevents me from reading and studying my Bible. I can only sit for a few minutes before the pain forces me to be up and moving. Lord, how can I ever study Your Word again?*

> *JOURNAL: Lord, call me forth from the grave. My enemy has wrapped me in grave clothes and would seal me away in a tomb and make me believe that I am dead. But, there is no death where You are. There can only be the illusion of death. Where You are there is light and strength and life.*

> *JOURNAL: I am so disappointed in myself. People around me talk about setting goals, but my only goal is You. Over and over I have to crawl back to You. I know You will never let me go because of the precious blood of my Savior.*

> *I know You are putting me through the fire and I hate it and reject it as much as ever. I am so disappointed in my soul. How pushy it is. How hard it fights for its own way.*

> *JOURNAL: Lord, I have heard two stories this month about mothers who were ardently pro-life until their child was pregnant. When it happened to them, their commitment to Your word and Your love of the innocent unborn went out the window and they took their children to abortionists. How can this be, Lord? What kind of faith dissolves in the face of an unexpected pregnancy? I don't want to be condemning, but I can't help thinking of the scripture in Isaiah that says "...this people draw near with their words and honor Me with their lips, but they remove their hearts far from Me and their reverence for Me consists of tradition learned by rote." (Isaiah 29:13) What could I say to You if I had even thought of sanctioning the abortion of my own daughter's baby? How could I ever look toward Heaven again? Thank you, Lord, that killing the baby never crossed any of our minds.*

When we finally moved into our new house, Stacey was temporarily at home before taking a job in Louisiana, Laura was at home awaiting the birth of her baby, and John was in college, coming home on the weekends. Dai and Laura were the only "full time" children at home.

> *JOURNAL: Lord, I feel such anxiety and at the same time such peace. It's contradictory, but they are the only words I know to describe how I feel. I fear what might touch or hurt my family, my daughter, or her baby, but I feel peace in the assurance that my loving Father is in control... somewhere...somehow.*

Because of the nature of the situation, and because my own children are not the primary focus of the book, I will not go into great detail about Laura's pregnancy, except to say she grew up in a hurry and because she was so tiny, she had an extremely uncomfortable pregnancy, which she bore without a word of complaint. In early November she gave birth to a beautiful, healthy little girl she named Katelyn. It was not the way we would have chosen for our daughter to become a mother, but the Lord has been true to His word and has brought good from it, not the least of which is our precious granddaughter. Our friends and our church were wonderful and supportive of all of us and fulfilled their scriptural responsibilities for restoration and love. Laura chose not to marry Pat, but his daughter has his name and he is involved in her life and he pays child support.

> *JOURNAL: The rest He has for me is Sabbath rest: thinking His thoughts, speaking His words, turning away from my own pleasure (Isaiah 58:13). What pleasure would You have me turn away from, Father? Surely not the pleasure of communing with You, and when I commune with You it becomes my greatest pleasure. Turning my foot from my own pleasure puts me into Sabbath rest, the best place a human can be. It means, "Let Me be your pleasure, let me give you the pleasure only I can give." This is too easy! Surely it must be harder than this. I always saw Isaiah 58 as a discipline, something I had to work at. Not as a gift from You! How amazing this is. I have never grasped Your love like this. All the promises in the Bible center on our being in fellowship and communion with You. No wonder we don't see the miracles You promised. We stay in our flesh and beg You for the products of Your communion. I used to be so lost in You in prayer, I would lose awareness of where I was, when I walked and prayed. I had forgotten that.*

> JOURNAL: Lord, as an American, I was taught to value my right to speak my mind about everything, but I never thought of silence as a right. Asians value the right to be silent. They value the right to keep their thoughts to themselves unless they choose to reveal them. There is a power in that I had never realized. I have actually found quietness to be quite restful and have discovered I usually speak many more words than necessary.

Dai's problems with the girls had decreased over a period of months, (due largely to his Asian ability to keep his mouth shut) and slowly my second-hand prediction about becoming a family came true. We began to have shared history. Dai had shared our six uncomfortable months in the rental house, he was there through Laura's pregnancy and he was the only person in the family who remembered which cable TV company we had used before we moved. Little things had begun to add up to make him part of the family. He had continued to try to be a good brother. He offered to lend the girls money, shared everything he had and was a devoted uncle to Katelyn after she was born. "Dai" was the first word Katelyn said on purpose. The girls' appreciation of Dai grew until finally we saw true evidence of love.

One day at the mall, I overheard some of Laura's friends asking her who Dai was after they had seen them together.

"That was my little brother," she said with a smile. "You don't have a little brother!" one of the girls said.

"I do so! He's adopted," Laura told her. It had happened just as Kathy had assured me and I had assured Dai. He had become their brother.

> JOURNAL: Lord, I am so impressed with Dai's dignity and strength. He has come into a family that was already complete and found a place for himself in it. He has changed schools twice, joined a new soccer team, gone to a

new church, and even though I know he still feels out of place in our culture, he faces each new situation with a quiet strength I find very admirable.

The Lord has given us a unique blessing by bringing Dai into our family. Through him we have been able to experience things we never could have otherwise.

I used to be able to look at pictures of children in third-world countries playing in the dirt, poorly dressed, ill-fed, sick, and see a "condition." Now I see an individual child with a heart and a soul, with desires and dreams, hopes and fears; I see Dai. Now instead of sighing and turning the page, my eyes fill with tears. I know now as I never could have if not for Dai, that the language and customs which make people seem so different from me are only behavior they have learned from the people around them. They are still people exactly like Stacey, John, Laura, like Dai, like Hamp and me and our parents before us.

The Lord has brought me a third-world child who has learned to speak my language so he can tell me what he thinks and feels, and I realize that before he could speak English, he still thought and felt the same things; he just spoke them in Vietnamese. How alike we all are underneath our culture. How wonderful that the more Christ grows in our hearts, the more alike Christians become, because we are all being conformed to the same image—Jesus. He tears down all the cultural walls we thought were so strong and impenetrable. Acceptance, encouragement, understanding, even salvation, don't require that we know or agree with the customs or culture of the other person.

When Dai came to us, his older sister Kim visited over holidays and school vacations, more and more often. Since she had been living at college and had no foster family, it was natural she should come to visit her brother in our home. But it was the gift of God to us all that she has become like a member of the family. Our relationship with her has brought about several things I never expected. One is that God has given Kim a family in America that loves her very much. Another is that our children have a sister they didn't expect. We all think of Kim as one of the daughters of the family. But the most unexpected result of my relationship with Kim has been a close relationship not only with her, but with their mother in Vietnam. It sounds strange to say that I am close to a woman on the other side of the world whom I have never met, except through letters that must pass through two translators. But Dai and Kim's mother has become my friend. With so much potential for mistrust and misunderstanding, I know that only the Lord could cause two women to be able to share two children and to respect and value each other, and to pray for each other as sisters.

I have learned through Dai's experience in our home that a person can be a total stranger and an outsider in his physical surroundings and still be "at home" with himself and Jesus. This is a great comfort to me, having always feared being totally alone.

I have also learned from Dai's experiences in our family that if one allows time for relationships to slowly take root, they will. So often people run away, because a situation isn't immediately comfortable. Dai did his part to build trust and acceptance, and hopefully waited for his relationships with the family to grow, and they did.

I praise the Lord that He can bring love from anywhere. I have a son from a place I have never seen, sent from a family I don't know. A boy He caused to open his heart to me and love me when he couldn't even understand most of what I said. I praise Him too for my family. They opened their hearts to Dai at first, then rode out the rough times with him until You had made us into a family. Not every "only son" would receive a boy just a few years younger into his family with open arms as John did. Not all daughters would have been so willing to move over and make room for another teenager in the family as Stacey and Laura did. There were fireworks for a while, but once they all understood each other's personalities, they got along better than most natural siblings, and it happened because they were all willing to share a home and parents and love, and they were willing to do that because of Your Holy Spirit within them.

> JOURNAL: Lord, even with the muscle relaxers, when I wake in the morning I can hardly get out of bed. How can I ever take another baby? I don't want this pain to control me, but I don't see how I could physically hold up under the pain and loss of sleep with another baby. If I am doing something to make it worse, please show me what it is.

When Dai had been with us for over a year and Katelyn was three weeks old, we were finally called about a foster baby. I had commented to Dai that he didn't know what our home was really like because we had not had a baby the whole time he had been with us. The social worker was calling from the Mississippi Gulf Coast area and knew nothing about us. She had been given my name as a possible foster mother for an eight-month-old Vietnamese baby girl who had lung problems. Her parents had tried to care for her, but the language barrier and high tech equipment needed to care for her were more than they could handle. Plus, they had three other small children. When the social worker told me the baby was Vietnamese, I started laughing because it was so like the Lord, to bring us a Vietnamese baby for Dai.

How sweet of the Lord, I thought, to leave us without a baby until Dai was settled in the family, then bring a Vietnamese baby for his first experience with a foster baby. How good too, to bring such a specific type of baby to let me know our ministry wasn't over in spite of the pain in my muscles. The fact that we had never been asked to take a Vietnamese baby made us feel she had to be for us and our prayer about her was along the lines of "Lord, if we aren't supposed to take this baby, please stop us," and, of course, He didn't.

JOURNAL: Lord, don't let me be like the girl in the Song of Solomon (Song of Solomon 5:3). She washed her feet and went to bed and when her beloved knocked on her door wanting her to get up and let Him in, she was torn between her love for Him and her clean feet. She said in essence, "I'll get my feet dirty if I get up again. It's too late, I'm comfortable now, I can't get up to let You in." Lord, don't let me refuse Your desire for me because I have achieved a degree of physical comfort and it is too great a temptation just not to get up and let You in. Please don't let me wash my feet and lie down until my bed is a casket.

11

THUY

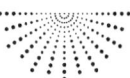

The baby's name was Thuy. The Vietnamese use only about a hundred names, so her name was as common in the Vietnamese community as Elizabeth or Ann in America. And she was the only baby we never called by a scriptural name at all. We gave her the scriptural name Miriam, but didn't use it because she was already hearing two distinct languages and we didn't want to confuse her even more. Of course we nicknamed her "Thuytee Bird."

I knew Thuy would be terribly set back in her language skills by hearing Vietnamese, then English then Vietnamese again, so I prepared myself to mother her by asking Dai to write down in Vietnamese some phrases I often say to babies. I thought if I said some of the same things her mother said to her, she might not be totally

Dai and Thuy were perfect for each other.

confused by everything she heard when she went back home. When I practiced repeating the phrases he had written for me in Vietnamese, Dai chuckled at my pronunciation and said, "I don't think this baby know you speak Vietnamese to her, Mom."

When Thuy arrived at our home, Katelyn was one month old, and even though Thuy was seven months older, they were almost the same size. Thuy was small and thin compared to American babies, but not much below average for a Vietnamese child. She was pale and had to be on oxygen 24 hours a day. She received the same breathing treatments as John Mark and Ben. Except for her fine black hair which stood straight up on her head, she looked like a little Chinese doll.

Like most of the babies, she was listless for the first several days, but gradually began to respond to us, especially Dai. Like other sick babies she liked to sleep on someone's chest, so she spent hours sleeping on top of Dai while he lay on the couch watching TV. Thuy was the perfect baby for Dai to learn about foster babies. She was not brain-damaged, she was a happy, alert baby and she even looked like the babies he was used to. He had younger brothers and sisters in Vietnam, but he had never even held a baby as small as both the babies were when Thuy came to us, but he took to it amazingly.

> JOURNAL: I know wonderful truth! The natural conditions of life are totally unable to alter what the Holy Spirit is doing in the spiritual realm. A natural pain or trouble in no way affects what He is doing at that moment. The power continues to flow no matter what happens around you, unless you shut yourself off by putting the natural between yourself and God.

Having two babies in the house this time was much easier than when we had Ben and Daniel, because Katelyn was a normal baby and Thuy only had respiratory problems. Also, Katelyn had her own very skillful mother to take care of her and was no inconvenience to me at all. It goes without saying Laura needed no oversight when handling a baby. It was noisy once in a while when both babies were crying but having experienced Ben and Daniel together, Laura and I hardly noticed.

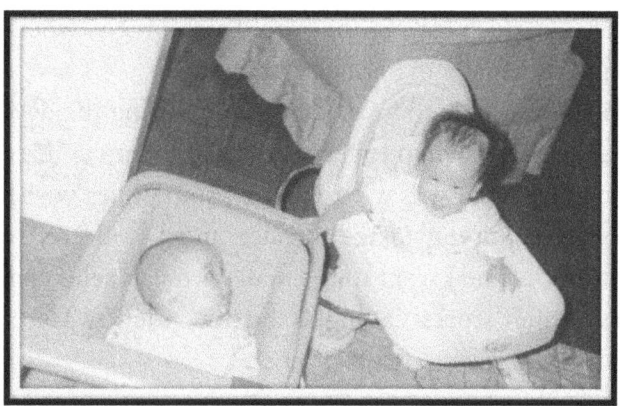

Oh boy! Katelyn's here. Thuy and Katelyn had great fun together.

Before long Thuy was strong enough to crawl over to Katelyn's infant seat to pat her or give her a toy, and as Katelyn grew they enjoyed playing together immensely. So much so, I couldn't help thinking what happy sisters they would be if allowed to grow up together.

> *JOURNAL: Lord, my neck hurts, but not as it did. It has improved greatly since we took Thuy. Even the stiffness and aching in the secondary muscles is better. I take this as grace from You to continue with your babies. Please help me stick with the exercise program I am on to control the pain, and bless it to my body.*

Dai often played with Thuy and she adored him. He let her play in his room while he studied, and lie on his bed with him while he played basketball with a miniature ball and a hoop over his door. Thuy would lie on Dai's bed watching him throw the ball until the hypnotic repetition put her to sleep. When she was older, and Dai baby sat for us, he would pick her up and head for his room as we were leaving, saying, "Thuy, don't you want to watch Dai throw the ball?"

"She always sleep for me," he would say smugly, when we came home. She was usually in her bed fast asleep.

When she was able to be off of oxygen during the day, I started taking her with me when I went shopping or to run errands. Her exotic looks drew crowds everywhere. I sometimes wished I could just take her shopping in the stroller and be allowed to simply shop. But every time I went to the mall with her, sales clerks ran to the doors of their stores, calling to the other clerks, "Here is Thuy!" So they all could rush to play with her.

> JOURNAL: *The sacrifice of His death was hard for Jesus to face (Hebrews 5:7,) but the loss of all worldly things brought unspeakable glory and joy for Him. It put him back where He belonged, with the Father. Oh Lord, give me a sacrificial spirit to give up what profits me nothing, that I may draw near to You.*

Thuy's time with us was uneventful in terms of dealing with problems. She made good progress and was a happy, almost healthy baby. She was seldom sick, and by the end of the eight months we had her, she was standing up, preparing to walk. By early spring, she was off her oxygen and ready to go home.

I called the social worker and suggested she have Thuy's parents come to our house for a weekend to get reacquainted with her and to learn how to care for her. Of course such an ideal situation would have been impossible if the Lord had not provided Dai to translate.

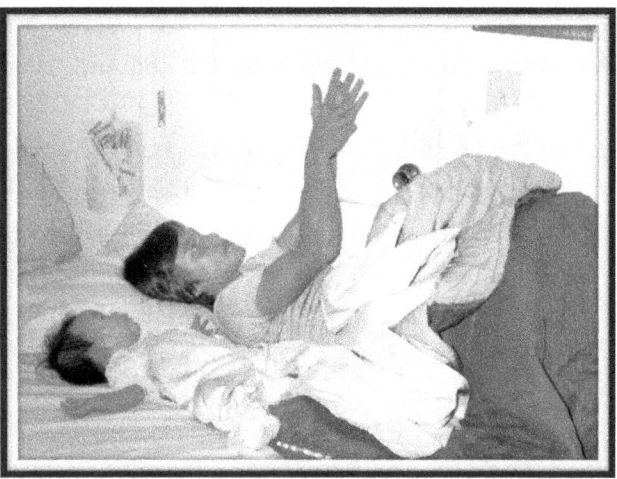

| Dai throwing the ball up to put Thuy to sleep.

As I made plans for Thuy's parents to be houseguests for three days, I had a nagging worry in the back of my mind. Some reports of social workers and nurses had noted her mother was extremely hostile and difficult to deal with. One nurse even reported that on one occasion she had thought Thuy's mother was going to hit her. Never having dealt with a Vietnamese mother before, I couldn't imagine what might cause her to be so belligerent, and I was afraid she might view me with the same hostility. She sounded like a person with a very unpleasant personality, but as there was no other way to prepare them to take Thuy home. We felt we had to give it our best effort.

> *JOURNAL: Lord, You know my frame, that I am dust, and You know how cluttered my mind is with childish things. I desire to be a child on whom You look and say, "Well, she's not very bright, but oh how she loves Me!"*

The weekend Thuy's parents were to arrive, Dai's friend Ugyen (Win) was spending the weekend with us. I had two boys to translate for me, which was helpful, but it also added another person to the household who was speaking a language I didn't understand. As a general rule, it didn't bother me for Dai and a Vietnamese friend to speak Vietnamese in front of me. Dai had asked me soon after he came to live with us if it bothered me. I had said, "No, as long as you don't point at me and laugh, while you are doing it."

"Mom, you know we never do that to you," he said with a smile.

But this weekend, I found it very stressful to be surrounded by so many people who were very possibly talking about me in a language I didn't understand. I suppose it was a little taste of what Dai had experienced when he began to visit us.

> *JOURNAL: Looking back in prayer journal A, I saw that I had written, "The Lord doesn't want us to work for Him, but to pray and spend time and prayer and praise, and then He will cause us to do things and cause things to happen in our lives that will bless Him and other people.*

When I finally met Thuy's parents, I was surprised to find her tiny mother a perfect beauty, who greeted me with a big smile, as if she was genuinely glad to meet me. Her husband was small also, and they, like Thuy, looked very Chinese to me. They were polite and cooperative and never stopped smiling. Yes, I knew Asian people smile no matter what they are thinking, but it made me feel better all the same. It was a relief to all of us that Thuy obviously remembered her parents and was happy to see them. But it was nerve-racking to need to get one of the boys to tell her parents everything I wanted to say to them, and vice versa. Interestingly, for a great deal of our communication, I found Thuy's mother and I shared a common maternal wavelength. We each seemed to know intuitively what the other was saying about the baby. The mother asked to bathe her the first afternoon they were here. I knew she wanted a chance to undress her baby and look her over for signs of neglect or abuse before she got too friendly with me. I was glad to provide the baby tub and towels, and pretended not to notice her careful scrutiny of her child as she bathed Thuy on the kitchen counter. Her concern increased my confidence in her as a mother.

> *JOURNAL: Lord, show me today when I put anything between You and me. Don't allow me to put up a veil, partition, and then wall between us. Stop me when it is a hint of a vapor, and let the pure light of Your power and love be unhindered in my life.*

The second day Thuy's parents were with us they disappeared, taking Ugyen with them! We had no idea where they had gone. This is a Vietnamese cultural trait that always unnerved me. Because there was almost nowhere to go, and they were almost always on foot, people in Vietnam thought nothing of leaving without telling anyone where they were going or when they would be back. They didn't realize Americans think this is odd and rude behavior. Dai had learned quickly in our family that comings and goings were expected to be done within certain time frames. They were gone for over two hours, and we had just decided they must have gotten lost, when they returned with a beautiful pot plant wrapped with colored foil and tied up with a bow.

It was a gift to us for caring for their child, but they never said that. They just put it in the center of the kitchen table without a word. I admired it and complimented them on their choice, but wasn't sure what it was for. When I moved it to another table, Thuy's father moved it back to the center of the kitchen table.

I finally whispered to Dai, "Is that flower supposed to be for us?"

Dai slowly shook his head with a perplexed smile, "I have no idea," he whispered back.

"Well, can't you just ask them?" I said.

"No, I don't think so," was his answer. "That would be rude."

I could feel myself slipping into culture shock. After two days of hearing almost no words I understood except brief conversations with Hampy and Dai, trying to give Thuy's parents enough liberty with her not to offend them, and at the same time preserve a semblance of her usual routine, I felt ready to self-destruct.

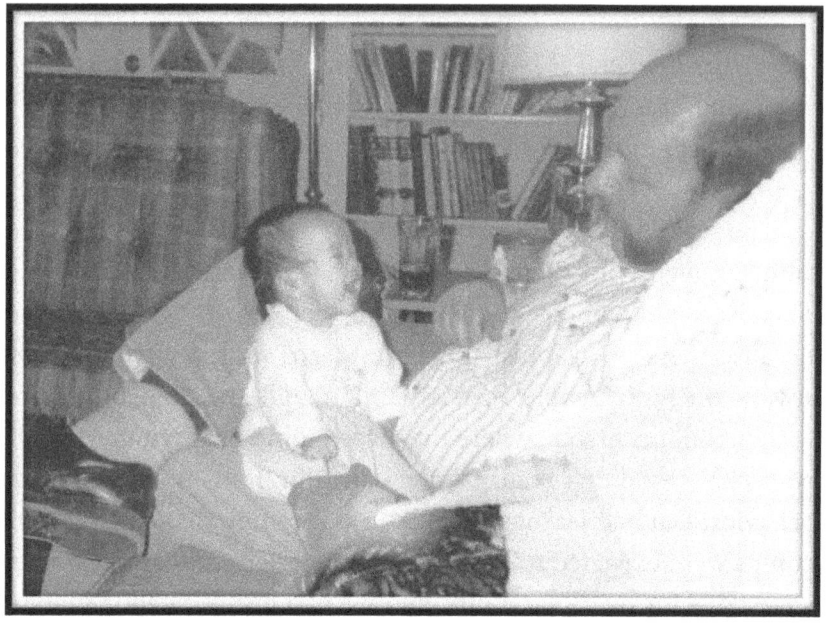

Thuy having a laugh with Daddy.

I knew it was a difficult situation for Thuy's parents too, and when it was finally time for them to leave, they looked as relieved as I felt. Of course it was hard for them to go, because they had to leave their baby, knowing it would be at least a month before we took her home to them. The social workers had told us it would take a month or more for the paperwork to be done to give her parents custody again.

While both of them had tears in their eyes when they first saw Thuy, her father now seemed to make a great effort to be strong for his wife. He hugged and kissed Thuy for a long time, then handed her to her mother. She squeezed her and kissed her quickly on the cheek as if afraid she might not be able to let go of her if she held her longer. As she gave me her child, Thuy's mother looked at me and a depth of understanding passed from her to me, which I had never experienced before. It circumvented the mind and went straight to the heart. We each knew exactly how the other felt. "I'll take good care of her, she will be fine," I said, knowing she didn't understand my words. As she looked into my eyes Thuy's mother nodded her head. She didn't understand the words, but she was confident she understood me.

> *JOURNAL: Lord, Thuy's mother was so unlike what I expected. She was cute and sweet and gentle. I like her very much. There was no trace of hostility or resentment toward us, even though her child had been removed from her care and given to us. It is clear to me now, her hostility and anger toward the nurses was due to culture shock, postpartum stress and fear for her baby's life. Of course, she was frustrated and angry. She knew her baby was sick enough to die, and everyone was telling her that her child needed things she didn't understand and couldn't give. Everything in America was so strange to her. In Vietnam, she was on solid ground as a mother, but here everything was frightening and foreign. She must have felt so very vulnerable. Lord, how insensitive we can be to the pain and fear of others. The Americans around her were offended by what they saw as her lack of cooperation and resentment of their help, because they didn't have empathy for what she was feeling.*

> *JOURNAL: Lord, I see that duty is something you feel obligated to do. It is something you can accomplish without any feeling of the heart, but motivation by love is totally different. How much further we are willing to go, how much longer we are willing to endure, how much less thanks we think we deserve if we act out of true agape love.*

Love runs with arms outstretched, while duty walks determined, and stoic. Christians can serve out of duty, and make the recipient feel unworthy and burdensome, but love makes the recipient feel worthwhile and valued. Lord, please let me serve with a loving heart.

of the black women in America, and I know what they are when their lives begin. I know they are beautiful and happy, wide eyed innocents. Their hearts are open and loving, ready to meet the world with a smile, until the day someone tells them who they are; until the shock and pain of unjust rejection begins to harden and embitter their hearts. God have mercy on a society that blights the hearts of its own children.

It was evident very early James had a great need for concerned parents and a live-in big brother. He had many abnormalities and insecurities. He had mild cerebral palsy and presented many early symptoms of brain damage. He didn't reach for toys, didn't respond to our attempts to communicate with him and constantly looked at his hands. For months he simply lay where we put him and looked at his hands, which he held right in front of his nose, as if there was nothing else in the world. He took no notice of anything around him unless he was put in a position which frightened him; then he would react with anxious crying. He became very upset if he was held facing away from the person holding him, and always wanted to be held with his face close to ours. For a long time, the only way to calm him if he was particularly agitated, was to put our cheek against his as we talked to him. I felt sure this worked because he could feel our skin and hear and feel the vibrations of our voice right next to his ear. This was one of the "tells" which concerned me the most. Normal babies don't need so many reinforcements of contact or comfort. He cried for hours every afternoon and evening the first few months, and he was so tense and slept so lightly it was impossible to switch on a light or open a door without him jumping or flinging himself onto his back in terror. Both responses were followed by frantic screaming.

JAMES'S EYES WERE BADLY CROSSED, AND WHILE IT SURELY AFFECTED his vision and was not something to be pleased about, we at least had the satisfaction of knowing we could have that corrected when he got to be eight months old. As soon as he had attained the awaited age, we went to the pediatric eye doctor. It was then we discovered something we had not considered, because he had so many strange behaviors.

"This is probably the most near sighted baby I have ever seen!" the eye doctor said, looking into one of his eyes.

My mind took off: This was why he looked at his hands so much. He could get them to his face and see them. This was why he wanted to be facing us when held. He couldn't see enough to make anything out when we held him facing a room, or worse, the out of doors. This was the reason he showed no interest in toys or his mobile—he couldn't see them clearly enough to want to touch them.

While this diagnosis complicated everything, it also gave us hope. Hope that many of his abnormal behaviors were not from brain damage per se, but from the fact that he was almost blind. From then on, we had to consider each new inability both ways. Was it his eyes, or was it his brain?

THE DAY FOR EYE SURGERY WAS ONE OF GREAT EXCITEMENT FOR US. Everything went perfectly. Then there was the healing period and examination for glasses. Finally, the day came when I could go get his glasses and put them on him. I was so excited. I couldn't wait to see his face when the world came into focus! I was even ready for him to be afraid at first.

I put him in his car seat, left the door wide open with the window down, so he could see the leaves on the tree I had parked under on purpose, moving in the breeze. He could see the other cars in the parking lot, the red color of my car, and me, clearly for the first time. I put the thick little glasses on his face. Breathless, I watched for a reaction. James looked around him in apparent amazement, didn't like what he saw, grabbed the glasses and threw them into the front seat. There aren't a lot of days for foster mothers to cheer and do a victory dance, but I had been anticipating one for months. I just stared at him in disbelief. I remembered how surprised I had been when I first saw the leaves on trees in the fifth grade. I was so disappointed in James's reaction, my eyes filled with tears for a moment.

Driving home with James's world as foggy as it had been before, I decided he would have to get used to seeing the world by degrees. I was sure he would quickly realize his brain was showing him wonderful things to be touched, and played with, and the faces of those whose voices he had learned to depend on.

FOR ENDLESS MONTHS, JAMES SEEMED TO MAKE ALMOST NO progress. His glasses were of no use because he wouldn't wear them. He snatched them off and tried to twist and break them each time I put them on. Then he would throw them as far as he could. He broke them several times. He was also resistant to baby food, and would hold his tongue out, leaning over the tray of the high chair until the food finally just slid off. Of course he didn't have this aversion to pieces of wood, clumps of dirt and dead bugs. The therapists decided he had a sensory aversion in his mouth, and most foods just didn't feel right. He was over a year old before I convinced him baby cereal was food, and belonged in his mouth. At two and a half he would only eat a few soft foods, rejecting anything with a strong taste, texture, or anything that required chewing. He did make one mysterious exception—he would eat crackers. The fact that he wouldn't chew was even more frustrating for me because he had been teething since he was six months old, and had a mouthful of teeth.

For more than a year, James seemed to have no interest outside of his hands, but he had graduated to feeling things with his fingers.

He seemed not to like the sensation of something touching the palm of his hand, but he did start using his fingers to flick things back and forth for hours. He often lay in his crib or play pen looking at his hands or flicking a moving part of a toy, happy it seemed, to be left alone, content to have no other stimulation, sometimes for several hours.

The family comes full circle. Katelyn, Laura's daughter kissing little James while John is holding him.

God did give us one great encouragement during that frustrating first year. James had one asset which seemed to deny all the dire expectations his symptoms suggested. It was his capacity for laughter! Even when he was very young, he laughed a wonderful, infectious laugh if someone tickled him. And to hear James laugh, was to know there had to be a little person somewhere in there, with more intelligence than he showed. His laughter was a strange contradiction to all of his withdrawn, disconnected behavior.

When he had been with us for a year, and still woke at every sound, we took James out of our room and put his bed upstairs in the room just above ours. Dai's room was next to ours, so there was no one upstairs to bother him, unless some of the other children were at home for some reason. James's sleep and mine both improved dramatically with the move upstairs, and I hoped my fibromyalgia would improve, but it didn't. I was a little worried about not hearing him when he awoke, but James took care of that by kicking his feet against the mattress of his baby bed as hard as he could. It sounded like cannons going off over our heads. It was so loud I put blankets under the mattress to try to muffle the sound. By the time he outgrew his kicking, I had found one of our baby monitors misplaced in our moving, and used that to keep tabs on him.

> JOURNAL: What a joy to know there is nothing of my pitiful flesh in what You have done for Your babies, and yet some sadness too, that I have nothing to offer You. You are all that is worthwhile and good in me.

When he was about fourteen months old, something seemed to click in James's brain and he began to make progress. He finally started to crawl, after months of my crawling on my knees and one hand, holding him in a crawling position with my other arm. Beth even came out of retirement to assist with this skill by playing with James and making him crawl. For a long time whenever he scooted or rolled over to her, she would growl him a warning and move away. She was eleven now, and too old for baby foolishness. Then one day I heard James screaming with laughter and Beth barking a high pitched bark. He had apparently caught her in a good mood, and she was running and bouncing around him while he chased her laughing. When he was laughing too hard to crawl, he threw himself on his back and just lay there laughing like a completely normal child.

Playing with Beth and crawling were not the only changes that came around that time. He started to prefer Dai and me much more than other people. And instead of receiving hugs and kisses passively, he started to bury his face against our necks and squeeze us tightly; often putting his lips to our cheek when asked for a kiss. He began crawling over to me as I sat at my desk and holding up his arms to be picked up and cuddled. I had never expected to see these things because he was so violently opposed to so many other things, and autistic children often are unable to form attachments or show affection. I believe it was the Lord who gave him feelings of love and relationship. When he was adept at crawling and had access to the lower level of the house, we discovered James understood the meanings of many more words and phrases than we had thought. He loved to push the button to turn on the TV in the living room, even though he knew it was not allowed; likewise banging the rocking chair against the wall in the den. When he did something not allowed, and we asked him to stop, he would either obey us immediately or turn his head to look at us out of the corner of his eye, as if to say, "Excuse me? Are you talking to me?" If his refusal to obey resulted in discipline, he would often throw himself on the floor and cry, stopping completely to look at us every few seconds to see if we were sufficiently impressed with his distress. This was clearly acting in relationship.

"Congratulations, James," Hamp said calmly, looking over the side of his newspaper. "Manipulation is a clear sign of intelligence."

If I took James by his shoulders and slid him away from the cabinet, he often swatted me on the leg. He was normally affectionate sometimes, and abnormally violent at others. He hit and kicked me when I restrained him to change a diaper or comb his hair, but if I spanked his hand, he usually removed his hitting or kicking to something that wouldn't fight back, like the counter, or cabinet. When he was sick or tired, he wanted me to hold and cuddle him.

When he learned to pull up, James's favorite place in the house was the dining room window. It looked out onto the patio. In warm months there were flowers and green grass to look at, and sometimes the cats lounged there in the shade. But he didn't like the window. In fact, even with his glasses on for a minute, he didn't seem to notice anything outside. He only wanted to play with the plastic tab used to lift the screen off. He seemed unable to deal with the stimulation of his actual surroundings. He clearly preferred the blurry haze which required him only to focus on the few things really close to him. If this was the case, the cause was obviously brain damage.

> JOURNAL: I am a good example of the scripture, "My grace is sufficient for you, for power is perfected in weakness" (II Corinthians:12-9). At first glance it seems strange and almost inefficient for God to pick me to mother His handicapped babies, because of my "only child" background, my doubter mentality and my body's inability to tolerate sleep loss. But it shows the world it is His power alone that has made me able to accomplish His desire in me and not my own strength.

When James was two and a half, the search began for a family for him. I found there were so many contradictions in his behavior, I was hesitant to make any predictions about his development. He was eighteen months behind on almost everything, but how much was his brain and how much his eyes, it was impossible to tell. He had never spoken a word, but he was making a wide range of creative sounds in preliminary efforts toward speech. He was walking by then, but he hated it, and pinched my hands bloody when I held his hand and made him walk short distances. He would still eat only the softest and blandest foods, and refused to chew anything but toys and crackers. Consistent with drug damage was his slowness to play appropriately with toys, but that could be his poor vision. Maybe he didn't see well enough to find a way to play with a toy. There were only a couple of things he used appropriately, and one was a ball. He quickly learned how to roll and chase a ball, and he had no difficulty whatever finding it, even when it had rolled far beyond what we thought he could see.

Both James and Dai had gotten glasses that year. Dai is showing James his so, maybe, James will wear his.

His mental development was progressing because he understood and obeyed simple instructions, like "come here," or "don't do that," unless he was in a bad mood or feeling frustrated. Even then the look on his face left no doubt that he understood he was defying us and had decided to fight. Once when I held his hands to show him hitting me was unacceptable behavior, he bit me very hard. When I retaliated with similar aggression of my own, he quickly decided he should use biting only as a symbol of resistance. He never bit me hard enough to hurt again, but would gently put his teeth against my hand, then scowl at me ferociously to show his anger.

I FINALLY REALIZED I HAD TO MAKE A CHOICE BETWEEN TRYING TO keep James's glasses on, so he could be more visually stimulated, and the issue of his hostility and acting out with others. I chose the latter, deciding his new family would have to be able to get near him to put his glasses on. Our efforts in this direction produced in James a considerable degree of self-control, which would stand him in good stead when he was adopted. I hoped as he was affirmed and encouraged by his new family, he would develop sufficient desire to see more of the world and wear his glasses.

James's high degree of mobility and two-year-old behavior made writing a book while caring for him a real challenge. Eighty percent of this book was written with him pulling on my sleeve, pounding on the key pad, or emptying my desk drawers. Once when he had spent the whole morning trying to pull my papers off the desk, I spanked his hand and warned him not to touch my things again. In a few moments, a slight movement caught my eye and I looked down to see one tiny brown finger slowly advancing toward my white papers. It was so cute I had to laugh, but it encouraged me too. Surely there is much hope for a brain damaged child who tries to avoid detection by inching one little finger onto the desk instead of his whole hand.

BECAUSE JAMES HAD BECOME A VERY AWARE LITTLE PERSON, THE knowledge that he had no idea he was not our child, caused the old specter to loom darkly around the corners of my mind again. When the time came for the search for God's family for him, I found that years of facing this pain had caused a strange division of heart and mind in me. When I tried to explore my thoughts about James's inevitable feelings of loss and abandonment, I found my mind was numb. I was almost unable to think about the pain James would feel when he was taken from us. Apparently my mind knew after all those years, there was nothing new to be thought of to protect the child from the pain he must endure when he loses the mother he thought was his.

Strangely, this knowledge had no effect on my heart. My heart seemed able to cover my pain about the loss and fear the babies feel, and store it away out of sight. But it can't give it up. It is always there for me to stumble over, if I allow my thoughts to stray too close to it. And often for a moment the pain and tears that result are almost as fresh as if I had just kissed one of the babies good-bye. Sometimes my eyes just tear up for a minute, but other times I weep uncontrollably for several minutes, overwhelmed again with the fear and sense of loss every child must feel who loses his mother. Then the Holy Spirit gently takes the pain and asks again, "Do you not know there is much to be done that can only be done by those who are willing to hurt and to bleed, and don't you know the children are more precious to Christ than to you? He has shown you that you can trust Him and His purposes. He is in control; rest in Him. Give them to Him.

> JOURNAL: I see there are pains, like the pain of separating from child after child, giving them to strangers, which go into a person's soul. My mind and heart deal with it the best they can. But my mother's soul holds on to it. Lord, will there come a day while I am still on earth that I will look for the pain and find it gone? Or is it a "holy hurt" I will carry until that day I stand in Your presence and am healed forever?

One afternoon I received a call from a social worker at Catholic Charities with the news they had found a family for

James in a home in which they had already placed a child several years before. She gave me the mother's number and asked me to call and tell her about James. They wanted him right away.

I called the mother and when we got down to the things I was afraid would turn people off, I made myself tell her. I told her of James's violent behavior toward me. I told her how he had slapped me so hard he had knocked my glasses off and mussed my hair because I was tying his shoes. I told her how he kicked me in the face with his shoes and pinched my hands bloody. He also had several very odd proclivities which might make the new family think he had been molested. Never fear, she told me, she had a child who did everything James did and she knew how to handle it. I had written down all of his oddities and read them to her. She laughed at them all. They were nothing. She was sure she could have him normal in no time. By the time we hung up I was seriously concerned about this woman. She was clearly delusional. I was not without experience myself, and James was a violent, stubborn little boy I was sure was autistic and she was going to have trouble with him. I went upstairs where James was playing, barricaded in his room with toys on the floor and a tape player playing children's nursery songs. I picked him up and sat down on the single bed close to his crib and held him close. I looked out the window and prayed that God would not let him go to a family who was not prepared to deal with him.

Nothing happened to prevent his adoption with this family because they had been so successful with all their other adoptions. Their state did have super services for special needs children which were not to be found in Mississippi at that time. Nevertheless, when a social worker told me the mother wanted to meet us at the airport, take James and leave with him, I thought, Does this mother know anything at all about children? How could she have a house full of adopted mentally handicapped children and not know you don't just take a child away from the only mother he ever knew and walk away? How could she not know that?

I told the social worker, "No way on earth would I do that to James. We are going to stay around at least a day or two to let him feel safe there and to see that we think these parents and siblings are safe and happy. And tell her we will not hand him over at the airport. He will ride with us to their house in our rental car." I stayed upset about this placement from the first phone call.

Hamp to the rescue: He thought it would be a good idea to invite his mother to go with us. Then we could take a few days' vacation and see the sights with her. It did help to have her there after we left James, but I don't remember anything of the trip to his new family. I think my mind just shut down so I could get on the plane to take him to them. She has told me James screamed a lot on the plane, but I wouldn't remember that anyway. I do remember the arrival at the airport. The new mother wanted to hold James immediately even though that was not the plan the social workers in their state and ours had worked out. The plan that had been worked out was everything I wanted, because they knew I was right. It was what was best for James. I refused to let her hold him. He was tired and crying.

Our rental car was not there, so we couldn't get away from them at least for a few minutes. Hamp had already told the father of the family more than once that James would ride home with us, not them. He was angry with the new parents for wanting to pounce on James, and irritable from fighting an overstimulated three-year-old all day on the plane. Finally, he whispered to me, "Keep them away from me or I'm going to do something I will regret."

Having never heard my husband say this, I pictured James's new father lying on his back on the floor.

"Don't say anything else to Hamp; he's really angry. Leave him alone or he's going to take all of us back to Mississippi," I told them in my most serious tone. I was afraid of what he might do. I had seldom, if ever, seen him that furious.

Eventually we got a car, and after Hampy grabbed the steering wheel like he wanted to twist it off and shouted, "AHHHHHH," we followed them to their house with James in our car, not theirs. They still didn't have a clue about how important a change this was going to be for James. At their home I discovered most of their adopted children were half grown and suffered some degree of brain damage, but nothing in the same universe as the family who had adopted Micah. The child she said was like James was a four-year-old little white girl who seemed very calm and not prone to the hyper movement and unpredictability of James. Maybe she was sedated. We stayed at their house for several hours. It was very large and very messy. There were clothes thrown everywhere in the areas she referred to as rooms for different children, walking on clothes as you walked through one to the other until it was time to turn around and walk on the piles of clothes to get out. I know children have to have small sleeping quarters in huge families, but the others I had seen were at least in some kind of order. The others understood their children needed order for their brains not to be overwhelmed. No one knows exactly what sensory input a brain damaged child is reacting to, or even receiving. Just presenting James with so many different colors all thrown on the floor was enough to make him react badly. They all have to be able to depend on at least some things they use always being in the same place, their room, their toys, their bed, the bathroom, etc. James's brain was programmed for our house and the people he knew there. Every single thing here was different, and they didn't seem to know that was important for him.

 I had been in big adoptive families before, and I knew the older children were great potential playmates and babysitters for James, but with all of them being mentally handicapped in this family, I couldn't tell if they could help pattern James's brain for more normal behavior. There was another little black boy smaller than he to play with, or rather next to. Who knew if James would ever develop the ability for reciprocal/interactive play? The older children helped the mother with food prep and cleaning up the table and dishes, but I couldn't see how this set of parents could ever have time to help the younger children develop anywhere near their full potential. I knew from experience, whatever progress they did manage, would be considered their full potential and it frustrated me to the point of nausea for James.

We ate a sandwich with them and pleading James's and my exhaustion, left for the comfort of our hotel room. This was the first family we had taken a child to which I just couldn't find anything to feel good about. I called our social worker in Mississippi and told her my concerns. We had already discussed my lack of confidence in the mother. She had promised to keep in close contact with the family's social worker there and make her aware of my expanded concerns. I couldn't say, "I refuse to leave him here," because I couldn't be completely sure things wouldn't work out well there in spite of everything.

The next morning, we had to take him back to their house. James, who never dreamed we would leave him there, played on the floor with the other little boy, and let different teenage children hold him. I don't think I ever sat down; I don't think I could. Then James crawled over to the other little boy, whose back was to him, and whacked him on the head for no apparent reason. Of course he cried, and James just stared while the mother picked the baby up and comforted him.

"That is pure James," I told them. "You never know what he's going to do next, but very often it's aggressive."

"He'll be fine," his new mom said smiling. He just needs time to get to know his new brother. In a week they will be playing together like they have known each other all their lives."

No they won't! my mind screamed. My nausea was becoming very uncomfortable. "You know what?" I said to Hamp. "He is happy right now and he's playing with new toys. We should leave. These are the conditions I wanted to achieve before we left, and he is going to feel abandoned no matter when we leave. I wanted to leave James happy, and he was. It was all I was going to get, and I knew it. I had to get out of the house, or the people and place I had to leave my baby was going to make me throw up.

WE LEFT JAMES WITH HIS FAMILY AND WENT SIGHTSEEING. OR HAMP and his mother did. I was lying on the back seat taking nausea pills. We stopped around the middle of the afternoon because I had to know how James was doing. I called from a pay phone at a shopping center.

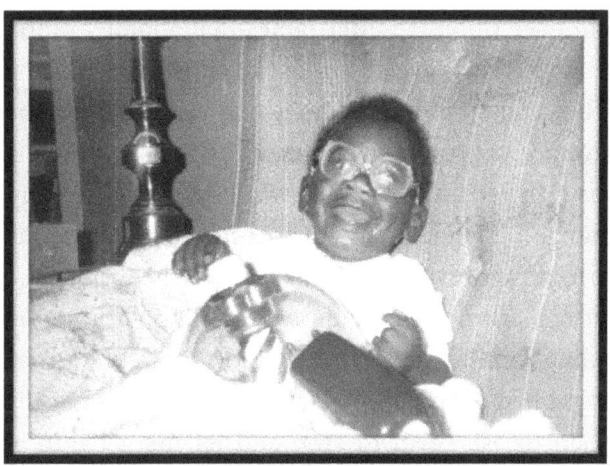

| James happy, even with his glasses.

"Oh, _____ is doing just great!" His new mother said. They were already calling him by the name they were going to call him, not working it in gradually until he got used to it. I wonder who James thinks she is talking to, I thought.

"He's sitting in a high chair right now, eating a hot dog and calling me Mama."

My stomach lurched. "Wow, what a miracle," I said weakly. I got back in the car and told Hamp and his mother what she had said. "If she really thinks that, she needs to be committed," I said. Hamp asked if we should call our social worker at home and tell her we didn't think he should be left with them. I lay on the back seat and cried for a while.

"You know, Sweet," Hampy said, "we've known lots of parents who were terrible at parenting. But they did take their children to the doctor, eventually, and got them to school, and clothed and fed them. Santa always came to their house with things the children wanted, they all had bikes. What I' m trying to say is, like you say so often about the babies: Normal is a huge wide range. And at each extreme, it's not what most people want. This family is nowhere near the center of normal like we want them to be. But they might have things to offer James that a family more like ours wouldn't. Also, they have had most of those kids since they were babies. They must be doing something right, or they never even would have been considered for James by social workers here."

He was right. My mind agreed wholeheartedly, but my stomach was unchanged. The next day I was just as nauseated, but we went to a tourist attraction we had only seen in the distance. There is a picture of me sitting on a fallen tree smiling with my mother-in-law standing behind me. When I look at it, all I remember is feeling as if I had terminal flu. Hamp had to help me get up. Eventually, I had to ask them to stop and let me get into a bed. My fibromyalgia had flared up every time we placed a baby for adoption, especially if we had to fly to do it. But this was different. Three years of my life had gone into getting James to the place he was in emotionally and mentally and he loved me and knew I loved him. I had hit the wall and I wasn't going through it. I remember a big double bed, kicking off my shoes and jeans and sliding between the sheets. "Thank you, Father, thank you, Father," I said and went instantly to sleep. I slept until the next morning. My mother-in-law stayed with me and Hamp went back out to take pictures of places I wouldn't get to see.

The next day I ate, which I should have done before, and felt better. Sleep is the best thing for fibromyalgia, and I had finally gotten enough.

At home, I was depressed about James for a long time, but his new mother sent me a professional photo, saying in her note he was doing fine, and I could believe the picture. Who knew if what she thought was going on, really was? That was the last contact I had with her.

| Gotcha! Daddy and James at three years old.

13
SARAH

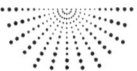

At the time I wrote the first edition of this book, we still had baby James, and I expected him to be our last baby. I was fifty, and had done some research and found the Kohathites of old were exempted from the burden of carrying at fifty. I didn't think I could tolerate the pain of another baby. I could even contemplate sleeping all night, and having control of all of my time with a certain degree of pleasure. I had not told the Lord, "I am through now," but I thought it was time for me to turn God's babies over to younger hands and especially younger shoulders and backs. It seemed, however, that God and I were not on the same page this time.

THAT NOVEMBER THE LORD SURPRISED ME WITH MY WORST nightmare of a baby—another trach. I knew this meant no sleep, carrying suction everywhere I went…all I had been through with John Mark, only I was a lot older. It was an eight-month-old little black girl, the sicklier one of a pair of twins. Her sister was fine, but this baby had a severe stenosis, or narrowing in her trachea (windpipe—the tube you breathe through). She had suffered nearly constant pneumonia since her birth, and had been in the hospital, as often as out. The doctors had put in a tracheostomy a few weeks after birth to keep her airway open. The last time she went to the hospital, doctors called her social worker and said if they didn't get her to someone not on drugs who would take very good care of her, she would die. Her crack addicted mother knew how to give her excellent care, she just wasn't doing it because of the drugs. And each bout with pneumonia had left her baby weaker and weaker.

"Isn't there someone in the extended family who can take her?" I asked the social worker. She said there wasn't.

"Tell them to try to find someone else, and call me if they can't."

I hung up feeling pretty safe. Surely God wouldn't require me to take such a hard, dangerous baby at my age, knowing how much pain I was in. I put the baby out of my mind. If there was anything God knew, it was who could and couldn't do what.

About a week later, a nurse called and started telling me all about this same baby.

"Are you serious? There is no one else to take her?" I asked with dismay.

Then it came out: all the other members of the family were caring for the mother's other children, plus they were all afraid of the responsibility of the trach. Clearly, if I didn't take this baby, she would be returned to her birth mother and probably die.

After I hung up the phone, I folded my arms, put my head on them, and cried for about ten minutes. Not for the baby, bless her heart, for me—just for me. Remembering the pain I endured to care for John Mark made me feel sick. The restriction of not being able to leave the house, unless someone very capable was with her was to be dreaded. Taking her and all of her equipment with me just to run to the store, was more than I could face. Our children were all grown and on their own, and even though Dai was at home for now, he would be off again before long, and I would have no one to help me but Hamp. He worked very hard in the heat and cold, and was usually ready for bed by 9:30.

ONE MORNING I CAME TO MY DESK TO PRAY AND LOOKED AT THE bare forsythia bushes outside the window. I had prayed beside this window for years and never paid any attention to them. The leaves are green and yellow in fall, but in January or February, the height of dreary winter they burst into beautiful yellow blooms. They don't even have leaves—just flowers. As I prayed, I found myself looking at the bushes and musing, "Can I be like that? Now that the fresh, green strength and beauty of youth has faded, will I be able, by Your Spirit, to bear in the winter of my life a more startling witness for You, because of my season of life?"

A few weeks later I came to my desk by the window to pray. To my astonishment, the forsythias were in full bloom! It was November. I had noticed no beginnings of yellow flowers in the past week, or days. Yet there they were, in full bloom. It had rained hard the night before, and I thought maybe that was what pushed them into early bloom. But tears came into my eyes, as I realized the bush was telling me the water of the Holy Spirit could make anything bloom anywhere and anytime He wanted, even me. The forsythias have never bloomed in November again.

During the next week, everything I saw or heard said, "Take the baby." It was Daniel all over again. Everywhere I went, God was there ahead of me saying, "Take the baby."

QUICKLY IT WAS THE WEEK OF THANKSGIVING. I SPENT THE WHOLE week walking and praying. I knew from experience if this was my baby, the Lord would make me want to take her. Hamp wanted to take her, but he knew from John Mark how hard it would be, so he prayed for me and let me fight it out with the Lord. As I prayed, the Lord told me some very interesting things, and gave me wisdom I had never heard.

"You can't focus on yourself and your needs when you hear my call. You must trust Me to protect you. A divided house cannot stand, nor can a divided heart."

How many Christians commit themselves to things that are easy for them, leaving the really arduous works of Christ for just a few to carry. John 3:8 says, "The wind blows where it wishes. You hear the sound of it, but do not know where it comes from or where it is going. So is everyone born of the Spirit." The Lord may call on us to do things even we and other believers can't understand.

I also realized these are the vastly important days of my flesh, in which I will seek to serve Him, or I will seek to serve myself. That was the only real question.

BY THE END OF THE WEEK, THE LORD HAD CONVINCED ME I WAS TO take His baby. I didn't know how I would survive, but I would take His baby. Within hours of my decision to obey the Lord, He spoke to me about my constant pain. I was standing in our bedroom when He said quite clearly, "Try Elavil again." Elavil, I thought, I tried that years ago. It had terrible side effects. I can't take that! I couldn't see how I could possibly take it, but it was so clear I called my doctor and asked her for three of the lowest dose to try.

I tried one that night and the next morning I woke feeling sixteen years old. I couldn't believe it. Oh, the blessed freedom from pain! Those who have never had to live with a constant backdrop of pain every minute of the day can never comprehend what it means to be free of it. And what a confirmation of Philippians 2. If I had not obeyed Him, I feel sure He would not have told me to take a medication I had already turned my back on. I think it was exactly like making me laugh on the plane with Micah. He gave me what I needed because I was obeying Him.

I have many pictures like this: Katelyn holding Sarah. They loved each other so much.

Later I prayed, Oh Lord, I pray I will see this child as Yours, see her little soul and life as precious to You, no matter what the circumstances of her birth and background. Let me not forget I am Your instrument in this whole affair. Bless her family, the social workers, everyone involved, and let them all see You working Your will for Your precious little girl. As it turned out, the social worker I dealt with on her case asked many questions about the Lord and began attending church. She sent me a lovely card telling me she was praying for me when this baby went back to her home. She said she saw the hand of God in my life. What greater praise could there be?

Quickly the day came to get the baby, and for the first time I was going to go into the home. I had never had to do this, and I was really dreading taking a baby from her mother in her own home.

After a ride of several hours, the Catholic Charities social worker and I arrived in the city where the baby lived. My first request was to call the baby's doctor. I had already been told she did not have bronchopulmonary dysplasia, the dangerous condition which had nearly cost John Mark his life. The home health nurse who had been visiting the baby said she did not have it, but I needed to be sure. It was a frustrating conversation:

"Oh, I consider bronchopulmonary dysplasia her worst problem," the doctor said.

"What about asthma?" I asked, slowly shaking my head. "Oh, yes, she definitely has asthma," he said.

"Then why isn't she getting aerosol treatments?" I was growing more irritated by the second.

"She is getting them, four times a day!"

I turned to the baby's home health nurse. "Aerosol treatments?"

She shrugged her shoulders. "Nobody ever told me." None of this surprised me, but I still wanted to scream.

To top it off, I knew I couldn't be sure the doctor was right anyway. How often in the past had I gotten wrong information about the babies from doctors? A few months later, there would be a heated shouting match between this doctor and a doctor at the children's' hospital in which the baby had been treated for her many bouts with pneumonia. The hospital ENT doctor would point out that he had scoped the baby under anesthesia and "been in her bronchial tubes."

"This baby has not got bronchopulmonary dysplasia!" the doctor at the hospital would shout at the local doctor. Thank the Lord he was right. She did not have the life threatening problem. She didn't have asthma either.

After the call to the doctor, it was time to go to the baby's home and get her. We found the mother and two of her older but still very small children with the baby. It was cold outside, and the children were wearing coats as they ate their breakfast. It was ll:30 am. I was glad my new baby's twin sister was permanently in the care of a responsible, mature older sister of the mother.

The mother, a very pretty girl, I'll call Keesha, knew why we were there, but apparently had not told the other children. They stayed at the table while we went into the bedroom where the baby lay in a crib. They were used to social workers coming and going with the baby's ill health and trach.

When I first saw her, I thought, Oh, Lord, couldn't she at least be cute? The baby looked big and fat and her face so puffy with swollen eyelids, she looked as if she had Down Syndrome. In fact, I was sure then she had to be intellectually disabled. She had suffered enough oxygen deprivation to cause brain damage. Her hair was pulled up into a greasy little pony tail full of flakes of cradle cap. She smelled terribly from her trach strings. They appeared not to have been changed in weeks. The stench of them was almost unbearable. As my senses struggled with all of this negative input, the Holy Spirit whispered, "Give her a beautiful name to live up to. Name her Sarah." Great idea! I thought. Thinking of Sarah, Abraham's wife and an exceeding beauty, helped my perception of her immediately.

It took about an hour for us to find and gather up all of the baby's medications, equipment and clothes. Everything was covered in dust, dirt and hair and most of it was on the floor. All the medicine bottles were sticky and had dust stuck all over them. I didn't want to take any of it home with me, but it appeared I had no choice. Drugs had exacted a terrible toll on this mother and her children. I couldn't look at the suction machine, and was glad fresh equipment would be delivered to our house as soon as I got there with her.

When her siblings saw us taking all of her possessions out of the house, they jumped up and started crying. "Don't take our baby! That's our baby! Please don't take our baby!" Their frantic crying nearly broke my heart, but I couldn't think of a response. When we got everything but the baby in the car, I told the social workers they would have to take her out of the house. I couldn't do it. Their social worker stepped up. On her way out, she stood in front of the mother, holding Sarah, wanting to give her a chance to kiss her good bye if she wanted to. Keesha took her and sat on the couch. She sat the baby on her knees at arm's length and just looked at her for a minute. Even though her face remained expressionless, tears began to run slowly down her cheeks. A few seconds of watching that young, defeated, addicted mother and her suffering, confused baby looking into each other's eyes quickly filled my eyes to overflowing as well.

I sat down beside her and put my arm around her. "Keesha, I promise you I will take very good care of your baby. I am really good at taking care of sick babies, and I promise you I will take care of her as if she were my own child." She half nodded without looking at me, then wordlessly handed the baby back to the social worker. The other children were still crying frantically. I got down on one knee and put my arms around them and said, "I will bring your baby back. I promise you! I am just going to take care of her while she is so sick. When she is all better, I promise I will bring her back to you. While she is with me, you can come and see her at my house any time your mother wants to bring you, okay?" They nodded without looking at me, their little eyes still pouring tears. They didn't know me. Not much in their lives was stable or dependable. Why should they believe a strange white lady?

BACK AT THE OFFICE THERE WERE PAPERS TO SIGN, PRESCRIPTIONS TO get and arrangements to be made for the equipment to be delivered to my house. Before I started on the Elavil, I would have been so stressed out and exhausted, I would have been asleep on Keesha's couch before we ever left with the baby, but I felt fine.

I couldn't bring myself to take the suction machine the mother had been using, and I wasn't looking forward to the long drive home with no suction to clear her airway. I was surprised when she quickly fell asleep. Then I only had to keep her trach strings as far away from my nose as possible. I held her, because I was afraid her trach would get plugged and I needed to be able to get to her as soon as possible to try to open it without a suction machine. After several hours' drive we reached Jackson, transferred Sarah and all of her belongings and medications to my car. Then I began the forty-five-minute drive home through rush-hour traffic.

As soon as we arrived home and had unloaded the car, the home healthcare van came up the driveway. I was glad I remembered all of the equipment, and how to use it. By this time, Sarah had awakened and was frightened and upset to find herself in a new place, surrounded by white people. I offered her some formula, and she drank just a little before beginning to scream again. Hamp had already commented on the smell from her trach strings. I couldn't put clean ones on without washing her neck. I decided to pop her into the kitchen sink. So off came the old trach strings, and in she went. She was not pleased. I did manage to get her and her hair reasonably clean, wash her neck and put on clean trach strings. Next we cut her hair, an enormous faux pas, but I didn't know it at the time. Finally, we had a clean, sweet smelling, very indignant little girl. She was too tired from all the stimulation and excitement to protest for long though, and soon she was sound asleep.

That's when we first heard the gurgling and wheezing sounds coming from her chest and upper airway. I got my stethoscope and listened to her lungs and bronchial tubes.

"Oh, she sounds awful!" I said to Hamp. "It's a good thing we have an appointment with the doctor in the morning." With our experiences with John Mark in mind, instead of putting Sarah in the crib in our room, I decided to set up a port-a-crib in the living room with the mist machine, all of her medications and equipment so I could stay up with her and sleep on the couch if I got a chance. I didn't want to keep Hamp up. I just couldn't feel good about being more than a couple of feet away from her. Even for a few minutes. There was so much congestion in her chest and she was so stressed out from being in a completely new environment, she was ripe for a deadly infection.

Before I fell asleep the first time that night, I thought, Where will Jesus lead me except closer to him?

SARAH AND I CAMPED OUT IN THE LIVING ROOM FOR SIX DAYS AND nights, and I stayed right by her nearly all the time. Someone commented that one end of the living room looked like an intensive care unit, and it did. But it was the Lord's provision for my being able to arrange things to make caring for Sarah as comfortable as possible for us both.

Sometimes prayers seemed to come from deep inside me, and I have no idea what I'm going to say. I think perhaps these are prayers of the Holy Spirit, who alone can utter my feelings or needs at that moment, things for which I have no words. This prayer is one of those.

> *JOURNAL: Lord, I praise You for seeing Sarah in her mother's womb, seeing the stenosis in her trachea, and stretching out Your mighty hand to her. You saw her, Lord, a tiny little girl the weaker of two exactly alike, and You valued her so much, You made me want her. You made a place for her to be nurtured and cared for and loved. Man*

would say, "She is only a sickly girl, and there is a perfectly good one, already strong and healthy, let this sickly one go. She is also poor, black and the child of an unmarried, drug addicted mother, who already has several children. We have plenty of children like this; we don't need any more!"

But You said, "No, no, she is here. She is Mine, and she is beautiful. I will provide for her. I have a servant, who is willing to obey Me if I just encourage her a little and tell her it is I who ask it and not man."

With every passing day, we saw more of Sarah's personality. On the third day I kissed her on her forehead, and she smiled. Before long, she was smiling at everyone, reaching for toys, and turning her head to watch people. She was very behind in her development, due to her constant sickness, and the lack of stimulation, but she was surprisingly intelligent. As we stimulated and moved her around, held her and patted her back to loosen congestion, gave her the aerosol treatments and medications she needed, her chest cleared dramatically. The fluid retention around her eyes, in her face, and even her body, left as well. Within just a couple of weeks, she turned into one of the cutest babies I had ever seen. Her nickname could only be, "Sweet Baby Darlin'." It was impossible to call her anything else. She smiled all the time, and never complained about anything, except maybe a really serious diaper.

SIX WEEKS LATER, SARAH WAS NINE MONTHS OLD, AND HER VISITORS were her mother, the brother and sister I tried to comfort when we took her, and the driver. Her mother's first words when she saw Sarah were, "Oh, they cut your hair! I can't believe they cut your hair!" I wondered what all the fuss was about and assured her I had every expectation it would grow back. I told her I only knew how to take care of little black boys' hair. You comb it, you wash it, you cut it, end of story. I had cut Sarah's just like theirs, and it looked adorable. She was far too pretty for anyone to think she was a boy, and I loved her hair short. It wasn't long before African American friends told me little black girls' hair is never cut until they are at least several years old. It just isn't done, because it grows so slowly. Well, it was too late now, so not being able to keep it short as it grew, I got by for several months just pulling it back from her face with a barrette.

Sarah working hard to move her mouth like the therapist is.

She looked exotic and beautiful with it like this, but I eventually had to try to learn to part her short curly hair into sections and then attempt to force it into little braids and get a tiny rubber band around it. Or worse, an elastic band with two colored balls on it, which took a magician to get to loop through each other and to secure.

> *JOURNAL: AGAIN, AGAIN, AGAIN—it was not the power of the Lord to do miracles, which saved people! It was His power of self-sacrifice to die on a cross! Try to remember this!*

Sarah was a different kind of child in every way, from any I had known before. She was the most angelic, sweet tempered child I ever knew. She was incredibly intelligent, understanding things I would have thought impossible for a child her age.

She was behind in her development, but she progressed by leaps and bounds. In no time it seemed, with physical therapy and Hampy, Dai, Laura, Katelyn and me, encouraging her, she went from being unable to sit up, to crawling, then walking, and she learned to understand language extremely rapidly. She almost always understood what we said, even though she could not speak herself because of the trach, and so lacked the reinforcement of using the words herself. I found myself thinking, over and over, I can't believe I could have missed ever knowing and loving this fantastic little girl.

In addition to doing physical therapy with her the first few months, we also had to get our speech therapist, Miss Peggy, back to help her learn how to eat, and to strengthen her facial and mouth muscles. She needed to be ready to use them when she regained her ability to speak. Because she had only sucked a bottle and had no ability to make sounds with her mouth, the muscles in her face, tongue, lips, and throat were extremely weak. It just took a lot of effort and time, to take her battery operated suction machine, tubes, sterile catheters, and sterile water, plus a normally equipped diaper bag everywhere we went, and to have to stop often at inconvenient places to suction her, plus the constant need to suction her all day and often numerous times during the night. But she smiled at me and cooperated all she could when I had to suction her in a hundred different places and times.

 *JOURNAL: Every obedience we omit obscures some truth we would have learned if we had obeyed.*

Sarah was so smart that often we could see her trying to figure out how to communicate with us. When she reached toddler age, if she couldn't get what she wanted because I couldn't understand, she would put her head to one side and frown, then smile, as if making the only faces she could think of would somehow help me understand. Not far into her speech therapy, she started making strange motions with her hands to Peggy. She would hold out her arms, open her fingers wide, then close them over and over, grinning the whole time. Peggy and I nearly became obsessed with trying to think what on earth she was trying to tell us. Then one day I passed through the den on my way to the washing machine while she was watching *Blue's Clues*. She watched it every day. As I passed by the TV, Steve was making Sarah's motions with his hands and saying "Blues Clues."

"Sarah! Is that what you are doing with Miss Peggy?" I said.

She grinned and nodded her head, then jumped up to run over and hug my legs. I choked up as I put down the laundry basket and stooped to hug her. It was such a simple thing, but so important for her, and so hard. The next time Peggy came, I told her what I had finally discovered. Sarah was in the high chair for her speech lesson. She leaned toward Peggy, smiling and nodding in agreement, anticipating the look on Miss Peggy's face when she understood what she had been trying to tell her.

Peggy and I both had tears in our eyes while she hugged Sarah over and over. "You knew what you were telling me didn't you darling? I should have known. I've seen *Blue's Clues*. I should have known," she said, "but I never even thought about that."

The problems of an extremely intelligent child who could not tell us her thoughts or feelings were frustrating as she got older, and entirely new to us. John Mark had gone home at a much earlier age, and while he was a very intelligent little boy, Sarah's comprehension was extremely advanced for her age. She continuously exhibited understanding and desires that we just didn't anticipate. Once after Sunday school, I went to check on her in the nursery. She was over in a corner, busily pretending to cook with pots and pans on a toy stove. The nursery worker, one of several wonderful women who worked permanently at the church and all of whom had tremendous empathy for our babies said, "She really loves that stove! I'll bet she has plenty of cooking toys at home."

I stared at Sarah for a minute, then said softly because I was ashamed, "No, I'm sorry to say I have never thought about her wanting to pretend to cook." The next day I bought her pots and pans and dishes and got Katelyn's old toy kitchen, out of the attic. Sarah was in heaven. She played with them for hours, sometimes smiling, sometimes frowning, she was concentrating so hard on her work.

I had taken Sarah with the assumption I would be caring for her alone, except for Hamp. But Laura and Katelyn moved home for seven or eight months pending Laura's marriage. As the Lord had known before hand, there was not only another mother here to help with Sarah, but her child was here to play with her. Madison was much younger, but she loved to play with him, and when he was a toddler they were wonderful playmates. One of Sarah's favorite treats was for Laura to let her come upstairs and bathe with Madison. She would get her pajamas, diaper and tooth brush, and scamper up the stairs to be bathed and play in the water with Madison. They would sit on the counter wrapped in big towels in front of the mirror, where they could see their reflections while Laura helped them brush their teeth.

SARAH CLEARLY COULDN'T UNDERSTAND WHY SHE WAS THE ONLY person she knew who had a tube in their throat, which had to be suctioned, and who couldn't talk, even though she had plenty to say. One day after watching me suction her in the nursery at church, Hamp said, "Sarah is embarrassed she has a trach and has to be suctioned. We need to do it where no one can see us as much as possible." I hadn't noticed the look on her face, because I was always looking at what I was doing under her chin, and pushing buttons on the machine and tubing. But the tears in Hampy's eyes for only the third time in twenty-nine years proved he had seen something I had not. It was another thing she couldn't tell me, and she was too sweet a child to fight me to let me know she didn't want it. From then on, I made it a point to protect her from curious eyes while suctioning.

Often when she would hear me singing worship songs at my prayer time, Sarah would come and sit in my lap. She would lean against me to feel the vibrations, sometimes putting her hand on my throat. I always told her I was talking to Jesus or singing to Him. Sometimes she would sit there for thirty minutes or more. When my back hurt from sitting, I would walk up and down, carrying her with her head on my shoulder. Her little hand patted me as I prayed or sang. It was amazing how quickly she picked up what we said about Jesus. She was in Sunday school every Sunday, and in the church nursery before that, where she heard Christian children's songs and of course she heard us talking about Jesus.

> *JOURNAL: Jesus took off His very glory to become one of us, to lift us up out of the mud. When I picture Him, who embodies all beauty and purity, stripping off his beautiful "God robes," dropping them on Heaven's floor and jumping into the pit man had made of His world, wading through the mud and filth, our contamination clinging to His purity, and His straining to pull us out of the grip of corruption and death, I cannot but weep. He did this for us all and we choose to put Him in a glass case and to marvel at his beauty. We refuse to take the human hand He came to extend to us at such cost to Himself to guide us back to Him and his Father.*

Sarah and I had not been learning sign language very long when it was time to begin her trips to the hospital to be scoped. This was to check the status of her trachea to address having the trach closed. That would restore her speech and allow her to breathe normally. The first trip was to see if she had any reflux. This could ruin the stint they hoped to put in to open and strengthen her trachea. Even though this was not technically surgery, she had to be put to sleep for the procedure and spend the night in the hospital. We had to come back so often, we soon became a fixture in the outpatient surgery department. All of the nurses soon knew her by name, and greeted her with hugs and kisses. She distinguished herself here, in yet another way. My babies have always had to be stuck with needles for one reason or another, but I never had one who after the first time it was done, never cried again. She looked concerned and pressed her head against me, if they had trouble getting a vein, but she never cried after the first time.

For the first procedure, we went to the hospital at six a.m. a few days after they had first drawn blood. She wasn't upset at all to be back where they had stuck her arm with a needle. She was too busy looking at the people and smiling at them all, looking at what they had, playing with the curtains, and especially the nice loud, metal lockers. She let me put her into a steel crib, with very high sides on it almost like a little jail cell without protest and even submitted to being undressed and put into a tiny hospital gown. I left her socks on to keep her feet warm. She had a favorite teddy bear and some toys to keep her company while we waited her turn. As with all surgery, she had not had anything to eat or drink since midnight the night before. They always took the babies first except this time. We had such a long wait. She got hungry in the surgery holding room before the anesthesiologist came to get her. I had been hoping they would put her to sleep before this happened.

"In a little while," I told her as she signed "bottle" "bottle" over and over again. She was getting very frustrated because I always understood and gave her a bottle when she signed for one. I told her I knew what she wanted, but I didn't have a bottle, she would have to wait. I stood by the crib with my arms around her, praying they would come.

A nurse came by and put a tiny plastic cap for Sarah to wear during surgery in the bed with her. I tried to distract her with her teddy bear, but she would have no part of him. She was hungry and thirsty, and she was getting mad. I had never treated her like this, and she couldn't understand it. Her face was a little thunder cloud when the surgeon came to talk to me. He tried to talk to her, but she would have none of him. She turned her back, crossed her arms, and tossed her head. This was her self-conceived manner of expressing the greatest display of anger she could conjure up. On the few occasions I saw it, I knew the Baby Darlin's ire was thoroughly aroused.

As she repelled the doctor's advances, without thinking I said, "She's mad because she can't have anything to eat."

Eat! The minute I said it, Sarah thought that was the problem. She was signing the wrong word. She began signing, "Eat, eat, eat, eat."

You idiot! I said to myself under my breath. "Honey, I'm so sorry, but there is nothing here to eat," I told her.

That did it. She grabbed the teddy bear and sailed him across the room. As I straightened up from retrieving him, the shower cap nearly hit me in the face, and before I could pick that up, she sat down and pulled off first one sock and threw it out, followed quickly by the other. She was pulling on the fitted sheet when I took it to keep her from throwing it out too. Sarah threw herself down and began thrashing around and crying. I tried to hold her, but I couldn't. I thought later how intelligent she was to have thought so quickly of something to do that would express her intense frustration and anger. She could have cried, but that wouldn't have told me how she felt. Throwing everything she could find out of the bed with a big scowl on her face told me exactly what she wanted me to know.

Finally, an anesthesiologist came with a surgical glove, blown up into a balloon and managed to distract her with it long enough to carry her to surgery. One of the nurses who had been there the entire time, commented, "I am so glad they finally came for her. That was the maddest little girl I've seen in a long time!"

THE SURGEONS FOUND SARAH HAD A LITTLE REFLUX AND WOULD need medication to protect the stint when they put it in, but there would be a lot of overnight procedures before she was ready to have the trach closed. We went through over a dozen of these procedures before we were through.

That night, and all that followed in the hospital with Sarah, proved to be surprisingly easy. I managed to engineer an acceptable way to sleep on the slippery plastic extend-a-chair and never had trouble sleeping. The time we spent in the hospital was for the most part enjoyable after she got out of recovery. We walked to McDonald's in the hospital building and to the gift shop to look for treats and toys. She loved to go to the pool and fountain in the atrium of the Methodist Rehabilitation Hospital, which joins UMMC outside the McDonald's. She always drew smiles, which she instantly flashed back as she danced through the halls in her little hospital gown, with the I.V. line taped to her foot flapping with every step.

AT HOME, SARAH WAS A JOY ALL THE TIME, BUT ESPECIALLY WHEN SHE got up in the morning. I can still see her dancing down the hall into the sunshine, her whole body twisting like a happy puppy, running to meet the new day. This from a child forced to be silent when everything in her keen little mind was simply dying to be able to talk and sing.

The second summer we had Sarah, when she was two, she rode

for seven hours in her car seat on a trip to Florida and never cried once. She slept in a crib in the hotel room as if she was at home and loved to look at the gulf and seagulls from our balcony or on the deck. She had the same effect on the people there as at home, coming out of the Waffle House with an official Waffle House hat on, and the manager of the local Shoney's running after us in the parking lot to give her a Shoney's teddy bear.

Ms. Peggy and I had tried several things to enable Sarah to make sounds, but none of them had worked. The doctors said she might get some air around the trach tube and over her vocal cords when she got bigger.

Sarah's kitchen. Katelyn was always willing to play there with her, just because it made Sarah happy.

But they couldn't promise anything until the trach opening was closed. They made no promises it could ever be done. It was strictly a wait and see situation. Then one night Sarah and I were in the kitchen together, when I heard a little vocal sound. I spun around and looked down at her. She had a surprised and happy expression on her face.

"Sarah!" I said. "Did you make that sound?"

She nodded her head, still grinning "Can you do it again?" I asked.

She opened her mouth and made a raspy little noise again. This time I could see almost all of her teeth. I knelt down and hugged her.

"You are going to be able to talk! You are going to be able to talk and sing like everybody else, do you know that?"

She nodded her head, hugging me as hard as she could. She understood what it meant much more than I did. I called Hamp to come to the kitchen.

"She is going to be able to talk before they close the trach," I told him. "She's getting air over her vocal cords right now. Listen. I looked at Sarah expectantly, and she made the sound for Daddy.

Hamp jumped back as if she had frightened him. "What was that! Where did that come from? Did my little girl, make that sound all by herself?" Sarah ran to him and he scooped her up in his arms. "Talking, that's what she's doing. She's talking. You are going to be talking so much we will be telling you to be quiet," he told her. The grin had never left her face.

This was one of the most important and wonderful moments in her life. If I had had my way with God, we would have missed it.

ONCE SARAH KNEW SHE COULD MAKE SOUND, SHE PROGRESSED rapidly. Within a couple of months, although her voice was raspy, she could be understood easily. Now that she could talk, I thought she would benefit from a preschool a couple of days a week. She had been with me constantly for months, and I didn't know how she would react. We went one afternoon to look things over and meet the teacher when there were no children there. As soon as she spotted all the toys, she made herself right at home. The teacher also was fine with her. It must have been staying in the church nursery.

My first day of school when I was six, I clung to my mother and cried. Then I threw up. Not Sarah, she went right into the room full of children she had never seen before and found what she wanted to play with. She took it to a table next to another child and never looked at me again. I had to get her attention to tell her goodbye.

"Goodbye, Mommy," she said cheerily without looking up.

She went to preschool two days a week and every night when I was getting her ready for bed before a "school day" I would tell her, "Oh boy, school tomorrow!"

And she would say, "Oh boy! School!" Her little eyes shining with anticipation.

SARAH LOVED EVERYONE AND GREETED THEM ALL WITH A BIG SMILE, but she especially loved her daddy. When it was time to change her trach every week, I waited until Hamp was home to hold her. It hurt, and sometimes bled. One of my most precious pictures is of her wrapped closely in his arms, right after her trach change.

Her face still unhappy and tear streaked, leaning her head against his neck, taking comfort from the only daddy she had ever known. He is leaning his head toward her, telling her, "It's all right. It's all over now."

> JOURNAL: Daniel 2:22 (Daniel's word to Nebuchadnezzar, interpreting the dream) "He knows what is in the darkness." He knows what lies ahead. He knows

what we will need to obey him. He knows the comfort and protection we will need in what to us is the scary darkness of the so totally hidden future.

Finally, after a dozen or more trips to the hospital to remove granulomas and to see if it was time yet, the day came to schedule surgery to close the trach permanently. Hamp went with us to help entertain and chase Sarah during the long waits before we went into surgery. They didn't allocate a room for us until she came out of surgery.

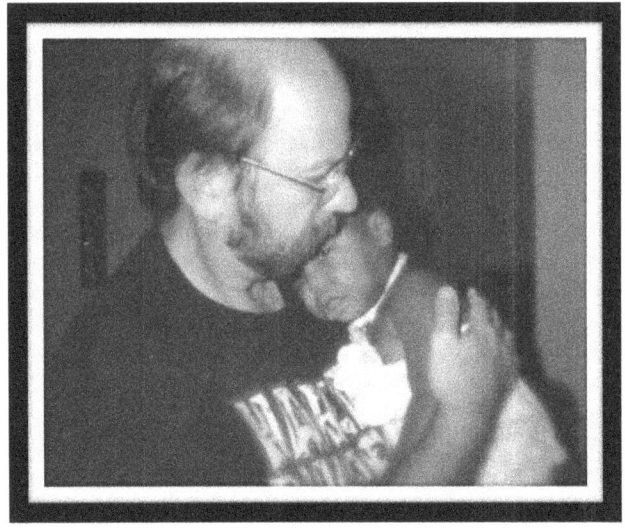

Sweet "Baby Darlin" being comforted by Hampy after she had a tracheostomy change.

The doctor, who had just arrived after studying under the doctor in Cleveland, who had closed John Mark's trach, explained Dr. Cotton's new procedure. They were going to take a little piece of her rib, and make a stint to hold her trachea open. The tissue of the trachea would grow to the stints and soon she would have a strong, normal trachea like everyone else. I was worried about the pain from the incision to take the piece of her rib, but the doctor said most children never noticed it. He was right, she never even looked at her side.

After all of my trips to the recovery room, I was no stranger to the sight of blood. But I nearly cried when I saw Sarah after the surgery. She and her gown were covered with blood. Her nose was full of blood, her trachea was oozing blood and bandaged, and she had a big bandage on her side. I gently set about cleaning up what I could without waking her. I expected this to be the first time she would wake up in pain. She did awaken in pain, and she was terrified. She looked at all the tubes and blood stains, then looked at me in alarm. When she felt the bloody bandage with her fingers, she realized she couldn't talk again and began crying as if her heart would break. She started fighting to get up, and even my getting as close to her as I could, telling her everything was all right didn't help. She knew her voice had been taken away, and she wanted to go home. She was pulling at me and looking into my eyes for answers.

"You will be able to talk again, Sarah, I promise. You can't talk now, but by Wednesday you will be able to talk. It's gone, Sarah!" I put her fingers on the bandage so she could feel that the plastic appliance I suctioned her through, was gone. The bandage was flat. I counted out the days on my fingers. "You will never lose your voice again. It's fixed now, after three days, you will be like everyone else." I kept repeating it for three days.

When we went to the hospital for this last surgery, I was in despair. I had told DHS I wanted her taken home as soon as possible after she had the trach closed and could talk to defend herself. Every day that passed, she was putting her roots deeper and deeper into our family. That is how God made children. They attach as tightly as possible to their mothers and extended family, so they always know where they belong. I knew I was right, but I could barely do anything without bursting into tears. I found myself crying just walking down the halls of the hospital whenever I was away from Sarah. That first night, while she was asleep from pain meds, I was picking up one thing after another and putting it back down.

I couldn't focus on anything. I was trying to make up my couch for the night, when a nurse came silently up behind me and spoke. She startled me so I burst into tears again. She knew me from other babies I had brought to her floor. She put her arms around me and I sobbed on her shoulder, "She thinks I'm her mother! And I want to be! How could I have let this get so far, without telling her!"

"She's gonna be all right, honey, she's gonna be all right. You got her all well now, and she's gonna be all right. You got to trust God with her now, just like all the others," she said softly.

That night was long and painful with me demanding more pain meds for her and crying most of the night, thankful she didn't hear me.

Two days later, when she could whisper again, we were lying on the little couch in her hospital room. She was on top of me, when she propped her elbows on my chest and said with a big smile, "Mommy, I so happy."

"Why, Sweetheart?" I asked.

"I so happy you my mommy!"

My heart felt like it just turned to blood and began to pour out of me onto the floor. I wanted to die, right there, and take her with me to Heaven where no one could ever hurt us. I burst into tears.

"Mommy, why you crying? Mommy, don't cry!" she said.

"Sarah I'm crying because I'm not your mommy. I wish I was, but I'm not."

I can still see the look on her face as she finally heard the confirmation of what she had hoped was not true. She had always known Keesha was her first mommy, and her siblings were connected to her in a good way, but she had apparently hoped that somehow in some way she didn't understand, I was her mommy, and she belonged more to me. She threw herself down on me and began to cry as hard as I was. The things her family had been telling her were true. I didn't know what they had been telling her, but it was a good thing someone had handled my love for Sarah better than I had. At least they had prepared her as much as they could. More about that in a minute.

After a few minutes, I felt I had to stop this or we would both lie there and cry the rest of the day, and it wouldn't change one single thing. "Look, your oxygen is 99!" I said, sitting up and reaching for tissues. I diverted her attention and mine for a while by getting her some toys to play with.

I had already requested Sarah's mother be brought to spend the night with her, so I could go home and sleep in my bed and relax my muscles as much as possible. Late that afternoon, Hamp called to say his uncle had quite unexpectedly died in his sleep, while taking a nap. He had just been found by a neighbor. He was in his late seventies, but it was still a shock, and Hamp wanted to know when Keesha was coming, so he could wait for me to go and be with his mother. I called Keesha to be sure she would be there by 6:00 and was informed she was not coming. A cousin of hers was getting out of prison that day and they were going to have a party for him.

"You can't go to the party, Keesha," I told her. "You promised you would be here. Now Hamp's uncle has died and he and my family need me. You come down here like you promised."

I called her social worker for help to make her come. She said she would get on it, but obviously couldn't guarantee anything. While I waited for her mother, Sarah slept and I paced the floor. I got my journal and wrote from Psalm 8:4 & 6: "I am reckoned as those who go down to the pit. I have become as a man without strength. Thou hast put me in the lowest pit, in dark places, in the depths." I felt as if spiritual and earthly reality had had a meltdown in me and I didn't know to which I was reacting. How could it be possible that this beautiful, loving child must lose the parents she wants and the life, too? How can men have advanced so far in technical, electrical and medical ways, and yet be so completely ill equipped to protect our precious, helpless children. You brought her to me, Father. It seems a lifetime ago. I remember the first time she smiled; I kissed her…Oh, God! What will I do without my baby?

I cried most of the afternoon, consumed with how I would live without my baby, and what would happen to her in the poverty stricken, drug-laden area where she would grow up. Six o'clock came and went. Her mother didn't come and it was too late for anyone to do anything. I had no choice but to go home, get something to sleep in and clean clothes, and turn right around and come back. I was diligent to try not to let the babies keep me from my family responsibilities. Now my husband had lost an uncle he had known all his life and my mother-in-law had lost her only brother, and I wasn't there because of a baby. Keesha had given me no choice. I was truly angry with her. I didn't feel I deserved this kind of treatment from her after saving her baby's life and carrying the weight of taking care of her for over two years. Christians are not to keep an account of wrongs, but I felt what I felt; angry and frustrated. But I was also in a lot of pain and so terribly exhausted. I was also so sad and depressed I could barely face the long drive home in the dark and rain and the drive right back.

The rain felt like one more assault as I crossed the parking lot to my car. I drove home staring at the road ahead, not even thinking. The pain of what Sarah had said, the shock of Hampy's uncle dying, the only confrontation I had ever had with Keesha, and feeling like I had a terrible case of the flu from the fibromyalgia, all combined to overwhelm my brain. As I pulled away from a traffic light, my empty mind was filled with a picture just above the deserted street. I saw the muscular, tanned arms of Jesus. There was a white robe on the arms and chest. My eyes filled with tears as they always do when the Lord manifests Himself. He pushed up first one sleeve and then the other with a definite sense of purpose. I knew exactly what it meant. He was going to do something. Then I saw Sarah and me standing in my kitchen facing each other. He put one hand on her back and the other on mine. It only lasted a couple of seconds, but the message was clear. He was going to help us. I didn't know how, but He was going to help us somehow. I knew it.

> JOURNAL: Lord, we open ourselves up to all kinds of ungodliness and when the consequences present themselves, we run screaming that we are being attacked by Satan. The truth is we have attacked ourselves, and just now feel the wounds.

It turned out that Sarah's family had been preparing her to leave us for a long time. They had been telling her she and they were black, while my family and I were white, so she couldn't belong to us, but to them. One day several months before she left, she came to me and put her little brown hand on top of my white one. I looked quizzically at her, but she didn't ask anything, and in a minute, went back to what she had been playing. It is hard to admit I was so stupid. I like to tell myself it was because she was the only baby for whom race was an issue. None of the other babies knew to wonder about the difference in our skin color, and since it wasn't an issue for us, I didn't realize it was very much an issue for her, especially because she understood what her family was saying.

Another day, not long after comparing skin colors, she came into the living room where Hamp and I were and asked, "Mommy, am I white?"

I was so caught off guard, I couldn't think of a thing to say. Finally I got out, "Umm hum, where is your baby doll? Isn't it time to feed her?" And I went in search of the doll. I was terribly upset at my stupidity. I realized someone had been telling her we were different, and I had not even prepared myself for it. She had given me cues with things like comparing our hands without saying anything, and I had not homed in on it at all. I had talked a lot about her and her twin sister. I had told her twins were special sisters. They were alike, and were born at the same time, had been inside Keesha at the same time, and they would always have a special love for each other. I had at least put a picture of her and her twin sister on the refrigerator door and spoken of it often. At least I had done that. I had also said a few times that she would go back to her other family one day in the future. I had waited for her to ask if she would ever go to them and not return, but she never asked. This was why she was so devastated in the hospital when I finally said the words, "I'm not your mommy." It was all my fault. She had given me chance after chance to tell her, but I couldn't bear to put the weight of that knowledge on her for the rest of her time with us, or I was just selfish and couldn't bear the pain of telling her, knowing how she would feel.

> JOURNAL: *This is a word from the Lord to encourage me at this awful time. "There are graces you know not of. Just as there is a grace for you with the babies that people who know you well can't see. Even though they are close enough to see first-hand the pain you are experiencing. So there are graces for all who belong to Me in every circumstance, even though others can only see the suffering. The grace is there, just as it is when your heart is breaking over Sarah. You cry, but deep inside you is comfort and peace from My Spirit which you may not even be aware of at the time. Don't compare yourself with other people and think you would crumble if this or that thing happened to you. You can't see their grace. This reminds me again that "The just shall live by faith."*
>
> *Often I can only see the grace when the situation is behind me and I look back and wonder how I ever lived through it. It's then that I realize how powerful His presence was with me. Even though I wasn't in enough*

control of my mind to realize it was He who kept me going, kept me sane.

It was spring, and just after her third birthday. We knew Sarah would have to go home soon. She had been with us much too long to make separation easy for any of us. Now she and I had to go to the town where her family lived for a meeting with everyone involved in her going home. There was even a psychologist. She was a nice older lady who would be working with Sarah at home to help her adjust to her family and to losing us. The Human Services office was exactly like all of the other Human Services offices in poor towns in Mississippi: concrete block buildings outside and cheap paneling inside with a white vinyl floor. The obligatory folding chairs were lined up against the wall and it smelled of poverty and institutional cleaner. Everything about it made my heart even heavier. Always before, I held my babies when we had to visit their county DHS worker, but Sarah had to climb up into one of the metal folding chairs and wait, like she belonged there. My bright eyed little girl didn't belong in this place. Neither did any other bright eyed little child.

Everyone else was already there when our social worker and I arrived with Sarah. She refused to go to Keesha until I insisted she show her mother a new toy she had brought with her. A few minutes after everyone in the lobby had seen her child wanted nothing to do with her, I saw Keesha slouch out the door and start puffing on a cigarette. She had told me the last time I had seen her, "I'm sick of all this s---. I want my baby home." I assumed she was bored with waiting and just didn't want to have to fool with all of this. But her older sister told me she was embarrassed because Sarah clearly didn't want to be with her. I was astonished. Her body language only had spoken to me of boredom and disgust at having her life so controlled by other people.

Eventually all of the adults involved were in the psychologist's office. When she told me I should begin immediately telling Sarah she was going home soon, and not coming back, I started to cry. I didn't stop until the meeting was over. I knew I had to tell her very clearly, but my heart just couldn't face it. I couldn't imagine what every day would be like if we both knew she would soon have to leave me forever. She would know what that meant. The psychologist having to tell me to do it was bad enough. I was already carrying around the weight of it, but having to face it in front of all those people was awful. I felt like a fool for not having done it, and crushed, knowing how she and I both would feel when we were separated. It was like being trapped in a fire and knowing you could only get out by walking slowly through, letting the fire burn you. Once I happened to glance toward the other women in the room and saw that every woman there was crying in sympathy for Sarah and me except the psychologist and Keesha. I was glad to see Jane, Sarah's aunt who would be taking care of Sarah and her twin, crying for us. She had been to my house to pick Sarah up and knew how much I loved her.

We made a video of Sarah's birthdays and Christmases, of her singing with Katelyn, playing in the bathtub, going to the zoo with Laura, Katelyn, Madison and me. I even taped her last day at preschool. We made sure everyone in the family was on the tape, so she could always remember us and how much we loved her. I also got photos of all of us and lots of her with us, for her to take with her.

Sarah seemed the same as always, even when she knew she would be leaving and not coming back soon. She was a little subdued, but not sad. I tried not to let her see me crying, and we acted as if everything was as usual. The only thing she did that showed she had any fears about going home, was to call me back one night after she had said her prayers. I was leaving the room after kissing her goodnight, when she said, "Mommy? Can Jesus take care of me everywhere?"

"Yes. Anywhere you go, He will be there with you." I whispered to God, "I hope You heard what I just promised that baby."

She smiled and nodded, satisfied. A few days later she asked, "Is Jesus everywhere?" Again I assured her He was. This child had been three years old for a month, and she knew the most important thing to be thinking about. She was the most intelligent, spiritually alert little girl I ever knew. She was projecting into the future and wanted to know if Jesus translated into black, into where she was going, and where she might end up in the future. Would He be there? That was her main concern.

At first it pained me to think she was worrying about this, but after she left, I realized if she was thinking about Jesus, instead of asking about her family, how far away from us she would be, or a million other obvious questions a child her age might think about, he must have made Himself real to her. It would have been a great blessing for me to have realized that before she left, instead of months later.

On her last visit with her family, after I got all of her things in the kitchen for them to take, she climbed up on my lap and said, "I don't want to go with them. I want to stay here with you!"

"They are your family, darling. You have to go; they love you and want to see you."

She took my face in her little hands and looked me in the eyes, almost nose to nose. "I don't want to go! I want to stay here with you!" as if she thought I didn't understand what she meant.

I had to tell her, "Sweetheart, you have to go." She threw herself against me and started to cry. We were both crying when she left that day.

The day came for Sarah to go back to her birth mother's family. Bringing all of her things to the kitchen and piling them up, I felt like I was building the gallows that would kill me in less than an hour.

I managed not to cry until I heard the car drive up. I choked back my tears with great effort and didn't open my mouth. I knew I couldn't talk without crying. Almost wordlessly the social worker and Keesha and I put all her little things in the car. I was glad they had brought her twin sister to be with her on the ride home. I felt sure no one would ever be allowed to separate them no matter what happened in the family they happened to be living with. I expected them to be shuttled from one part of the family to another and they were.

When everything was in the car but Sarah, Keesha and her social worker went out and left us alone to say good-bye. I took her on my lap, tears streaming down my face.

"It's time to go, Sweetheart," I choked out. I pressed my lips on hers for several seconds, wanting neither of us to ever forget that kiss and all the love we had shared for almost three years.

Sarah looked up at me, her little face dry and showing only concern for me. "Don't cry, Mommy. It's all right," she said, putting her hand on my cheek. "It's okay." There wasn't a sign of a tear in her eyes.

There it is! This is what Jesus was showing me He was going to do, I thought. Move quickly, while the Lord is providing supernatural grace to her to feel no grief. I quickly took her hand and walked out to the car with her and put her into the car seat, and patted her twin sister on the leg. I closed the car door fast, and stepped away from the car. Sarah waved solemnly as the car drove away. I went into the empty house and cried.

> *JOURNAL: Lord, Your word says that You "number my wanderings and put my tears in your bottle" (Psalm 56:8). If that's so, Your bottle must be very big to hold thirty years of my tears for Your babies. I always try to remind myself there are millions of women who have more to cry about than I. Those who watch their children cry from hunger and disease, and have nothing to ease their suffering. But surely there must be some place for me to cry before You for babies I have to call mine, who had no mother but me, who loved me and trusted me. They instinctively sensed my love meant they belonged to me, and I would never think of*

giving them away to someone else. But I did. I gave them to people they usually didn't even know. I left and never came back. Lord until my dying day is over, I will never get over the inexpressible suffering I feel for having betrayed the love of those babies.

14

ABIGAIL

The following spring the Lord spoke to me of another baby. It had taken me a year to get over losing Sarah, and I didn't know if I could face that kind of wrenching separation again. I knew it would take a real anointing. Then one beautiful spring day I went out to walk and pray and thought, this is a day to be strolling a baby. With no real sense of purpose, I found myself praying about whether I was to take another baby. I wasn't longing for a baby, but I knew with all of the sick children in the world, there had to be a child who was suffering where he was. One who would be better off with me, surrounded as I was by sunshine and flowers and birds singing and a spacious sun filled home. As I walked and prayed, the sense that there was, indeed, a child who needed me grew. I stopped walking and was standing in the quiet street surrounded by woods, crying and entreating the Lord's mercy on this child, whoever he was. I assumed it was a little black boy as usual. The power of the feeling diminished and I stopped crying and began walking again.

"The baby is white."

I stopped in the middle of the street and said out loud, "White!"

That hadn't even occurred to me. It was consistent in the Lord, letting me know it was He speaking to me and not a conjuring of my own mind. I would have liked to know more, but it was enough. I knew that I knew, there would be a call about a white baby and we were to take him.

> *JOURNAL: It is clear from the natural world You want good to be cultivated and nurtured. And You want it to be a struggle. That is one reason why weeds and ugly, choking, thorn covered vines grow everywhere, both naturally and spiritually. All around us You give opportunities to bring Your light and love into the ugliness that runs rampant because of sin. You have created man as the one living being on earth capable of choosing to stand against the constant assault of evil and selfishness, death and futility which the world produces. I think that is one of the things the babies do. They shine a light of love, hope and compassion on a world that is losing hope in God because they don't see enough people allowing You to show Your power by obeying Your word to the best of their understanding.*

ABOUT A WEEK LATER KIM CALLED FROM CATHOLIC CHARITIES. "Carlene, we have a little girl almost three years old, who is very long and heavy, who has severe cerebral palsy. She can't swallow, she's fed through a tube in her side, and she has really dangerous esophageal reflux..." at this point I interrupted her.

"Wait, wait," I said. "What color is she?"

I had been called about children this big before, and for twenty-seven years I had always turned them down. I couldn't handle a child that size even when I was young. I had always drawn the line at about twelve pounds, knowing they would get heavier as they grew.

"She's white," Kim replied. "That's really different for you, isn't it; not only white, but a girl."

Oh, no. My heart sank. It was my confirmation this was the child God had spoken to me about. "Okay, go ahead," I said, pulling out a chair and sitting down to listen. This baby was going to need someone strong enough to carry her and move her around, plus a world of medical care and therapy.

I knew the Lord must be tired of hearing how afraid I was, but I knew exactly what lay ahead. The Elavil, which had gotten me through the first year or so with Sarah had lost most of its effect. Though it still helped, I was having a lot of pain and fatigue. Then Kim blew away all thoughts of myself.

"There is something else, Carlene. This child is a victim of Munchausen Syndrome by Proxy."

"Oh, dear God!" I said. "What is her mother doing?" I knew she was speaking of an emotional disorder in which a mother purposely harms her own child to gain attention for herself.

"She is blowing air into the baby's stomach with her feeding tube, shooting the Pediasure up her throat and out her mouth and nose, making her choke and vomit."

This struck a chord in me I had never felt. The shock and revulsion at the thought of a mother hurting her innocent, helpless child had always been a distant knowledge. To have it presented to me in the form of one of my babies shook me to my core.

"I'm glad you only told me she was white that day in the street," I told the Lord after I hung up. It was a while before I could start my "baby countdown" of information gathering. I had to sit and let it penetrate my mind just what I was getting involved in. There was a possibility I would have to deal with this mother in person. How could I do that?

My first call was to the hospital social worker on her case. We agreed to meet several days later for me to see her. It was clear he was sure I would not want to take her home after I saw her, and realized the difficulty of caring for her. But I knew something he didn't. I knew as I had with Matthew, the Lord had singled this child out for me from all of the needy children in the world. I could feel my willingness increasing by the hour. I knew when I felt willingness and even anticipation, in a situation which would stretch me beyond my endurance with a baby, I was right where Jesus wanted me.

ABIGAIL, OUR SCRIPTURAL NAME FOR HER, WAS HAVING PLAY THERAPY in front of a big mirror when I first saw her. She was unable to control her body or even hold her head up, but she was looking at herself in the mirror. When the therapist stamped her feet for her in time to the music, her eyes danced. I breathed a sigh of fleshly relief. I saw delight in her eyes and knew I could make emotional contact with her.

FOR THREE WEEKS I VISITED ABBEY ALMOST EVERY DAY AND SAW HER at her worst before I took her home. She arched backward like Micah, her arms rotated forward, fists and teeth clenched tightly. She made snorting noises as if she couldn't breathe, and she screamed...a lot. Because she couldn't swallow, she had a feeding tube new to me. Instead of through her nose to her stomach like Ben, she had a hole in her stomach. It had a snap on it to keep Pediasure from leaking out. To feed her, I attached the bolus with her Pediasure in it, to the snap by a tube which allowed liquid food to run from the bolus into her stomach.

Most of the nurses fed her in about one minute, holding the bolus up high, letting the Pediasure flow quickly into her stomach. A few minutes after feedings, she started choking, and acting as if she was going to vomit, but she never did. When put down, she would arch and scream. When I tried to hold her, the arching was so powerful I had to just let her lie across my lap, supporting her head in my hand.

Every time I left to go home with my neck and back throbbing, I would say, "Father, I have no idea how I am going to take care of that child, but I know I am going to."

> *JOURNAL: Father, have mercy on me, a sinner. In spite of all my sin and all my foolishness, Lord, please grant that I might stand, a tiny child on the edge of the great crowd of more worthy people who served you. Let me be content just to see Your lap from afar, and know that someday in the long eternity of time, You will get to me, and I may sit in Your lap for one brief moment, content at last in my Father's arms. (This is a spiritually mixed metaphor, and I don't know that anyone will have to wait for God's comfort. But it came to me in the form of a picture in my mind. It expresses a child of God longing for the comfort of her Father's arms).*

For the first time in all my years of taking babies, I never had any doubt I would and could take this one. I couldn't see how from where I was, but I knew it was the Lord and that was enough.

So far I have described a spastic, quadriplegic child who couldn't even direct her eyes where she wanted to look. A child who couldn't and would probably never be able to chew a bite of food and swallow it. She would never run and play, learn to dance and sing and be in school programs like most little girls. But Abbey was a beautiful child. Her hair was like spun gold curled into little ringlets, her eyebrows and lashes were the same peachy golden hue, and her eyes were emerald green. Her skin was like white porcelain.

> 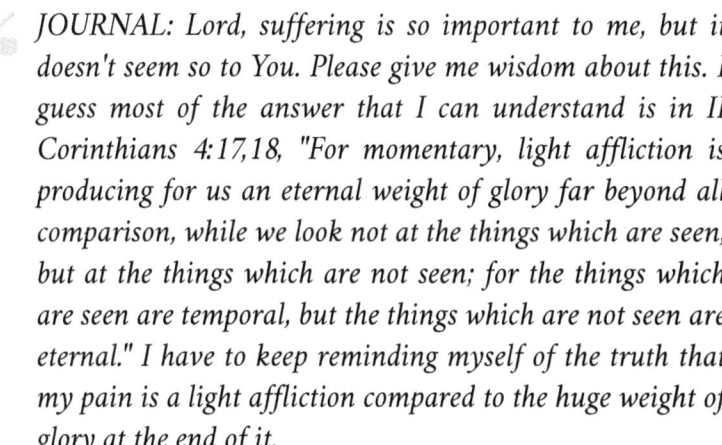JOURNAL: Lord, suffering is so important to me, but it doesn't seem so to You. Please give me wisdom about this. I guess most of the answer that I can understand is in II Corinthians 4:17,18, "For momentary, light affliction is producing for us an eternal weight of glory far beyond all comparison, while we look not at the things which are seen, but at the things which are not seen; for the things which are seen are temporal, but the things which are not seen are eternal." I have to keep reminding myself of the truth that my pain is a light affliction compared to the huge weight of glory at the end of it.

We bought Abbey a tape player, several music tapes and some toys so she would have familiar things to bring home to help ease the transition to a new place. At least that was the idea.

I saw Abbey's doctor twice before we left the unit for permanently disabled children. He was hard to deal with, very negative about Abbey, and seemed to think I was going to fail miserably in trying to take care of her. That didn't bother me. The doctors were always the most negative about a baby. But I got furious when he refused even to order physical therapy for Abbey when she came home. He said it would be a waste of time; she would never be capable of anything. I was beside myself. His arrogance was intolerable. I searched everywhere and called everyone I could think of trying to get help for her, but circumstances blocked me at every possibility. And Abby lost several important months of therapy because of him.

> JOURNAL: Unbelieving intellectuals who are taught by other unbelieving intellectuals can't handle the knowledge they absorb properly, because they handle it only in their

> natural minds. They can't see it in the light of God's truth. The Bible says the beginning of knowledge is the fear of the Lord.

Because Abbey was in an extremely dangerous and unusual situation, I called a friend who was a child advocate, and asked if she had any information on Munchausen. Actually, she did. She knew two people who could help me. In fact, one of the deputy sheriffs who was on the scene at the hospital when they secretly taped Abbey's mother abusing her, was sitting at her desk talking with her right then. She put him on the phone and he told me the following: The sheriff's department had Abbey put into a private room with a hidden movie camera. When viewed, the film was both shocking and sickening. The camera showed the mother caressing and talking to the baby until other family members left. Then she went to the door and looked to be sure they were gone. She got an empty bolus tube, pulled the plunger back filling it with air, and attached it to the tube which attached to Abbey's feeding button. She pushed all of the air from the bolus into Abbey's stomach, making it puff up like a balloon and causing her to scream in pain. Pediasure spurted from her mouth and nose and she began to choke and vomit. The mother then rushed into the hall screaming, "She's vomiting again!"

"What happened?" I asked, meaning to the mother.

"Well, we went in and arrested her," he said. "We took her to the station and talked to her and she confessed."

"She confessed? Then why is she probably up there right now with her, and why were they going to take her home with them!?" I knew they were coming to see her at odd times from the nurses.

"Well, that's the strange thing," he said. "We've got a written report by a woman doctor from the hospital, saying what she was doing was not life threatening. That put the brakes on everything. They had to let her bond out because the doctor said it had been considered non-lethal abuse."

"Anything that causes a person to aspirate into the lungs is dangerous! It can always cause pneumonia!" I said, "How could any doctor say that!?"

I asked to see the paper, and at one point I did, but I can't remember when. It was a messy, yellow copy that had been under one or two other copies. It was the 1990s and everything was still being done by hand. It was filled in hastily by a doctor with a pen. It did seem to say it was not lethal abuse and the name seemed to be Bev something. It was really not clear enough to base a decision about a child's welfare on it.

The mother would have to wait for a court date to go before a judge, but in the meantime she was allowed supervised visits with her child. I couldn't change that, but I could find the woman doctor and find out how on earth she thought it wasn't lethal abuse. The first call I made was to the Chief of the Department of Pediatrics and a neurologist, Dr. Owen Evans, at the hospital. He recognized Abbey's legal name at once.

"Oh, yes," he said, "I've been taking care of her all her life."

I told him the plan was to return the child to her family. "My God! Do they want to kill her? That is insane! If that child goes home she will die!"

I asked if he knew of a woman doctor who would have signed a form saying what the mother had done was not life threatening.

"Absolutely not! No one in their right mind would say such a thing. They have this woman on tape shooting air into the baby's stomach." He had seen the tape and described it to me again. "Of course it will kill her. It nearly has already!" He left no doubt he feared for Abbey's life.

I HAD ALWAYS INSISTED ON ACCESS TO MEDICAL RECORDS OF BABIES who were severely compromised. Knowing what I knew about Abbey's background, before I even began to try to help her, I had to get all the records from as many hospitals as I could as quickly as I could. There was just too much information in too many places for me to just pick up from the time the child was put into my arms. Records were scattered among four or five hospitals and she was "tagged" in them all. Her whole body was controlled by Cerebral Palsy, life threatening esophageal reflux, inability to eat or drink and probably other things we didn't even know about. Doctors see so many "hopeless" cases, they sometimes fail to even consider hidden potential in a child who presents as poorly as Abbey. She was tagged as completely helpless and isolated in her own very small world. She was also completely defenseless. She could be abused every day for the rest of her life and never be able to fight back or tell anyone. It made me sick.

IT WOULD TAKE WEEKS TO GET RECORDS FROM ALL THE HOSPITALS they knew she had been in. But the one in which she was born and had been brought back to over and over was fifteen minutes away. Hamp and I hired a nurse from an agency to stay with Abbey for about three days, the length of time I estimated it would take for me to go through the thirty-six-inch stack of folders on her in the medical records department.

The first day I went to read records, I met our dear Joyce. I opened my kitchen door and there she stood, all five-feet-one-inch of her. She was wearing a white nurses' uniform and a big smile. She would stand by me through everything I had to go through for years to come. She and Abbey fell in love with each other the minute they met. She became a second mother to her. I felt no anxiety leaving Abbey with her, even when neither of us knew much about what to expect from her.

Reading what I understood in Abbey's files, I found much needed medical information, as well as proofs of Munchausen which neither my social workers nor the social workers in her county knew anything about. When doctors see the same child over and over for the same complaints, they tend to just look at what was done the last time, especially with a severely brain damaged child. Add the factor of Munchausen mothers being some of the most seemingly loving and nurturing mothers on earth, it is no wonder normal, decent people never think for a minute the mother could be harming her child and making her child suffer so she can gain attention for herself. Although I thought just being bored sitting home all the time with a handicapped child might not be as much fun as being surrounded by sympathetic nurses and doctors and the drama of them running to care for your child and comfort you. There had even been an exciting ride in a helicopter to get Abbey to the hospital.

My friend who had put me in contact with the sheriff's deputy also called a psychologist friend of hers in Colorado who was considered the country's leading Munchausen by Proxy authority. She sent me a copy of an article she had written for a medical journal. I read the papers she sent me with minute care, looking for anything that would help me understand what had happened in this family. Finally, I found a statement that was a definition I could at least comprehend, if not relate to. She wrote, "Where most mothers have empathy and compassion for their children, these mothers have something else." It was obvious from the records that this mother was desperate enough for attention to repeatedly do terrible harm to her child in order to get it. I didn't understand, but it was the only thing that even began to make sense to me. This girl showed motherly concern for her child. She knew how it was supposed to look. Yet she was also capable of the terrible abuse she had perpetrated on her. She was so convincing, the social workers in her home county simply wouldn't believe it, and going back to her parents was still the written plan filed in her case. I sent copies of the incriminating evidence from her medical files to her social worker in her county, but they were lost and re-sent at least once. When I called, no one seemed to know where her file was, who had her case at the time, or if they had received our information about the abuse and the tape. I don't believe I ever spoke with a new case worker for Abbey who had been told she might be in danger from her mother if she was sent home.

WHEN ABBEY FIRST CAME HOME, IT WAS VERY HARD FOR HER TO play. She could only swing her spastic little arms at things with her hands tightly fisted with her thumbs tucked under and useless. The harder she tried to reach for the toy, the more her back arched and pulled her away from it. This was the "overflow" which had occurred with some of the other babies, when they tried to do something. The damage in their brain set off abnormal stimulation to other parts of the brain, causing unwanted parts of the body to move. It brought tears to my eyes just watching her trying so hard to play, only to have her efforts put the toy farther away from her. But the evidence that she wanted to play and was willing to work hard to get to a toy was extremely encouraging, and confirmed she was much more aware than she was able to show. It also proved she could not have gotten the stimulation from her family which they said she had. They had therapists coming to the house to work with Abbey, and to show them how to help her, just as I eventually did. But she had not shown in the hospital or at our house at first, that she knew how to use any toys.

EVERY MONTH OR TWO I TOOK ABBEY TO SOME SOCIAL WORKER'S office for a supervised visit with her family. Abbey's mother, I'll call Jean and father, I'll call John, were always there, and sometimes her siblings came. The whole family lived with Jean's mother, Martha, and the man who had lived with her like a husband for years, Bill. Abbey had her mother Jean's coloring, very fair with light hair and eyes; so did Martha. Abbey's father, John, had olive skin and brown eyes. Abbey's siblings looked like John.

The first visit in our county, a social worker from Abbey's county was there, as was Kim, my Catholic Charities social worker, and a social worker from DHS in my county. Martha, Abbey's grandmother and Bill, were there too. I had never seen them before. As we were all getting out of our cars and walking toward the door, I glanced up and saw Bill, also known as Abbey's "grandfather." I stopped in my tracks. Dear God! I thought. Abbey looks just like this man! I couldn't stop looking at him. He looked down. I assume I was greeted by the other social workers in the office, and the one who would sit in on the visit, but I didn't hear or see any of them. The image of the man's face next to Abbey's filled my mind. They looked just alike. Once we were sitting across the room from each other I scanned his face carefully. I had thought the unusual set of Abbey's ears and prominent forehead were due to her developmental damage. Her cheekbones were very high and prominent. Brain damaged children often have something odd looking about their features. It's one of the ways doctors know immediately to look for other abnormalities. But Bill's face looked just like Abbey's. It was obvious to me it was a genetic trait and not at all related to her brain damage. All the reasons I had come up with for Abbey's abuse faded in the glaring similarity I saw between Bill and Abbey. Jean was very possibly harming this child because she had been abused by this man, and Abbey was the result. I had long since decided Abbey's mother was at least mildly challenged intellectually, and it was hard to tell about her husband. He never spoke. But grandmother Martha seemed fairly intelligent, and though "grandfather" Bill said very little, he carried himself with the assurance of a man with normal intelligence. Later, when Kim and I were alone, I asked if she had noticed the similarity. She had.

I tried to set aside this obvious new information for the time being, and fixed on observing Abbey's mother with her. They were acting like any family who hadn't seen their baby in a while. They kissed and hugged her and handed her around. Whoever was sitting next to her on either side stroked her leg or held her hand. Abbey was all smiles. She knew them and had no idea any of them had harmed her. They asked about ear infections, her cough, which she didn't have with me, her reflux, etc. I kept thinking, I can't believe this mother has been harming this child and the rest of the family didn't know about it. After they left, I was alone with the social workers. We all sat silent.

I finally said, "I can see why nobody in her county believes us. They would have fooled me. I've read the reports in her hospital records, and I still have a hard time believing what I just saw wasn't totally sincere." They all agreed. I knew there had to be a lot of cunning on the part of the mother, and a lot of denial, if not complicity on the part of the rest of the family. I didn't know then that the wife of an abuser always knows what her husband is doing on some level. That grandmother had to know if her common law husband was abusing her grown, married daughter. This was one possible reason for Munchausen I never heard anyone speak of, but I couldn't help thinking it had to play a part in her torturing Abbey.

> *JOURNAL: Lord, let me not look at the evil of man and wonder about You. Let me dance for joy on the earth, so great is my delight in my God, and let me remember the admonition of Paul in Philippians 4:8-9, to think on the lovely and the good things, and the peace of God will be with me. There are many wonderful people still in this world, many who serve You with their whole heart. People who can be trusted to be upright when no one is looking but You.*

At the hospital I had seen Abbey choke and gag after feedings. I also had been told she couldn't swallow anything. That meant the only place I felt safe putting her was in the crib in our room, with the head of the bed elevated. We used gravity to keep her food in her stomach and not backing up into her esophagus. Abbey stubbornly refused to be propped up on anything. When propped with a bed pillow, she would arch until she was flat again. My fear of her choking and aspirating Pediasure into her lungs and developing pneumonia was so great that I saw no way to get her out into the rest of the house. I even tried a towel, to see if she would tolerate any degree of head elevation. She would not!

I had no choice but to make her bed as happy a place for her as I could. I bought a bright happy bumper pad and put a mobile and busy box on the bed, and a mirror for her to see herself. I noticed that when I put the mirror on the crib, she smiled, even though neither her head nor her eyes were completely turned toward it. She was seeing herself through her peripheral vision and seemed unable to turn her head or eyes at will. Sometimes she could do it and other times she couldn't.

ABBEY SEEMED FAIRLY HAPPY IN THE BED FOR A FEW WEEKS, BUT I grew increasingly frustrated with having to leave her in the bedroom by herself all the time. Not to mention she kept arching herself into a half cross ways position and getting stuck there, which made her feel trapped and she screamed for me to come release her. This isolation from the rest of the family was not good for her and I knew stimulation was the key to development. She was never going to learn anything just lying in her bed. I finally called Les and got her a feeding machine like Ben had so I could feed her as slowly as I wanted. After we started using the machine, reflux became a thing of the past. I still watched for it, but it didn't happen. I finally decided it was more beneficial for her to be around people and be helped to play and watch children's programming on TV even if there was a risk involved. If it turned out she really couldn't be kept safely out of her bed, I thought I would know it soon enough. We all watched her constantly.

As time went on and she never had one of those horrible, life threatening, episodes I had been told about, I became suspicious. She should have had at least some bad reflux, but she never did, so I bought a tumbling mat and cut it into two pieces. It folded in the middle, so it was easy. I put one in the den and one in the living room. She could be with us, see and hear us all the time and I alternated days, so she had a change of scene of sorts. One and a half of the walls of the living room had long windows so she could see outside easily, even from her preferred position of flat on her back, on the floor.

IT WAS A DIFFICULT SUMMER WITH NO THERAPISTS TO HELP ME. Abbey lost the therapy she could have had for those months, except what I could give her. My range of motion experience with other babies came in handy for us, but I had a real problem with her length and weight. She was a slender little girl, weighing between twenty-seven and twenty-nine pounds for the time we had her, but she was long, and it was very difficult for me to manage the combination of weight and length. The doctor and the social worker at the hospital had both told me Abbey would not be eligible for home health care after she turned three. Her third birthday came 2 months after we got her. They both had said the school system would have to pick her up and she would have to go to the school. This was clearly impossible. I put off calling them until I couldn't wait any longer. I dreaded a long drawn out fight over policies and spending hours on the phone.

I should have known better by this time, I really should; but I had believed them both without question. When I contacted the school system in late summer, to let them know how hard it was going to be to feed and medicate Abbey if they made her come to school, I found to my disgust that she did not become ineligible for home health at three. She could have been having therapists come to the house all summer, plus a teacher from the school system.

It seemed to take forever to get all of the testing and paper work done for home health therapists and a teacher from school, but we got Joyce Williams, the nurse we had paid for ourselves earlier, now paid for by Medicaid, to come and stay with her several times a week. This allowed me to leave the house without having to have Laura there. We also got Ms. Peggy back to help her try to learn to swallow and gain some use of her lips and tongue. Ms. Vickie came to do physical therapy and brought wonderful switch toys to play with. We also got Ms. Freda, a special education teacher from the school, to work with her and help reinforce the things the therapists did with her. Of course I was supposed to do the same things with her whenever I could, but I seldom was able to do much because she was so big. The fibromyalgia had sapped my strength more than I had realized, and I only did what I could that didn't put her in danger of being dropped or hurt.

> JOURNAL: Lord, I am in pain. It is so frustrating and hard to keep from becoming depressed when I face how little I can do for this child. It seems everything she needs from me causes me enough pain to force me to stop trying to do it. Help me to focus on the frustration and mental or emotional pain You suffered every day just living among sheep so near sighted You had to draw them mental pictures before they understood what You were telling them.

Some of the therapy we used for Abbey involved things that were done every day anyway, or that were easy. I put flavored and scented lip gloss on her lips for her to taste and smell. I held her hand around the brush to brush her hair and watch in the bathroom mirror. I also had to keep her off of her preferred side, which I accomplished about as much as getting James to wear his glasses. I profited with Abbey from things I had learned through years of caring for other children. She had scoliosis, a curved spine, which could eventually kill her by compressing her internal organs until they couldn't function. The doctor didn't have to tell me what a priority it was to keep her off that side as much as possible.

To do this, when I saw her on the mat on her preferred side, (which she arched back into within minutes of my moving her) I had to move her and give her a reason to stay on the non-preferred side. I regularly moved her toys to the other side of her body, so she couldn't see them anymore, then bent down, took one of her legs and swung her body around, so she could see what I wanted her to look at. I also had to keep her facing the videos and children's programming on TV the same way. My leaning and bending seemed endless, between fighting her preferred side and keeping toys within her reach. I also had to sit on my feet and ankles to change her diapers and clothes and to give her meds and feed her.

From the beginning, it had taken all my strength to do simple things like pulling a top over her head. It didn't help that Abbey fought me desperately for some reason. Her whole body would stiffen, her jaws locked like a vise and she would make sounds of frantic distress. She hated anything touching her face. Washing her face was done with Abbey bent backwards, eyes closed, teeth clenched, pulling her head toward her heels unless you could block her with your body. I learned to sit on the toilet lid with her on my lap, wedged between the toilet tank, me, and the vanity. It was the only way I could get to her face to brush her teeth or wash her face in front of a mirror and in a normal sitting position. How a child views the world around him is extremely important and I refused to do everything for her while she lay on her back. I wanted her to be able to see herself in the mirror, hear and see the water running for her toothbrush, and to watch herself brush her hair.

When Ms. Vickie started coming twice a week, she brought switch toys. All Abbey had to do was push the big flat circular switch with any part of her body, and the toy part, which was attached to the switch by a long cord, moved. Her favorite was a cute black and white cow with a little pink tongue and a tail that swished when she stopped to moo. She walked toward Abbey as soon as she pushed the switch. Abbey started out pushing it with her right knee and, after months of trying, with her open hand. The cow would walk a few steps, stop and moo, then walk some more and moo some more, until she got to Abbey. The cow helped her overcome her fear of having something touch her face. She liked her so much that she would let the cow walk right up to her and push against her face, and if Abbey opened her mouth, sometimes the cow put her nose right in, and instead of pulling back and clenching her teeth, Abbey would laugh.

This was a huge milestone for her. I couldn't believe she would let the cow touch her face, much less put its nose in her mouth, but she loved it. Then one day a page from her hospital records floated through my mind. Her mother had put her hand over Abbey's mouth and nose to cut off her air supply and make her oxygen levels drop in PICU to bring the nurses running. Who knows how many times she may have done it to render Abbey unconscious and blue to precipitate a trip to the hospital. She had probably done it to her while pulling clothes over her head, with washcloths, and towels, using the cloth to muffle her screams before she pinched her nose and held her mouth shut. I had failed to make the connection between what her mother had done to her and my trying to pull shirts over her head or wash her face. I had never tried to hurt or frighten a baby in my life, but those things must have terrified Abbey. I am sure that's why she trusted the cow to get so close. She knew it wasn't a person, and she controlled when it started and when it stopped.

It took some doing to find the best way and times to feed Abby, and to figure out a way to keep her from pulling the tube loose from the snap on her tummy. Her spasticity drew her arms in and down, with her fists against her stomach, which repeatedly scraped off the cap on the feeding tube where it coupled with the button on her belly. If she was being fed, within the time it took me to walk to our bedroom and back, there was Pediasure everywhere. Her clothes were soaked and it was all over the mat or mattress or carpet. I finally had to firmly tape the tube to her stomach, which I thought would irritate her skin and hurt. I remembered how Nathan and Ben had hated the tape on their faces, but she didn't mind it a bit. Every time I had to pull the tape off, she actually laughed. Such is the way of brain damaged children. One never knows how they will perceive anything.

After months of total confusion, we developed something resembling a routine. My day began with hearing her making little noises in her bed about 7:30 to let me know she was ready to get up. Abbey woke early and lay quietly or played with toys in the bed, not demanding to get up until about 7:30, which was a godsend. Usually babies were up by 5:00 or 6:00 every morning. Not only that, but she usually slept all night. When I got up, I would tell her "Good morning," which always got me a big smile, and I pulled up the blinds by her bed. She would immediately turn toward the light and smile some more. We had turned her bed so she could look out and see the tree tops and the sky. The sunlight came gently in at that window, just enough to be cheery. I always told her the same words, "I am going to take my shower, and I will be back to get you up soon." Then I would put on one of her music tapes, probably her favorite, *Sesame Street*. For months I sang "Rubber Ducky" and "Doing the Pigeon" in my sleep.

After a very hot shower and some major stretching, I was able to pick her up. Following a diaper change in bed, we went to the bathroom where I helped her wave "good morning" to Abbey in the mirror. The little girl in the mirror smiled back at her. Then we washed her face by putting a small corner of the washcloth in her hand and my guiding it over her face. By this time, she did not object at all to having her face washed as long as she was allowed to help. In fact, she looked proud of herself. Then came the detested brushing of her teeth. Even a Brushy-Brushy, singing toothbrush which had finally won James over to dental hygiene was not welcome in her mouth. Eventually we had to resort to little flavored sponges on soft sticks. Then I would dress her and we would go to the mat she had not been on the day before, and she would start her feedings and medications for the day.

I bathed her during the day and often Joyce did it for me to save my back. All of this was hard, but it was not impossible. Sometimes we interpret very hard as impossible, but I think it is impossible for us to want to do it, which is a whole other thing. For those who don't already know, Christians often have to beg God to make them willing to be willing to do His will. There is nothing wrong with that. He already knows we don't want to do it. We may as well face it and get on with it.

> JOURNAL: *Those of us who are surrounded by man's artificial light cannot see the true light. That is why most miracles happen to the poorest and lowliest among us, not to the great rulers of the world and of the church. This is why He withholds His riches from most of us. We are blinded by the light that is generated by power and influence.*

We discovered because the only position Abbey would accept was flat on her back, she did have enough reflux to cause ear infections, and we fought them the entire time she was with us. She usually showed no signs of discomfort until late afternoon. The air would be rent with an ear piercing scream, followed by a long sequence of others, and we were off to the after-hours clinic. Hampy always drove us to the doctor, even though I often encouraged him to stay home and relax. He was up at 5:15 every morning to read his Bible and eat breakfast at a local diner. He worked from 7:00 to any time between 4:30 and 8:00, depending on what he was working on. But he never, ever, let me go out at night alone if he was at home or had time to get home. So we spent many an evening waiting in lobbies and examination rooms for a doctor to come and pronounce her ear or ears infected. The answer seemed obvious. Sit her up. But believe me it wasn't that easy. In fact, it was impossible. Abbey had a top of the line Medicaid covered kid cart, a fancy combination wheel chair, car seat with a big aluminum base which raised her to table level when she was in it. But I couldn't get her in it. If she would let me put her in it without hurting herself badly, I could have just strapped her into her kid cart and elevated her head in increasing increments until she was sitting up. But because she arched so hard to avoid being made to sit up, I was afraid she would hurt herself. Besides, unless she was feeling exceptionally reasonable, I couldn't get her into the chair. I had to lift her into the chair then hold her there with one hand while I separated her legs around the wedge which kept her legs from scissoring with the other hand. Then, with Abbey arching backwards and to the side, away from me, I had to fasten all the complicated straps for which I had no extra hand. She was just too big and too determined not to stay in the chair. One good arch would just pop her out before I could get her fastened in. It was the same getting her into her car seat, except it leaned back enough to help me a little bit, but I still had to put one foot in the car, twist my body toward the car seat, hold all her weight out with my arms extended, then lift up to get her bottom into the seat. My hands, neck and hip joints would never be the same.

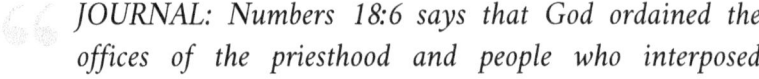

JOURNAL: Numbers 18:6 says that God ordained the offices of the priesthood and people who interposed

themselves into the area of sacrifice who didn't belong there were to be put to death. IT IS A HOLY PRIVILEGE TO BE ALLOWED TO SACRIFICE TO GOD.

In this chapter I speak much more about my struggle with pain from fibromyalgia. This is because it seemed to grow worse by the day with Abbey. And because some people considered the burden beyond God's asking. I was fifty-four and had mothered over forty of God's babies after my own precious three babies. I had looked up the age at which the Kohathites or holy carriers retired. It was fifty. Still, knowing that, when I was called about Sarah, I knew I was to take her. We can only take the Old Testament types so far, and while I felt I was at the end of my "carrying ministry," the Lord made it crystal clear I was to take her. It is part of being human to wear out and become too old for a particular activity, but I was still very capable of caring for Sarah, not so much with Abbey. I knew as I said at the beginning of the chapter, that my body was not up to caring for Abbey, but the Holy Spirit was, and I knew He would pull the rest of me through, sometimes through other people and sometimes by giving me supernatural strength.

TWO WOMEN ANSWERED REQUESTS IN CHURCH BULLETINS TO HELP me take Abbey to doctors and the hospital to see specialists because I just couldn't carry her that far without dropping her. I didn't realize how weak my muscles were until Joyce began coming to help me take Abbey to the hospital. Tiny little Joyce, who was a little older than I, and very petite, trudged for what seemed like miles to me across the parking lot, into the hospital, through endless halls, with me asking every few minutes, "Don't you want me to take her for a few minutes? I know you must be exhausted."

Only to have her say, "No, I'm fine. She's not so heavy to me."

Joyce was always cheerful, always laughing at Abbey and playing with her. She bought her a blue velvet dress and new shoes to wear to church at Christmas, not to mention all the toys. She brightened many a day for me and I don't know what I would have done if the Lord had not brought her to me. What a blessing she was, and still is to me, and what a blessing she would be to me later, when I needed her more than I ever dreamed. God knew we were going to need a nurse we couldn't afford to pay; one with an unselfish and constant love just months after Abbey left. If I had refused Abbey, I never would have had Joyce to lean on, physically and emotionally. It's amazing the blessings we can look back and realize we would have missed if we had refused to obey the Lord.

> JOURNAL: Hosea 11:3-4, "Yet it is I who taught Ephraim to walk, I took them in my arms, but they did not know that I healed them. I led them with bonds of love. I became to them as one who lifts the yoke from their jaws and I bent down and fed them." Lord, what a picture of what You have done for Your babies and me. How it comforts me to know You compare Your love and pain over Your people, to that of a mother's feelings for her child.

I had long since given up on finding the female doctor who thought Abbey's abuse was not life threatening. Then one night at church, Jason Miller, a pediatrician friend solved the mystery for me. He had asked me how Abbey was doing, and as we talked, I mentioned Dr. Evans's name.

Finally, he said, "I might just give Bev a call about her." "What did you call Dr. Evans?" I said, grabbing his arm.

"Well, his name is Owen, but everyone calls him Bev," he explained.

"Jason, that explains why the sheriff's office thought a woman doctor had said the abuse wasn't life threatening. Someone must have misread the poorly copied report he had written, and thought he had said it wasn't life threatening. I couldn't find a woman, because it wasn't a woman!" I could have talked to Jason for an hour without him saying the doctor's nickname. It had to be the Lord, telling me that no female doctor would surface and dispute the danger of Abbey's abuse. Dr. Evans must have been so used to being called "Bev," that it never occurred to him that it was his name on the misread report.

NOT LONG AFTER THIS I AWOKE ONE NIGHT TO THE FAMILIAR SOUNDS of vomiting. I jumped up, my heart in my throat. It was finally happening. Abbey was vomiting! I just knew she was going to choke and maybe even stop breathing. Without stopping to turn on the light, I rolled her over, turned her head and lifted her upper body a little. I wanted as much as possible to come out her mouth and nose and not go back down her throat. When she stopped heaving, I switched on the light, expecting her to be blue. But she was fine. My fear changed to confusion. She wasn't even upset. As I was cleaning her up and watching her every breath, she began to heave again. I took her to the bathroom, but nothing came up. I continued to watch her, but it became more and more obvious she was fine. There was no coughing or gagging or choking. It made no sense. If this baby couldn't swallow, and had choked and stopped breathing before when she vomited, she should at least have coughed and choked until she cleared her passages, but she didn't need to. My growing suspicions were confirmed. Abbey didn't have horrible esophageal reflux disease. She had a slight problem with reflux, exacerbated by her refusal to sit up. Her mother had been nearly choking her to death by shooting air into her stomach way more often than any of us had suspected. Even the doctors who knew about her mother still thought Abbey had horrible, life threatening reflux. But she didn't. Her mother's abuse had caused Abbey to be diagnosed with a terrible deterrent to adoption; and it wasn't even true. It was all her mother's doing. It was almost impossible to believe the suffering Abbey had been subjected to.

> *JOURNAL: Because I am no longer capable of giving Abbey the degree of care I want to, I feel guilty a lot of the time. But I have realized I am giving her the things that matter most. No one is ever going to choke or suffocate her, or shoot air into her tummy while she is in my care. I am giving her the awareness that she is safe and no one is going to hurt her. I am giving her, with the help of Hampy and Joyce, more stimulation and more concern for what she wants than she has ever gotten before. Abbey is safe, comfortable and happy. I have given her that. Maybe that is all God wanted me to do.*

I took Abbey to see Dr. Evans. He was pleased with how much healthier she looked and the state of her reflux. I asked him to write DHS in her home county a letter, telling them his opinion of their plan to give her back to her parents. He got a Dictaphone and dictated the letter right there in the examining room. I asked him to please state clearly his opinion if the court gave Abbey back to her family, he believed she would die. He said just that. I knew this letter would be very important when we went to court.

I made sure to make a copy for myself in case DHS's copy got lost, like so many things sent to them.

IN DECEMBER, A THERAPIST TOLD ME ABOUT AN EYE DOCTOR AT THE School for the Blind who evaluated exactly how children's eyes functioned to see in spite of disabilities. He told the parents how to help their child learn to use their eyes more effectively, if that was possible. I made an appointment immediately. He told me Abbey could see out of the upper right quadrant of one of her eyes but he couldn't be sure about the other. He gave me some excellent ideas to help her. He suggested some paper that looked like strobe lights when you shine a light on it and move it. It was really fascinating. Great sweeps of neon color seemed to roll across the paper. Abbey liked it and it did attract her eyes, but what she really loved were the icicles I bought her. It was right before Christmas, and in Wal-Mart I noticed some really long blue and gold and red icicles attached to cardboard cards. I left them stapled to the cards and just waved the beautiful, sparkling, brightly colored icicles for her to watch and reach for. The night we bought them, while Hamp put the groceries in the car, I was twirling around the parking lot, waving the icicles in great sparkling circles.

"I thought those were for Abbey," he said, grinning at my uncharacteristic exuberance.

"Do I need to go back in and get some for you?" He was laughing because I am not usually one to dance around a parking lot waving icicles in both hands. I wish I were. But they were so beautiful I couldn't help myself.

"Well, if I respond to them like this, think how Abbey will act when she sees them," I told him as I got in the van. I held them in my lap so I could run into the house and show them to her first thing. She laughed when I ran them over her head and down her body and it wasn't long before she was reaching out and grabbing for them as they went by. I dragged and draped them all over her to make her aware of her whole body. They also helped her learn to focus better. Hand-eye co-ordination did not work for Abbey, and she usually tried to grasp or reach for something without looking at it. The flashing, sparkling icicles drew her eyes as nothing had.

JOURNAL: I am as timeless as You. You have put me into time, as Jesus came into time. But He was aware that the greatest place was timeless, and He was going back to it. He

> said where He is, there I will be also. I can never be farther away from Him than I am right now. I can only be closer.

> JOURNAL: There is no difference between what You see in me today and what You have always seen in me. You have always seen the flesh and sinfulness I only see now. You see the sin that will remain in me until I die. Sin I will never even be aware of in this life.

After months of waiting, we were notified finally there would be a court hearing regarding Abbey's future, in her home county. This was a tribute to God's perfect timing again. Had we gone to court a few months earlier, I would not have been allowed to say anything in court. But in July of that year, a new law had given foster parents the opportunity to say what they thought should be done for the child they had taken into their care, and anything else they thought important. No way were Hampy and I going to miss that hearing.

To prepare for success, I FAXED copies of her hospital records to the social workers in her home county and to the judge, showing clearly that her mother was the source of her suffering, plus the letter from Dr. Evans stating as Chief of the Department of Pediatrics at UMMC, that it was his opinion she would die if sent back to her family. This letter was my ace in the hole. I knew no judge in his right mind would open himself up to culpability for a child's death with such an expert testimony in writing right in front of him.

I HAD NEVER BEEN TO FAMILY COURT BEFORE AND IT WAS JARRING. The ante room was packed with angry, exhausted parents and sullen teenagers. The door was wreathed with cigarette smoke from the parents and kids outside smoking. There was actually screaming coming from inside the courtroom as some parent and teenager raged at each other right in front of the judge. We looked around and found everyone we knew should be there. Abbey's parents looked terrified, especially her mother. I knew she was scared to death the tape of her abuse and her confession were going to be shown. They should have been, but they weren't. They were still locked in the evidence room in Jackson. I also knew that judge was going to hear everything Abbey's mother had done to her before he and I parted company. I didn't know how it would be accomplished, but I was not going to have another chance to save her. This was it. I had to do it now.

I had no information about the judge, nor had I ever addressed a judge in court.

The judge plopped down in his chair and started asking questions which had no relevance to Abbey's case. It turned out the prosecutor had requested termination of parental rights on all of the couple's children. Hampy and I hadn't known if one child was removed from parents' custody because of abuse, all of the children were subject to removal as well. Apparently because Abbey was separated from her siblings for abuse, he decided to temporarily disregard the other children and focus on her.

About ten minutes into the hearing, he said, "Wait a minute, wait a minute, is there something wrong with this child?"

I wanted to stand up in my chair and scream with frustration. I had sent copies of every bit of evidence I had to his office and to his prosecutor, and neither of them had even seen it. The judge put the social worker from Abbey's home county on the stand and asked her questions with no bearing on the case, and wouldn't let her tell him anything. He asked the mother a question and she just looked at him.

He threw himself back in his chair in disgust and roared, "Does anyone know the IQ of this mother?" The social worker did know that, and it was much lower than I would have thought. He let the social worker say the psychologist who had evaluated the mother thought she wasn't smart enough to perpetrate MSP on Abbey.

I turned to Hampy and whispered, "I could train a dog to hurt a baby if he knew he would get a doggie biscuit for it!!"

I was getting more and more furious and frightened. He put Kim on the stand and even she was unable to give him any real information because of his jumping from subject to subject. He wouldn't let her say anything except based on what she knew of the case, she felt Abbey should be taken from the family and put up for adoption. At some point he commented that nobody was going to adopt a child like this. He asked Abbey's parents if they had anything to say. They didn't.

My experiences with authorities dealing with foster children's lives had led me to bring my own copies of everything I had sent them. And as soon as I saw how this hearing was going, I opened my brief case. When the judge asked me if I had anything to say, I was on my feet before I knew it. I waved the stack of papers in my hand in the air and told him I had hospital records proving the mother had perpetrated Munchausen Syndrome by Proxy on Abbey, and I enumerated every single one of them. I told him how many babies I had cared for and that she was by far the hardest. I then listed the number of times she had to receive medicine a day, how many times she had to have therapy, how many times a day she ate and what was involved in feeding her. I told him I was barely able to care for Abbey, and this family absolutely was not capable of giving her what she needed, Munchausen Syndrome by Proxy aside. The judge glared daggers at his prosecutor.

"Mr. So and So," he said, "Do you have copies of any of these papers?" The prosecutor fumbled through his papers. He knew very well he didn't.

"I sent copies to everyone here I knew would be involved in deciding what happened to this child," I told the judge, making great effort to cover my outrage.

"Mrs. Singleton, would you allow Mr. So and So to make copies of your papers?" the judge asked, his eyes narrowed and his teeth clenched.

"Yes, sir," I said, "But I have to have them back. I'm not sure I won't need them again." I wanted him to know how little confidence I had in people with such power knowing so little about what they were doing. The prosecutor meekly took my papers, copied them and brought them back. The judge spoke to the grandparents, who were making all kinds of promises about the care they had and would give Abbey. It was time for my Ace in the hole. I pulled out my letter from Dr. Evans and gave it to Kim, who handed it off to the bailiff.

"He needs to read this," she said.

He took it to the judge, who stopped in mid-sentence and read it.

"Well," he said, "Dr. Owen Evans," and he read his title, "says he thinks the mother is capable of Munchausen Syndrome by Proxy, and says if we give this baby back to this family, she will die. I am inclined to agree with Dr. Evans!" Here he scowled pointedly at the young social worker who had provided the information from the psychologist about the mother being incapable of the crime. The judge asked the prosecutor another question about Abbey. When it was clear that he hadn't a clue, the judge said sarcastically, "Ask Mrs. Singleton. I'll bet she knows!" He was furious with the prosecutor and Social Services for having bungled their jobs so completely.

He asked Hampy if he had anything to say.

"Yes, sir, I do," he said. "I just want to tell you this child is very adoptable. There are lots of families who will adopt this little girl." He went on to mention Daniel and Micah as babies much more devastated than Abbey, and told him they had been easily adopted. A few minutes later, the judge pointed at Hamp.

"Mr. Singleton, you say there is a family out there somewhere who will adopt this little girl. You find them and I will court order her into their home!"

Hampy said, "Well, we've found that Social Services is really so slow…"

The judge cut him off. "Human Services is out of this! This is between you and me. You find a family, have your social worker notify me and I will court order her into it!"

My heart took flight. The weight that had dogged my steps over what would happen to Abbey went with it.

The judge turned back to the parents. "You have two choices: You can come back in here in two months and surrender all parental rights to this child, and I will let you keep your other three children, with some very strict restrictions, or you can come back in two months and I will take all of the children and have them placed for adoption for their own safety. It's your decision." He went on to say the mother was never to be left alone with any of the children again, and if he ever saw them in his court again, the children would all be taken. He banged the gavel and began to shuffle papers. He was through with us.

I SAT IN SHOCK FOR A SECOND, THEN SAID TO KIM, "DID HE SAY what I think he said?"

"If you think he said for Hamp to find her a home and he would court order her into it, you did," she said with a grin.

"I didn't think judges did things like that!" I said. "Hampy, did you hear him say you were to find her a home? Did he really say that?" I just couldn't believe it.

"That's what I heard," he said.

I slipped through the crowd in the ante chamber and caught up with the prosecutor, who I already knew was having a bad day, but I had to know.

"Did he really say that?" and I repeated what I had heard.

"Yes ma'am, he really said it."

"I didn't know judges did things like that," I said, still incredulous.

"They usually don't, but he's the judge. He does what he wants," he said.

As we were driving back to Brandon, I told Hamp, "I have never, in all the years I have walked with the Lord, seen Him work in the midst of such incredible chaos. I couldn't even keep up with what was going on. You never knew where that judge was going next. He jumped from one question to another before the first question had been answered, but the Lord was just as steady and in control as ever. He stopped him and made him hear Abbey's case today; he made him remember he had to give the foster parents the opportunity to speak. The Lord had everything in hand, while I had been as equally ready to hear him give her back to her parents, as take her away.

IN DECEMBER THE JUDGE GAVE HAMPY THE JOB OF FINDING A FAMILY for Abbey, and told her family she was not coming back to them. On December 21, I called Human Services in Sarah's county to see if I could find out where she was. The aunt who was going to raise her had died unexpectedly not too long after Sarah had gone home to her. I found it out quite by accident at the hospital with Abbey, when I ran into the driver who had brought Keesha to visit Sarah. I was shocked and crushed. I had counted so on her love for Sarah. Someone gave me the phone number of the person who had her and her twin and I called them. After I spoke with the adult who had custody, they asked if I wanted to talk to her. Of course I did.

When Sarah heard my voice, she said, "How you doin'!" just like a grownup hearing from an old friend. I asked if she was happy and she said she was. I asked if she still had the video of us and I mentioned Katelyn. She said she still had the tape, then asked where Katelyn was. I told the custodial adult that we had wanted to send money for Christmas as we had the year before, but didn't know where to send it. They gave me the address and I was able to get a check in the mail in time for Christmas. I hadn't realized what a weight had been on my heart about Sarah since I heard her aunt had died. I was so relieved to know where she was and to feel she was safe. I was happy I could get some money for her and her sister there in time for Christmas. I didn't know that would be my last contact with her.

> JOURNAL: Mercy should be the foundation of sacrifice. God had to have mercy on us before He sacrificed His Son for our sins. Several times in Matthew Jesus quoted Hosea 6:6, "I desire mercy more than sacrifice." Why are so many people willing to give money, but will do almost anything rather than show mercy? Because they don't have faith to minister to people and let the Lord control the outcome? Are they afraid they will be forced to become personally involved and really have to give of themselves? Mercy can't be faked and sacrifice is relative. What may seem like a sacrifice to men, may not be, but true mercy that is acceptable to Christ, cannot be shown selfishly.
>
> Mercy Seat means a lid, a place of covering (of sin). I never realized that, or I forgot it. How wonderful! The Mercy Seat in the Holy of Holies is a lid of covering for sin. Come before the Mercy Seat in the Holy of Holies. Come to God's temple, and seek the lid of covering. This lid was a provision from God for His people until the Messiah came and shed His perfect blood to cover our sins, and wash them away. "Blessed are those whose lawless deeds have been forgiven, and whose sins have been covered. Blessed is the man whose sin the Lord will not take into account." (Romans 4:7)

> JOURNAL: (Colossians 1:16-17). You could have caused

the world to be destroyed as it deserved with one word, but You chose to die for us instead.

Taking the judge at his word, Hamp and Kim and I started looking for a family for Abbey. After contacting several agencies, Betty Watters at Catholic Charities remembered a family who had adopted a little boy with cerebral palsy several years before and decided to give them a call. The mother's response to Betty's inquiry was, "Can we come get her tonight?"

They had been looking for another child, preferably a girl for several years and had kept their home study up to date in the event a child became available for them. There had certainly been plenty of handicapped children available for adoption before Abbey, but the Lord had chosen their family for her. Needless to say, with a family so excited over the prospect of adopting a beautiful little girl, there was a flurry of picture sending on the internet and many e-mails back and forth between the prospective mother and me, and it wasn't long before the mother presented herself at my door, anxious to meet her new daughter.

Since so much paperwork was already done, it was only about a month before we were ready to place Abbey with her new family. This family had a child with disabilities already, so they had therapists, doctors, neurologists, etc. just waiting to treat Abbey as well. The only thing they couldn't find for Abbey was a nurse to come in and stay with her as Joyce had done for me. Medicaid was approved, but they couldn't find a nurse, so our sweet Joyce, who was so committed to Abbey's being happy in her new family, and who could hardly bear to part with her herself, agreed to drive several hours each way to go and spend the night with the family and stay for two or three days a week for months until everyone concerned felt Abbey no longer needed her. Undoubtedly Joyce's sacrifice of driving for hours each way twice a week made Abbey feel much safer and calmer in her new home, and helped her adjust to her new family more easily. When Abbey left and I no longer had Joyce in my house several days a week, there was a double void. I really missed having her to talk to and she and our whole family have remained very close friends.

ABBEY'S NEW MOTHER CAME FOR SEVERAL VISITS AND BROUGHT A grandson she and her husband were raising, who was about twelve. He and Abbey had hit it off immediately, and the adoptive mother brought him with her when she came to take Abbey home. On my strenuous advice, she had made a bed out of the back of her van and Abbey rode to her new home lying down, with her new step brother to keep her entertained. Her new mother called to tell me she made it almost all the way home before she started crying. And of course it wasn't long before Abbey saw her favorite person, Ms. Joyce come through the door of her new home. It couldn't have been better orchestrated for Abbey's emotional adjustment.

I REGRET THAT THERE ARE NO PICTURES OF ABBEY TO SHARE. I TOLD her whole story. She *cannot* be recognized.

AFTERWORD

Abbey was extremely hard to care for, but the knowledge that whatever sacrifices I had made, God had saved her from her mentally disturbed mother, and that made it more than worthwhile. I pray that someone will step up to take my place now that I must retire from taking babies because I can no longer trust my body to be up to the task.

Sometimes when I see news reports on drug babies and AIDS babies, and children who simply have nowhere to go, my flesh tells me I should have done something to affect more children than just the forty plus I have. Then I remember the vision of the two orange trees. Maybe my sense of inadequacy is that Americans think in terms of numbers and not individuals. Doesn't God's love for His people always come down to the smallest and weakest individual? Didn't Jesus come for each and every helpless one of us (Matthew 25:40)? And what about Ebed-Melech, the black man who got Jeremiah out of the well? (Jeremiah 39:16-18). It says in the midst of the destruction and chaos of the Babylonian invasion of Judah, God stopped to speak to Jeremiah about Ebed-Melech.

"Go tell Ebed-Melech he shall have his life as a reward. He will not fall into the hands of those he fears, because he has trusted in Me," He said. Surely if the God of the universe cares so much about the fear and trembling of one little man, He sees and cares about every need of every child on earth.

> *JOURNAL: Where would America be if all of the intelligent, capable women were focused on the children of their generation. Surely all of our children would be loved, educated and provided for. God has not given men and women new roles. God has made no new creature to nurture and mother. We have structured nurturing right out of our culture and replaced it with counselors and therapists we pay to help us overcome our lack of nurturing as children.*
>
> *Lord, I hear women constantly complaining about the pace and emptiness of their lives. They are overworked and often heartbroken and frustrated over their lack of time to nurture and mother their children. What a job the media, fueled by Satan has done! They have made women put aside what means everything, to run after what means nothing.*

It was old-fashioned in the world's eyes to stay at home to feed and nurture, to watch over and comfort both my own children, and all these others. But it was also scriptural, and fruitful and satisfying to the depths of my soul. It is ironic that by staying home for my own children, then God's babies, I have had experiences outside the home most working women never have. I was president of the P.T.O. at school, room mother for countless classes and Girl Scout leader for my girls' troops. I also taught Sunday School and Bible studies, directed Mother's Day Outs and Vacation Bible Schools. In addition, I have also been on the Board of Right to Life of Jackson, serving in numerous board positions. I have written and produced pro-life radio and television ads, and been interviewed on television and national radio concerning abortion and special needs children's issues. I served with Hamp on the founding board of Adoption Ministries of Mississippi, and I was on the founding board of The Mississippi Center for Public Policy. We also served the ministry of Open Doors with Brother Andrew, hosting fund raisers and sharing our home with Bible smugglers. In addition, we were able to open our home to missionaries home on furlough for weeks at a time.

I listed so many things to make a point. Obviously, I never could have had the time, energy or flexibility to be so deeply involved in so many worthwhile endeavors if I had been working at an outside job eight hours a day. There are clearly millions of women who have no choice but to work, but those who can and do stay out of the secular work force are more available for Christian service than any other group in our society. They are able to minister fully to their own husbands and children, and also reach out to other children, neighbors, the sick and whomever else the Lord may bring their way.

Many years ago when our children were small and times were financially hard for Hamp's fledgling business, I overheard him tell another man that coming home at the end of the day to a warm, well-lit house, with his wife in the kitchen cooking, and the sounds of his children playing, made the day of hard work worthwhile. I was surprised by his sensitivity, but I knew what he meant. I sometimes came home as a child to find my mother out and the house dark and cold. I had long forgotten the chill and gloom of an empty house, especially in the winter. I wonder what difference it makes whether our families come home to one kind of house or the other. I think it means much more than we could ever dream. John told me in his thirties that he remembered a particular day when the sky was bright blue and the flowers were in bloom and he was playing in our front yard with his sisters. He knew I was in the kitchen cooking and any minute his daddy's truck would come over the hill. He said he stood still in the yard, acutely aware of all of this and feeling an overwhelming sense of happiness and security. He never forgot it, or when he felt it. He was four years old.

> JOURNAL: Lord, just as you showed me the difference between love and duty, now I see how important it is to understand the difference between reason and obedience. Romans 12:1 says, "Present your bodies a living and holy sacrifice...which is your spiritual service of worship." The sacrifice of our whole self is what God considers reasonable. Nowhere did Jesus say, "Now don't be unreasonable about your devotion to me. Keep your life in balance, keep your spiritual life in its proper place." He said, "Whoever does not love Me more than father or mother is not worthy of Me" (Matthew 10:37). And, "Whoever shall lose his life for My sake shall find it" (Matthew 10:39). Nowhere in the Scriptures are we directed to think things out and decide issues based on human logic or reason. Isaiah 1:18-20 says, "Come, let us reason together...though your sins are as scarlet, they will be white as snow...if you consent and obey (Me) You will eat the best of the land, but if you refuse and rebel, you will be devoured by the sword." God's reasoning says, "Do it My way or suffer loss."
>
> Proverbs 3:5 tells us not to lean on our own understanding, but to acknowledge God and let Him direct our steps. In I Corinthians 2:1-5, Paul resolved to know nothing among the philosophical and debate loving Greeks of Corinth, but Jesus Christ and Him crucified. So their faith would not rest on the wisdom of men (his good arguments and presentation) but on the power of God. This was an absolutely spiritual approach, and totally illogical.

> *Surely if believers desire to see Your power and Your beauty, we must stop qualifying when, where, how and to what degree we will serve you. Is there a sacrifice too costly, an obedience too lowly? Jesus didn't think so when He sacrificed His status and glory as God, and entered a human body, taking the form of a bondservant. Nor yet when He sacrificed that life, and willingly obeyed His Father to the point of death on the cross (Philippians 2: 6-8). And in John 13:3-15, He showed the disciples the essence of what Christian humility was to be when He girded Himself with a towel like a slave and washed their feet. Then He told them clearly they were expected to do the same.*

I cannot end this book without some comments about my husband. Married women who are mature in years and in the Lord will realize without being told that Hamp must have been a man of great faith, patience and godly wisdom, or the things recorded here, could never have happened. There are tensions and stresses with children and parents, differences between spouses concerning spiritual maturity, cooperation, authority and a host of other issues that make marriage and child rearing a challenge for Christian couples. For the benefit of those readers without such experience, I must explain that through all of these human realities Hamp was the earthly support for our family's ministry to God's babies, and the spiritual covering as well. A man generally surrounded by Christian men who drew very definite lines with God about how far they were willing to go with their money, time, meals, sleep, etc., Hamp drew no lines in the sand with Christ. When there was no money provided for a baby's need, Hamp paid. When I frantically woke him at two in the morning to take me to the hospital with a baby, he jumped up and dressed. Once when I had to spend the night in the emergency room with Matthew, I curled up on the examining table and went to sleep. Hamp sat up, drank coffee and watched over us both.

He was a godly husband to me, a godly father to our own children and Dai, and to over forty little people, who will remember him when they see him in Glory. He held us all together with his strength and faith.

I have always known there were other couples God was calling to minister to His babies, and the wives were ready to say, "Yes, Lord," but their husbands were unwilling to make the sacrifices. What blessings and spiritual growth Christian families often miss because of the immaturity and lack of commitment on the part of their fathers.

It would have been easy when writing this book, just not to mention my battle with the pain of fibromyalgia, but a witness must tell the whole story. If I had made it appear I had suffered no physical effects from the work the Lord had given me, it would have created a misleading picture.

Some Christians believe I haven't been healed, because I don't have enough faith. But after all these years of praying to be delivered from pain, I have come to see it another way. David said in I chronicles 21:24 that he would not offer a sacrifice to God which cost him nothing. In this light, I see that my physical pain, probably rooted in a genetic predisposition, may be a price of the sacrifice of my obedience in mothering God's babies, much like the emotional pain of giving up child after child. Before Aaron left us, the Lord said, "How much do you love me? How much do you love My babies? Do you not know there is much to be done, which can only be done by those who are willing to hurt and to bleed?"

The sacrifice of Jesus on the cross was painful, spiritually and physically; indeed, just coming to earth in human form was a painful sacrifice. I know for certain, we must all learn obedience from the things we suffer, even as He did (Hebrews 5:8) as we seek to be conformed to the image of Christ. And didn't Paul bear the marks of Christ on his body from beatings and stonings he had received for obeying God and preaching the gospel? Don't believers suffer pain of all kinds just because they are Christians in countries that try to suppress the Gospel? Only in a country of affluence and ease could Christians not understand there is a price to be paid for serving Jesus. I still greatly desire to be healed, but endeavor to be content if I am not (Philippians 4: 11-13).

> JOURNAL: "Therefore let those who suffer according to the will of God entrust their soul to a faithful Creator in doing what is right" (I Peter 4:19).

Stacey, John and Laura are all grown now and have established lives of their own. They are unfortunately subject to the same pitfalls as other believers. But they have some things going for them which distinguish them from other members of their generation. By the grace of God, they grew up in a home where Jesus was exalted, where the God of creation, Jehovah, Yahweh, the triune God of the universe was not just acknowledged, He was worshipped. As they grew up they saw their parents stand like mighty warriors for Christ, and they saw us fall prey to our flesh and fail miserably. They saw the reality of being a Christian. Also in the awesome mercy of God they saw miracles. They saw blind eyes healed and babies damaged and sick unto death, live and grow and go on to be adopted into loving families. They also experienced the deaths of babies we had prayed as hard for as the ones who were healed. The experiences which gave them sure knowledge about Christ were at times constricting, difficult and painful. At the time it was impossible for us to see all that God was building into them. Now they, like Hamp and I, realize what a magnificent work of God they were blessed to have a part in.

The world and Satan pulled hard at all of our children when they were teenagers, and even though there were times of despair, the foundation laid which is Christ held them. He would not let them go. Even when it seemed there must never have been a relationship to Christ as we had thought. Even when it seemed the very sight of their daddy and me made them reject Christ more. He never let them go. They had all committed themselves to Him as children and I believe a child's sincere, personal commitment to Christ gives that child a link to God that nothing in his life will be able to break. It gives a child his own relationship with Christ, not dependent on his parents.

> *JOURNAL: According to Your instructions the Holy Place, where the priests routinely served You, had ten candlesticks and the golden candlestick from the tabernacle to provide light. You gave the priests permission to provide this light for themselves in the Holy Place, and You gave them sacrifices and works to do there. But on the other side of the veil in the Holy of Holies, there was total darkness. There, the priest who went in once a year on the Day of Atonement was alone with the holiness of God. There was nothing to light his way. He had to obey You blindly. Surely Christians are like this today. Most of us who are priests unto God (Revelation 1:6 and I Peter 2:5), go into the Holy Place (church) and feel comfortable and productive there. It is light; we have our Christian work to do and we feel content. Few of us are willing to venture through the torn veil into the darkness of total dependence on God, that is, into Your holy presence in a deeper way.*

> *JOURNAL: You are the light of the world and You are in us (John 8:12). We go into the darkness of physical uncertainty, but Your light within us will give us spiritual light.*

> *JOURNAL: Lord, because You wanted to restore us to full fellowship with You, You sent Jesus to pay the price for our sins and split the veil, giving every priest belonging to You*

access to the fullness of Your holy presence. Lord, I desire to enter into the Holy of Holies beyond the light and safety of the Holy Place. I feel you calling me to total abandonment to it, but I am afraid of what it might mean for my life. My precious Redeemer-Husband, please take my hand and draw me there. I want to come.

ABOUT THE AUTHOR

A native Mississippian, Carlene Singleton has lived the Christian faith in all its reality. Along with her husband, Hamp, and their three children, the family fostered a rainbow of children, the last dozen being special needs.

A nationally known advocate for all children, she has served on the board of Right to Life of Jackson, and the founding boards of Adoption Ministries of Mississippi and the Mississippi Center for Public Policy. She is a Bible teacher, advocate for special needs children on TV, radio and in newspapers, and speaks at conferences and Human Services events.

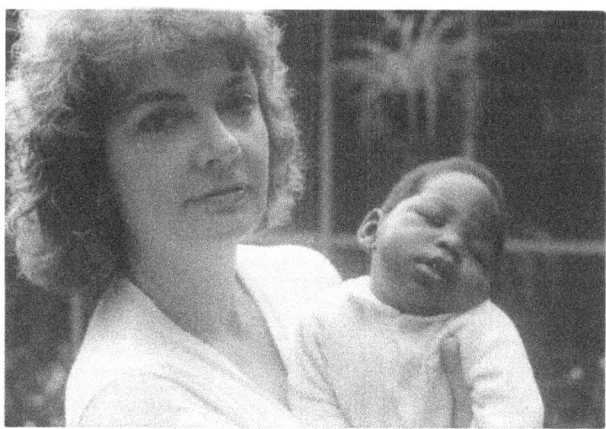

| Carlene with Baby Ben

We Carry Gold recounts her spiritual journey. You have to read the book to believe all she and her family saw and experienced.

IN MEMORIAM

John H. Singleton, (Hamp) left this earth way too early at the age of 56, succumbing to brain cancer February 20, 2001. That Christendom lost a giant was the consensus.

Ephesians 2:8-10

For by grace are ye saved through faith; and that not of yourselves: it is the gift of God: Not of works, lest any man should boast. For we are his workmanship, created in Christ Jesus unto good works, which God hath before ordained that we should walk in them.

Along with his wife, Carlene, Hamp lived these words day in and day out.

Carlene says of her husband, "He touched so many lives." The day he was laid to rest was a day to celebrate a life worth living, not his passing. His funeral incorporated people from all walks of life without discrimination on race, socio-economic status, or church affiliation. Joining in the celebration of Hamp's life were the Rev. Ted Bita, the pastor of Holy Trinity and St. John Theologian Orthodox Church; Roman Catholic Bishop William Houck; the Reverend Dolphus Weary, executive director of Mission Mississippi; Crossgates Associate Minister, the Rev. Claude Shufelt; and a close friend but not his pastor, the Rev. Donald Wheelock, a black Pentecostal minister, who delivered the eulogy; and the Rev. Barry Clingan, his own pastor.

Hamp was owner and operator of Precision Machine, Inc., a tool and die company in Ridgeland, Mississippi, and designer of a safer all-terrain vehicle. But his most important role was as husband and father, not only to his three biological children, but also to an adopted Vietnamese boy and foster father to more than forty children of multiple races, many having serious illnesses or disabilities.

During the service, Wheelock compared Hamp to a modern-day Abraham, saying that his quiet demeanor belied his deeds that spoke volumes for him. He was a man of few words, but many actions—most unknown to the general public—because he did not boast about his works but did all for, "the glory and honor of God." Those were Hamp's own words and what he would prefer to be remembered for.

Carlene relates that only three months after their last foster child was placed, Hamp was diagnosed with brain cancer. He lived less than two years. But the time he had on Earth was given in service to his Lord—being a father to the fatherless. All who knew him remember him as a quiet, immovable giant of faith.

Psalm 82:3

Defend the poor and fatherless: do justice to the afflicted and needy.

I only remember meeting this couple one time during their long spiritual journey, but I was touched by their testimony for the babies God gave them. In actuality, when I first met Carlene in the Red Dog Writers, I did not recognize her. When I saw the older pictures of her and Hamp, I recalled them speaking at a banquet I attended. It has been my honor to have reconnected with Carlene after a number of years and to have helped her relate the stories contained in this book and to remember a true man of God.

Janet Taylor-Perry
B.S., M.A.T. author, editor, educator

www.ingramcontent.com/pod-product-compliance
Lightning Source LLC
Chambersburg PA
CBHW071645090426
42738CB00009B/1431